LIFE OF A CONCORDE PILOT

*I dedicate this work to Mum and Dad, who have both
departed this world for the next, but gave me the most
wonderful upbringing since they adopted me at an early age.
I was born as a result of a secret, illicit affair in 1957 into
an unknown future – a life that, without Ron and Erica,
would have taken a completely different path. I've been
blessed. I have a wonderful family and have had a
glamorous, exciting and privileged career.
I hope that future generations of my family, and you,
dear reader, will find this story inspiring, moving
and, at times, amusing.*

LIFE OF A CONCORDE PILOT

FROM THE ORPHANAGE TO THE EDGE OF SPACE

JOHN TYE

FOREWORD BY
CAPTAIN JOHN HUTCHINSON

Cover illustrations: *Front:* Concorde in Chatham livery in 1998. (Courtesy Adrian Meredith). *Back:* John Tye (Courtesy Rosie Maggs)

First published 2023
Reprinted 2024, 2025

The History Press
97 St George's Place, Cheltenham,
Gloucestershire, GL50 3QB
www.thehistorypress.co.uk

British Library Cataloguing in Publication Data.
A catalogue record for this book is available from the British Library.

ISBN 978 1 80399 463 5

Typesetting and origination by The History Press
Printed and bound in Turkey by Imak

Trees for Lᵞfe

CONTENTS

PROLOGUE

'3-2-1, now.' Full power is produced instantly from four Rolls-Royce Olympus engines with 12ft flames leaping out of the back as the reheat ignites. The acceleration is phenomenal. A wisp of kerosene comes briefly through the air conditioning. The flight deck bounces up and down. I'm pushed aggressively into the back of my seat. Seconds later, '100 knots … V1 … Rotate.'

I'm airborne for the first time at the controls of Concorde, the world's only successful supersonic airliner. It's 18 February 1999. It's sunny. It's Seville, Spain. Thousands of people are clinging to the airport fence watching our every move. Three TV crews are covering us live on Spanish TV. It is, quite simply, fantastic.

How on earth did I find myself doing this?

A Word from the Author

I'm starting work on this in March of the year 2020. It feels as if the world is coming to an end. The sun is shining, but we have become used to expressions never heard before. 'Self-isolating' and 'social distancing' are not just common phrases, but courses of action being enforced upon society to prevent the loss of many lives. Coronavirus is sweeping across the globe killing thousands of people along its way. If you are reading this now, it will seem a distant memory and the human race will have survived.

FOREWORD

Sadly I never had the pleasure of flying with John Tye, as I retired (kicking and screaming) in 1992, some years before he joined the very special family that is the Concorde fleet. So I have only got to know him in the last twenty years or so, meeting at Concorde social gatherings at Brooklands or at the Royal Air Force Club. I realised from the outset that John was a 'doer', organising Concorde reunions at Brooklands (which bears comparison to herding cats!) and conducting video interviews for the archives with original crew members to capture their recollections of her entry into service.

Reading this book has simply served to confirm the impressions I had already formed about him. He is a very remarkable chap who has had to overcome many challenges in his life. His inspirational story is an example for any aspiring pilot who might feel discouraged by the obstacles that have to be overcome on the way. John exemplifies the determination necessary for success; obstacles are there to be overcome.

He tells his story with humour and reveals much about himself in the process, notably his compassion for the underprivileged and for those with disabilities, as you will see when you get to India with him or go flying with him on the British Airways Dreamflights. Above all, you will discover that he has had to overcome his own personal disabilities as well as various setbacks on his path to becoming a professional pilot, which I knew nothing about until reading this truly inspirational book. Having said that, I am sure he would be the first to acknowledge that he couldn't have achieved all that he has without the support of his wonderful wife Lynne. The Tye family are a very close-knit team – as will become clear as you turn the pages.

For any young person dreaming of becoming a pilot this book is an absolute must. It has been a privilege for me to learn so much about John Tye, whose life ethic can be summed up in the motto of the Royal Air Force: *Per ardua ad astra*.

Captain John Hutchinson

1

THE EARLY YEARS
(1957 TO 1976)

HOW IT ALL BEGAN

'Look at his lovely blue eyes. Can we keep him?' Allegedly the words uttered by two wonderful people in Sunbury-on-Thames as I lay in a pram in the sunshine in the summer of 1958. Erica and Ron took me in for a few weeks to give my foster parents a break. I never left them. Even at just a few weeks old, it was clear my legs were somewhat abnormal and there was concern that I might never walk properly. Forty years later, I was a Concorde pilot. How did that happen?

I never knew the full story of how I came into this world for another sixty years. I had a wonderful, stable, loving upbringing by Mum and Dad. I never knew them as anything else. Dad was an engineer with the Post Office, which later became part of British Telecom. Mum had previously worked at the BP research centre in Sunbury.

Karen had a tough start to her very short life. She was Mum and Dad's only natural daughter, born on 4 July 1957. She spent most of her short life in and out of hospital before sadly passing away just six months later, before I came onto the scene.

How any parent can ever get over losing a child is beyond me, and I'm not sure they ever did. Some fifty years later, they were to go through the same dreadful ordeal again.

Lucille was the bonniest baby of the bunch and I took a shine to her straight away when we visited the Barnardo's children's home in early 1962. I was only about 4 and didn't appreciate the responsibility at the time, when we went out to 'choose a sister' for me. It probably wasn't quite as simple as that, with much paperwork and vetting undoubtedly going on behind the scenes, but when she was formally adopted on 17 December 1962, our family was complete.

Family photos show us all growing up happily together in the three-bedroom detached house in Lower Sunbury that Mum and Dad had bought from new in 1955. They never moved from there and it still stands, virtually unchanged, with a lovely family growing up there now.

Lucille and I were three years apart. Despite my leg deformities, I learned to walk and run fairly normally, albeit with some issues. We would play together in the lovely back garden, building camps and forts under the apple trees, with occasional squabbles like any brother and sister, but life was good.

Our family holidays, typical for the 1960s, involved an eight-hour car journey to the English Riviera: either Torquay or Paignton, Minehead in Somerset, or perhaps a slightly shorter expedition to Bournemouth. As a 5-year-old, one of my favourite pastimes was sailing my toy yacht on the boating lake by Goodrington Sands with Dad. Such wonderful days with those memories revisited whenever I see that same yacht stored carefully in our loft.

I remember making sandcastles, watching Punch and Judy, riding on the steam train, and when I was a little older, riding the bumper cars at the fair. That long journey to the far-flung West Country would take all day in our Morris Minor, Austin 1100, or by the early 1970s, wait for it, a Hillman Avenger. We would break the journey with a picnic halfway, more often than not sitting among the stones at Stonehenge, which you could do in those days. They weren't fenced in until 1977.

Those early holidays were only some fifteen years after the end of the Second World War, but I was unaware of that bleak, deadly past. Our family had come through it largely unscathed. I knew little of Dad's involvement in the war, but as I grew older I learned that it was something rather secret. Now that he has gone, the papers that I have unearthed reveal little. He was a signatory to the Official Secrets Act and was, through his work with the Post Office, an expert in 'communications'. Sadly, he never spoke of it, but he was probably involved with Bletchley Park, communications in Churchill's war bunkers or, more likely, secret radar development work with the Telecommunications Research Establishment (TRE) in Dorset. That's all I know about his secret work. I intend to investigate further in retirement.

As a goofy 5-year-old with a crooked fringe, I started my education at the local junior school, Manor Lane, later renamed as Chennestone. They were happy days and I made many lifelong friends. It was quite normal in those days for us to be walking to school alone by the age of 7 or so. It was a quiet fifteen-minute walk through a small residential area, so relatively safe, even by modern standards.

I remember the headmaster, Mr Turnill, being quite strict, but that was probably a good thing, and Mr Williams, the deputy head, was everybody's favourite with a warm, friendly Welsh accent and a constant smile.

Our family home in Lower Sunbury was about 5 miles south of Heathrow, or London Airport as it was called then. As I write, the debate over a third runway at Heathrow is still ongoing and is likely to be for many years to come. When I was a youngster growing up, starting to develop an interest in those various flying machines of all shapes and sizes, London Airport had six runways. When the wind was blowing from the north-west, the inbound traffic would come right past my bedroom window as the planes made their approach to Runway 33L. Those cross-runways have long since been decommissioned to make way for new terminal buildings and cargo sheds.

Dad was a genius. Keen to support my developing interest in aviation, he built me a very clever piece of equipment. A small box with plywood sides and a couple of knobs on the front could be placed next to a normal transistor radio and it would convert the VHF receiver to a higher, air-band, frequency so it could pick up the communications between the control tower at London Airport and the inbound pilots. I'd spend many hours in the early 1960s sitting in my makeshift control tower guiding the aircraft safely in.

Constellations, DC-3s, Argosies and various other slow, noisy aircraft were commonplace, some with nearly as many vertical fins as propellers. As time went on, the BEA Vanguards and Viscounts gave way to the BAC 1-11 and then the Trident and intercontinental VC10 and Boeing 707. We would often have a wonderful day out to Heathrow taking the bus to the central area and watching all the movements from close quarters on the roof of the late Queen's Building.

My fascination for aircraft was firmly established by the time I was 6 in 1964.

Dad was very strict with me and did his best to keep me from going off the rails as I grew up. A challenge at times I'm sure, but I'm so glad he did. He was very intelligent himself and excelled in all things mathematical and electronics based. My air band radio receiver was just the start. By the time I was 8 I had a full set of Meccano and we would spend hours together inventing and building no end of clever things. The most memorable was a triangular-shaped robot with two electric motors. We made sensors out of hinged pieces of metal that, when activated, would turn the steering and set the robot off in another direction. This thing would wander around the lounge for hours and every time it bumped into the sofa or a wall, it would set off on another trajectory. If we'd thought to turn this technology into a lawnmower or a vacuum cleaner we would have become millionaires.

My train set won Dad many awards, not for its breathtaking realistic scenery, because there wasn't any, but for its technical wizardry. It was built, by both of us, of course, upon a 7ft × 5ft sheet of hardboard, which when not in use, could be stored against my bedroom wall. There were switches, diodes, resistors, transistors and many other electronic components all joined together in a logical order to make things work. I learned how to solder by the time I was 9, and how to hide burn holes in the carpet soon thereafter.

The trains would ease out of the platform on schedule, with plenty of empty seats in those days, and make their way around the board, their engines pulling hard to get up the hill to the second level. The centrepiece was a crossroads where two main lines crossed. Sensors would detect an approaching train, activate signals and the associated red light on the other line would bring the conflicting locomotive to a halt, thus averting disaster. It was all very clever and much more than a toy train set.

Dad would spend hours with me, particularly once homework accompanied me home from school. I'd have to sit at the table in the lounge with the TV off and work diligently until it was all done. If I had any problems with maths he would patiently explain it all to me. He would turn anything and everything into a mathematical problem to solve. I think of Dad often when I'm doing the same with my adorable grandson, Harvey. Being a typical boy, as I got older I got lazier, and homework became such a bore. Once I was shut in the room alone, I'd often put the TV back on quietly and sneakily catch up on the comings and goings in *Z Cars* or *Dixon of Dock Green*, the latest 'cops and robbers' shows. That was until I got caught! A severe telling off followed and the fuse was removed from the plug for the TV. Oh well, back to the homework.

Dad invented a computer.

The computer was, again, built from bits. There were things called relays and valves, many of which were to be found in telephone exchanges in the 1960s. Funny that. He laid them out on a board and, using an old basic keyboard, connected all sorts of electronic components together once again. When it had warmed up and the valves were glowing orange inside, you could get this ingenious device to do calculations for you. It was an early-day calculator but certainly not of the pocket variety. Dad was my hero because he could build and invent things and nurture the imagination of his young son.

Dad was a quiet, introverted chap – a boffin type really. He was very active in St Mary's church in Lower Sunbury and set up their first PA system, often tinkering with it mid-service to ensure the best sound reproduction, much to the vicar's frustration.

Hi-fi, as it was known then, was his other passion. He would listen to classical music and I still have an original wind-up gramophone with a fold-out horn on it, that he inherited, which must date back to the early 1900s. The sound quality is dreadful. Dad was what we might call a perfectionist, and over the years, he strove to achieve the best sound production from his equipment.

By 1972 he had conducted much research into sound waves, frequencies and amplitudes, resonance and materials to build loud speakers. Our lounge was transformed into a workshop.

A trial single corner-shaped 6ft tall monstrosity emerged several weeks later and, as a family, we were presented with an incredible sound from this unique speaker. This was rather like 001 in the Concorde assembly line though, a pre-production prototype. After much tinkering and even more research, Dad disappeared back into the workshop again. The lounge was, once more, out of bounds. This time special tools were bought. If he couldn't get what he wanted he would make it. Jigs and clamps filled the room and the smell of glue was overpowering at times. Eventually, two enormous wooden cabinets emerged, each 83in tall, 16½in wide and 12in deep. I know that because I'm sitting in front of them today listening to Dire Straits as I write, nearly fifty years after they were built.

Even to this day you'll struggle to find a better natural sound reproduction. The secret is in the piping inside. They are called transmission line speakers. Dad wrote a detailed technical article about how he had developed this technology across two editions of *Hi-Fi Monthly* in the autumn of 1974.

Around 1976 I became friends with the bass guitarist with Manfred Mann's Earth Band, Colin Pattenden. He certainly knew much about LOUD speakers and accurate sound reproduction. He was fascinated by my tales of what Dad had built and came around for a demonstration. Colin thought about the commercial opportunities for such a wonderful piece of furniture that reproduced music to the best quality imaginable. It wasn't long before we had a couple of Japanese gentlemen from Sony in our lounge for a demonstration. Perhaps this invention would make us millionaires even if the self-driving lawnmower principle had passed us by.

It wasn't to be as they weren't suitable for mass production. They agreed that the sound quality was better than anything else they produced at the time, but they were far too specialised to take their interest any further.

They remain unique and very special to me. They are enormous and some might be as rude to say an eyesore in our small lounge. My wife, Lynne, is most understanding.

In those days we didn't express our feelings and love for our parents like we do now and it wasn't until much later in life I told Dad how much I appreciated all that he did for me. If he hadn't inspired me, shown me all these clever things as a child, been strict with me and made sure I did my homework properly, I wouldn't have been in Seville in February 1999, counting backwards from three.

When he was an old man, inspired by the Mike and the Mechanics song 'In the Living Years', I did hug Dad, told him I loved him, and thanked him for everything he had done for me. He died three days after the Concorde crashed in Paris on 25 July 2000, the 114th (indirect) victim of that dreadful accident, as I'll explain later.

Lucille was growing up three years behind me. We got along well most of the time but, of course, being from totally different natural backgrounds, we lacked the bond of blood siblings.

We had lovely neighbours in Sunbury and Mark next door was a similar age, as were Peter and Elizabeth three doors away.

Their dad, who we called 'Uncle Jack', was another hero of mine. He had a garage full of tools and lathes and would make all sorts of things to amuse us. Pedal cars and go-karts would emerge from his workshop after many late nights and much noise. Jack worked at a place called BAC Weybridge, which I didn't know much about, apart from the fact it had something to do with aeroplanes. As I got older I learned more about what went on there and what he actually did. During the 1960s they were building a new supersonic airliner. Apparently Britain and France, which I learned was a country not far away on the other side of the Channel, were working together on this new invention. It was all very exciting and much of it was being built at Weybridge, just a few minutes' drive from our home. Jack was very involved in the design and development of the electrical system for Concorde. Who would ever have thought, that, forty years later, I'd be moving switches and sending 'wiggly amps' through those very electric cables as I piloted that supersonic marvel. Once Jack retired he continued as a volunteer at what was by now Brooklands Museum.

He helped maintain the VC10 and Concorde once she was exhibited there. It was an honour for me to see him, late in his life, enthralled by my tales of flying the very aircraft he helped design and build.

SCOUTING FOR BOYS

Robert Baden-Powell took some youngsters camping on Brownsea Island in Dorset in 1907. It was a great adventure and the following year he wrote a book, *Scouting for Boys*. In 1910 he left the army and founded the Boy Scout Association. I joined the 1st Sunbury troop, which had its headquarters in a converted school building in Lower Sunbury. It was the making of me. I joined just before my time at Chennestone finished, aged 10, and made many more lifelong friends.

We would meet once a week, on a Friday, and dash to catch last orders at the local fish and chip shop when we finished. We would go camping, learned to cook on open fires, build large structures out of wooden poles and ropes and have sports days and trips away. We would earn much sought-after badges as we qualified in first aid or orienteering, whatever that was.

I went on to become a patrol leader and by the time I was 15, I was developing my management skills keeping the young brats, I mean Scouts, in order and leading a team of six boys, pitting our skills in various games or competitions against the other patrols.

Our Scout Leader was a wonderful inspiration to us all. As we trod the delicate path into our teenage years, Ray had the perfect balance, keeping us in order, while letting us spread our wings and learn some valuable life skills along the way. Ray was sadly taken from us prematurely in his early 50s with that wicked motor neurone disease (MND). It was dreadful for us to see somebody who was so fit and energetic slowly waste away.

Before Ray lost his battle with MND he led us all into the grown-up Venture Scouts, now renamed Explorers. Our trips away became more adventurous with minimal red tape and bureaucratic hurdles. We would go camping and potholing in the Mendip Hills in Somerset and mountain climbing in Snowdonia. Lulworth Cove was another popular destination and by the time we were 16 or 17 we had our own cars or motorbikes and would often travel down to Dorset in convoy after school on a

Friday night. I drove a white Hillman Imp by then and anybody taking a lift with me had to share my taste in music. I had one cassette tape, *Bad Company* by Bad Company. All the way there and all the way back.

One of the highlights of the summer of 1975 was the First Sunbury Venture Scouts expedition to Corsica. We travelled by train and ferry to this beautiful French island in the Mediterranean, arriving at the picturesque port of Bastia, on the north-east corner.

We set up camp locally and made final preparations for our assault on Mount Cinto, the highest on the island at nearly 9,000ft/2,700m. I'd found Snowdonia a bit of a struggle, partly because of my leg issue, and this was three times as high.

It was wonderful walking through the foothills in the sunshine. We hardly saw anybody along the way but found it difficult to suppress a fit of giggles one afternoon when we passed a German couple going the other way … completely naked.

We set up camp each night in the hills and had a lucky escape one night when a team of noisy pigs came charging and foraging through the campsite. They ripped the tents apart, eating anything they came across but we'd had the experience and foresight to tie our food high up in the trees, so they passed the 1st Sunbury troop right on by.

As the air got thinner and the going got tougher, the group started to spread out a bit. The more energetic were striding ahead, while some of us were hanging back somewhat, with enthusiasm waning slightly. We were by now 18 and some of us had discovered beer, cigarettes and women.

The weather started to deteriorate with heavy thunderstorms forecast for the next few days. A planning meeting was called and we decided to split the group into two. The keen mountaineers would push on for the summit while the less energetic group would head back down and make for the west coast town of Calvi. We agreed we would meet there in a few days' time. As a former patrol leader, it was agreed that I had suitable leadership skills to steer our party downhill to safety on the coast.

We arrived in Calvi, found a suitable campsite and set up home. All we had to do now was to enjoy ourselves until the serious mountaineers returned. In between the showers the beach was lovely, the bikini-clad women even more so, and the beer was French and chilled.

Early one evening the heavens opened. The campsite was awash. The tents and most of our belongings were soaked through. I made an executive decision to lead the troops to safety. We abandoned the campsite and took minimal possessions into town. The lads looked upon me for leader-ship. I didn't disappoint.

We found a local hostelry that looked particularly welcoming. It had a red frontage, steps that led down to a bar area, and it was quite bustling for an early weekday evening. There were many friendly locals in there who found our arrival fascinating. The water from the torrential rain was flowing down the steps, so we had to roll our trousers up and keep our feet up on the chairs. The beer was quite expensive, but any port in a storm. Most of the clientele were young ladies but gentlemen of various ages and backgrounds came and went during the evening. While we thought we were worldly wise, in fact we were still quite young and naive and it was quite a while before this former patrol leader realised that he had managed to lead the 1st Sunbury Venture Scout unit to the local brothel.

I was introduced to motorcycles at the age of 16.

In fact, mopeds were all you could drive at that age, with a maximum 50cc engine size and a governed speed of 30mph. They had to be fitted with pedals that gave credence to the definition of moped. 'A small type of motorcycle equipped with bicycle pedals' was vague enough for the likes of Yamaha to produce the best-selling FS1E. They were quite expensive and several of my friends were treated to them by their generous parents. With their metallic yellow fuel tanks and distinctive exhaust scream they were the babe magnets of the day.

I saved up my pocket money and bought an old Raleigh Runabout, which was much more of a bicycle with an engine, rather than a motor-cycle with bicycle pedals. It was bright red with matching leg shields to protect you from the bracing wind at 29mph. The Post Office delivery riders had used them in the post-war years. It cost me £16 and I loved it. I was proud that I bought it with my own money too. Dad let me keep it in the shed at the end of the garden as long as I was careful and always closed the door. It was part shed and part greenhouse, and Dad's tomatoes were a delight to behold.

I had just turned 17 in the December of 1974 and had secured a part-time job as a banqueting porter at the local Elizabethan Hotel. I was invited to the staff Christmas party and now old enough to drink. Or so I thought.

Mum and Dad didn't drink. I'd seen them have a drop of something called 'whisky' every now and again, so as that's the only thing I'd heard of, I ordered one of those accompanied by something called 'American', which was supposed to dilute it and make it last longer. The drinks were subsidised, so very cheap. The more you drank the more you saved. I'd never experienced this strange feeling that slowly enveloped me but it was all rather pleasant. All right, I might have had the odd drop of cider or beer somewhere.

It was a Sunday evening and house rules were such that I had to be home by 10.30 p.m. on a Sunday. Fridays and Saturdays were more lenient with a 11 p.m. curfew and occasionally 11.30 p.m. for birthday parties or similar. Barely able to read my watch by now, I realised that I had to get cracking to get home in time. It was only about a mile to get home so what could possibly go wrong?

The magneto on my moped was getting a bit tired, so starting it was a real palaver, particularly on a cold December night. You had to pedal this thing round and round the car park to get it fired up. My balance wasn't too good for some reason, perhaps the cold air was getting to me, and I fell off a few times. It didn't hurt though and my good friends helped me out. They took turns pedalling it around until it fired into life and I was ready to get going. They even helped me on with my crash helmet and my imitation leather biker's jacket. I was all set to go.

It was a quiet lane that led up to the road home so I took it very carefully. Once in the hedge though, I had the presence of mind to make sure I didn't stall the engine knowing that my support team were now back in the bar and I certainly wouldn't be able to get this thing started again on my own. Keeping my right hand working the throttle then, I managed to free myself from the brambles and get back on my way. I was somewhat concerned as it must have been getting close to 10.30 p.m. by now.

I followed the road successfully, made the left turn OK into The Avenue, but our house was on the right, so this was going to be a challenge. Look, signal, manoeuvre was the order of events I'd been taught in my training, but it was the simple act of turning my head to look over my right shoulder that was my downfall. Perhaps a gust of wind had caught me at the crucial moment but I was fairly comfortable leaning against the fence of the house opposite ours having safely mounted the kerb and crossed the verge and pavement without any obvious damage. I was getting the hang of this now, but with the end in sight and success just about in the bag, I decided, most wisely, to push it from there. The entrance to the shed was only just wider than the handlebars so, under normal conditions, I'd stand behind the moped and walk it carefully in. This wasn't normal though and I must have stood behind it and flung it the rest of the way. Oops!

I'd hoped the sound of the glass smashing wouldn't be heard in the house and I could at least avoid the inevitable conflict until the next morning.

Nope! Dad was there to meet me as I staggered somewhat inebriated back down the garden path. 'Somewhat inebriated' was perhaps a bit of an understatement.

I was braced for an absolute rollicking, but all he said was, 'I hope you know you're going to have to fix that tomorrow,' or similar. All very reasonable under the circumstances.

I've never touched a drop since, of course. In actual fact, I couldn't stand the whiff of whisky for many years. I was bought a nice bottle of something special for my 60th and am working on it slowly and very carefully. I've seen what it can do to you if you're not careful.

Our group of Ventures, as we were known, all had bikes of some sort and once we turned 17 it was time to move up to mightier machines. Triumph Bonnevilles and Norton Commandos alongside big Suzukis and Kawasakis. Little old me saved up and bought a 1965 Honda 160, the smallest of the chapter.

Talking of 'chapters', the Richmond Hells Angels were a smashing bunch of young men. Yes, they looked pretty scary in their filthy, greasy jeans, big boots and leathers with their 'colours' on the back, but they had some wonderful motorcycles. With their Triumphs, BSAs, Royal Enfields and other great names, and with extended forks, raised handlebars and amplifiers instead of silencers, they sounded like a squadron of Lancasters as they cruised down the road. Every weekend in the summer they would gather on the island in the river in Sunbury. Us junior bikers would look up to them in awe.

We would drink cider in moderate doses. I'd learned one lesson already about drinking and driving. We'd smoke Players No. 6. They were the cheapest at the time and came in handy packets of ten. The Angels would sometimes smoke some other funny-smelling, home-made cigarettes, which were clearly rather precious as they had to share them around.

They were armed, of course, but only with fairly harmless bike chains and axes. The stories of sawn-off shotguns were clearly an exaggeration of the facts.

Around this time the charitable nature of the Ventures was coming out more. We organised Friday night discos to raise money for our Scout group. The headquarters building was very old and vital maintenance was coming up. We wanted to do our bit to help. The discos quickly became legendary and sold out quickly. This was good news but brought with it inevitable trouble. Gangs from as far away as Feltham would appear on fleets of Lambretta scooters and fights would break out. It wasn't pretty but our friends from the Richmond Chapter were keen to provide security for us and peace was quickly restored. Their visual presence was all that was required and our fundraising efforts continued enthusiastically. Not once was an axe or bike chain used in anger.

A group of us paid a total of just £8 for a BSA Bantam. A bargain between three of us. I'm not quite sure how we divided eight by three, but Dave (Spec), Pete (Kraut) and I bought it between us. We all had nicknames in those days and weren't sure where most of them came from. This rough and ready motorcycle certainly wasn't roadworthy and at 15/16 years old we certainly weren't either. We kept it tucked away behind the Venture Scout hut, an educational engineering project, you understand? It had no mudguards, number plates, lights or much at all really apart from a noisy 125cc engine and some dodgy brakes. We would take turns riding it over the gravel pits behind the Scout hut. We didn't have a helmet or a pair of gloves between us and, as it was a single-seater, those not riding would keep guard at the end of the road in case the police came along. Quite what we would do if they ever did, we weren't sure.

I lost control of this beast as I went through a ditch, up the other side and through an open gate into the adjoining school field. An immediate left turn was then required and that's where it all went wrong. The right handlebar struck the solid concrete post a split second after I'd taken my hand off it. My unprotected head continued its path and I hit the post just above my right eye.

The blood started to flow but I wasn't badly hurt. My main concern was how to get the bike back. The throttle cable and brake lever were hanging off and the handlebar badly bent. Scouting had taught us initiative, so I found a way of riding it back with the throttle cable wrapped around my right hand. The others had scarpered by the time I got the damaged machine back to the pits and I couldn't go home in this state, so I hid the bike and went to Nick's house nearby. He had really cool parents.

I wouldn't get such a telling off and his mum used to be a nurse so I was sure she could fix me up and nobody would be any the wiser.

'That'll probably need stitches,' said Nick's mum.

Luckily it didn't though; she was able to patch me up herself and by the time I got home I'd come up with some kind of tale about falling off my bicycle and hitting my head on a brick. The scar is still there today, mostly hidden by my right eyebrow.

EVENTFUL DAYS AT BIG SCHOOL

While all this Scouting for Boys was going on, my secondary education was progressing. I took the 11+ entrance exam and secured a place at Hampton grammar school, something I wouldn't have done if Dad hadn't taken the fuse out of the telly and made me knuckle down.

I started at Hampton in September 1969. Concorde had flown for the first time in March of that year and the Americans had landed a man on the moon in the July. Colour TV was just catching on for those who could afford it and appreciated BBC2, the first channel to broadcast this latest technology.

I had a new school uniform and was soon allowed to catch the bus on my own, changing at Hampton Station or walking the last mile if I missed the connection. I soon made new friends as most of my contemporaries had moved to the brand new Bishop Wand secondary school in Sunbury.

In September 2019 we were invited back, fifty years to the day since we had first walked down the long central drive at Hampton towards the imposing tower. It was wonderful to see old friends again and meet the new boys who were wearing the same uniform for the first time that day. None of us had changed in that time of course. I created a bit of a stir by wearing my school uniform, not the one I started with as an 11-year-old, but my sixth form outfit, which was only 44 years old. The black flared trousers were a little snug and the blazer tugged slightly but it went down well. In fact, it was the only time I ever made it into the school magazine.

Hampton was a good old-fashioned grammar school in those days, open only to boys who had passed the 11+. In the mid-1970s it changed to a fee-paying establishment and, as we saw on our recent return visit, has expanded significantly, with state-of-the-art facilities, creating tremendous opportunities for the boys.

We worked hard and played hard. The school had a long sporting history, with boys excelling in rowing and rugby in particular. My legs were quite strong in those days but my ankles were weak. The calf muscle in my right leg, in particular, was abnormally large, but my toes lacked strength and movement so my balance was poor. I couldn't run well even though a few laps of the enormous school field were compulsory on games afternoons. I fell over frequently and was always last. Sport wasn't for me.

Academically, I did OK. Maths, physics and geography were my A-level subjects and I achieved sufficiently good grades to be offered a place at City University to study Air Transport Engineering. I didn't go though.

The school Combined Cadet Force (CCF) was also the making of me. I joined the RAF section and was kitted out with a very itchy and heavy wool pair of trousers and a blouson, and black lace-up boots with toe caps that had to be polished to within an inch of their lives. Parade was a very disciplined affair on the school playground.

My interest in aviation flourished during this period of my life. I didn't like people shouting at me and making me march around the tarmac in all weathers, but I did like the idea of going flying. The school even had its own glider, armoury and shooting range.

The glider was fun, a very early single-seater that was launched by a bungee, rather like a large and powerful rubber band. It had spoilers fitted to the leading edges of the wings though to ensure it didn't get completely airborne. The wings would generate just enough lift to permit a short hop across the ground at an altitude of not much more than 3ft. We learned about the principles of flight and put into practice what we had learned in the classroom.

I definitely wasn't one of the group who found how to remove the spoilers and fly the thing over the fence into the girls' school next door, but it did happen. Once.

GETTING AIRBORNE – 1

My first flight ever was in a Chipmunk at RAF Benson sometime in the early 1970s. I remember not liking the smell of the rubber face mask and not taking too well to aerobatics, but having never even flown as a passenger in an airliner, it was wonderful to be airborne for the first time and look down at life in miniature beneath us. I took the controls and we played around the puffy white clouds and swooped low across the stripy fields, but all too soon, it was over. I was hooked though.

GETTING AIRBORNE (ALMOST) – 2

I had crashed the hovercraft into the bike sheds. Oops.

Wednesday and Friday afternoons were dedicated to games. As I've already explained, I really didn't take to any of these outdoor sports. I couldn't run without falling over. My legs were unstable and, to be honest, I was quite lazy. I stood on the boundary fielding in cricket a few times, but was never going to make a name for myself there. I spent much of the time watching the aircraft landing at Heathrow instead of the path of the ball. When the wind was in the west and they were landing on 28L, the southerly of the two runways, they would pass just over a mile to the north of the school field. I missed a few catches because I wasn't paying attention, but was watching these new enormous 747s coming in from all around the world.

The hobbies section of a local dairy, of all places, had started on a project to build a single-seat hovercraft. They had given up and kindly donated the box of bits to the Hampton Grammar CCF. My good friends, Graham Marley and Rob Brook, joined with me to form the Hovercraft Restoration Club. We were given special permission to work on this instead of doing games. We were in our element.

The bright-yellow chassis was intact and fitted with a sturdy red rubber skirt, unlike the girls at Lady Eleanor Holles school next door, who were gaining our interest around the same time. The box of bits included two chainsaw engines and various drive belts and fans.

The target was to have this thing working in time for a star appearance at the school open day at the end of term. We used bicycle brake levers mounted on a joystick for throttles, one for each engine. The first engine powered a downward-facing fan, which filled the skirt and lifted the craft off the ground, while the second engine drove the other fan, mounted facing rearwards behind the pilot, to provide forward thrust.

I set off on the first test flight late one afternoon on the grass area behind the bike sheds not far from the rifle range. Directional control in a hovercraft is a bit of an art, and I wasn't much good at art either. There was a rudder mounted behind the rear fan to direct the airflow as appropriate, but why can you never find a good hovercraft driving instructor when you need one?

With a tremendous amount of noise and flying grass cuttings (note to self: goggles required next time), off I went. All went well initially, but it wasn't long before the bike sheds started to become a bit proximate. Just to be on the safe side I thought I'd bring the beast to a halt. All I had to do was release both the throttles and the engine rpm would drop to idle. That was the idea anyway. In reality though, even at idle power there was enough airflow to keep the skirt inflated and some residual thrust from the rear-drive department. Releasing the throttles, in fact, just meant I hit the bike sheds at a lower speed than I would have done otherwise.

The damage to the bike sheds was fairly minor and with any luck they wouldn't even notice it.

Safely back in the workshop we discussed potential modifications.

To think that while we were doing this, the Concorde design and development teams, not far away at Weybridge, were having similar issues with their progress towards supersonic passenger flight; but I suspect there was a bit more science involved in their project.

It was simple really. We would fit an ignition cut-out switch. That would kill the engine immediately and ensure no residual thrust could carry us into further trouble. Off I went again. The magnetic effect of the bike sheds came into play once again so, somewhat smugly, I activated the new kill switch. It killed it all right, but we hadn't anticipated that the skirt wouldn't necessarily deflate symmetrically. The hovercraft stopped dead and the left side of the ship dived to the ground, flinging me out in the same direction in a most spectacular fashion.

It was quite an easy modification to fit a seat belt.

We worked long into the evenings approaching the open day to make sure our hovercraft was ready to display to all the guests. We were now ready for a final test flight but it was dark and we hadn't fitted any lights to our wonderful creation. The plan was to take her out for a proper run onto the main school field. It was a vast area, so less chance of hitting anything, with several rugby, cricket and football pitches. We knew we needed to see where we were going with big posts erected everywhere associated with these strange sports.

Graham led the way on his Honda 175 motorcycle with his headlight on full beam. All was going well and we felt we were well placed to perform a demonstration flight for the crowds at the weekend. With two unsilenced chainsaw engines going flat out behind a motorbike with a bright light, we fully understood why the neighbours had feared a gang of Hells Angels were ripping the school field to bits and called the police.

Luckily the police took no further action. It was all a simple misunderstanding.

Aircraft spotting was my favourite pastime and the school field was a perfect location. I'd spend all my tea and lunch breaks with the other enthusiasts in the best vantage points armed with our CAMs and 'poles' (telescopes.) The CAM was a paperback publication (*Civil Aircraft Markings*) with many of the world's civilian aircraft listed in order by their registrations. Some of the boys had enormous poles. Mine was quite small, and not quite powerful enough to read the registration letters from afar, but those with the better telescopes would read out the letters for us. We would underline them in our CAMs once a new sighting was confirmed.

Before I was old enough to go alone, Mum and Dad had taken me to the roof gardens on top of the Queen's Building at Heathrow to witness all the comings and goings from close quarters. Who could have guessed that I'd be working there in the not too distant future.

A biennial highlight was a trip to the Farnborough Air Show to watch all the latest flying machines being put through their paces, both military and civilian. The Red Arrows, of course, were everybody's favourite. I didn't know then that I would get to know the team well at the end of the millennium. Concorde was the star of the show in 1972 with test pilot

Brian Trubshaw putting on a fantastic display. Who would have guessed that … you know the rest.

The Vulcan Cold War bomber was another impressive machine. With a camouflaged delta-shaped wing and four Rolls-Royce Olympus engines, she bore a resemblance to Concorde and certainly made as much noise. It wasn't until many years later that I got to know the Vulcan display pilot, one Jon Tye, unrelated but now a good friend.

Concorde first flew in March 1969, exactly six months before I started at Hampton grammar. In the seven years that followed she was refined and tweaked. She matured and was made ready to go out into the big wide world, with the first commercial flight taking place exactly six months before I finished at Hampton.

It had taken exactly the same amount of time to make me ready for the big wide world, and I was a far simpler affair. Mum played a big part in that. I was now approaching the end of my teenage years and hadn't gone too far off the rails along the way. Cider, motorbikes and cigarettes were about as far as it went, although, like any teenager, I'd probably caused Mum and Dad a few sleepless nights. Lucille was doing well at Bishop Wand school and arguably gave them a few more sleepless nights along the way. She was in the Brownies as a young girl, but it wasn't really for her and by the time she was in her teens she was keen to join the army, an ambition she went on to fulfil, albeit briefly.

As in most homes, Mum held the family together. She had given up work to have Karen, the sister I never met, and took on a full-time job, looking after us all. The house was always immaculate. The parquet flooring in the hallway shone in the sunshine with the toothpaste in the gaps marking out a white staggered roadway to nowhere. Oh, hadn't I told you about that little mishap?

In the 1950s and '60s, pre-Amazon days, it was normal to have some household items sold at the door and each fortnight a nice man would come with the family supply of soap, washing powder, cloths and, yes, toothpaste. Money would change hands on the doorstep, all very legal of course, despite the fact that wartime rationing only ended three years before I was born. Mum would put these items out of my reach on the banister at the bottom of the stairs until she made her next trip to the only bathroom at the top of them. They weren't always out of my reach, of course, as I was a growing boy. The cap on the toothpaste tube was easily undone and the contents squeezed in a most artistic fashion into the parquet floor until I was caught red-handed. I can't recall if that was categorised as a 'wait until your father gets home' level of punishment, or was dealt with by just a mild ticking off from Mum, probably with a slight smile of amusement. It was nothing that a decent rug, and later when they could afford it, a fitted carpet, couldn't put right.

Mum spent most of her time, like everybody's mum in those days, cooking, cleaning, washing and gardening. She was always welcoming to my school friends and while reminiscing recently in our 60s, David reminded me how she would always offer you a cup of tea, regardless of your age, the size of your motorbike or the length of your hair.

All mums are special, but it wasn't until 2016 I appreciated how special she was, when she was awarded the British Empire Medal in the New Year's Honours List. I'll explain more later.

THE SUPERSONIC ERA BEGINS AND LOTS OF BROKEN CHINA

'3-2-1 Now,' announced Captain Norman Todd as he applied full power to launch supersonic commercial services at 11.40 a.m. on 21 January 1976. Sitting in the co-pilot's seat was Captain Brian Calvert and behind them was Senior Flight Engineer John Lidiard.

Much later in life I found myself in the same hospital ward as Captain Todd as he was recovering from a car accident. A party broke out when many visitors from the Concorde family arrived to celebrate an anniversary of some sort, perhaps that first commercial flight. Just over forty-two years later, I was privileged to spend time with John Lidiard and his wife Anne at their home in Bristol, just a month before he passed away. He had some fantastic stories to tell about the early Concorde days. I was there with a film crew to capture them all for future generations.

Here I was clinging to my precious piece of chain-link fence along with my good friend Graham (from the Hovercraft Restoration Society) on the perimeter of Heathrow, close to Hatton Cross. At 11.40 a.m. precisely, the gleaming profile of Concorde commenced her rapid acceleration down Runway 28L. The reheat lit up. The ground shook and thousands of people watched in awe as supersonic passenger flight commenced. A hundred paying passengers or invited guests were riding in luxury on their way through the sound barrier to the edge of space for the very first time, and we were there to witness this grand historic occasion.

Quite how we came to be there instead of in double geography on a Wednesday morning, I'm not quite sure, but we'll gloss over that bit.

I recently gave one of my Concorde talks to a local group and told that story, including the bit about bunking off double geography. Afterwards, a lovely elderly gentleman came up to me and said, 'Did you say you went to school at Hampton? My name is Tony Creber. I was your geography master!'

If somebody had bet me a million pounds that one day I would fly that very aeroplane, I would have laughed and not taken the bet. Another missed opportunity to become a millionaire.

The summer of 1976 was the hottest ever and the year we were taking our A-levels. Our whole future depended on the results and we had benefited from six years of the best education and opportunities, so the pressure was on. In hindsight, I'm not sure the deck at Sunbury outdoor swimming pool was the most effective venue for last-minute revision, but the sun was hot and the girls were pretty.

SCHOOL'S OUT FOR SUMMER

The title of Alice Cooper's big hit in 1972 and one that was played endlessly every summer at the end of the school academic year in the 1970s. It was time to move on to the next stages of our lives. Our days at Hampton had flown by. We'd learned much more than we realised at the time, formed lifelong friendships and we would remember some of the masters (teachers) fondly, particularly the strictest ones for some reason. Ernie (Mr Badman to you), for example, would command immediate respect and silence as soon as he entered the room, mainly because he would frighten the living daylights out of you. He taught maths and history and you would also learn how to duck and dive without hesitation, to avoid the flying board rubber that was coming your way after your momentary lack of concentration had been noticed.

While we awaited our A-level results it was appropriate to find some part-time summer employment to keep our motorbikes running and fund our developing social lives. I'd already had a weekend job as a banqueting porter. Remember the staff Christmas party? By the time I was 17 and still at school, a few of us were taken on at Hampton Court Palace. Well, the Tiltyard Cafe in the grounds to be more accurate. It was great fun, hard work and we had to work every weekend, but were paid double time on Sundays and bank holidays.

I was qualified to make sandwiches, load the industrial dishwasher, clear the tables, work the tills and chat up the girls. Pranks and practical jokes brightened up the long days. It honestly wasn't me who put one of our disposable paper hats in a tuna mayonnaise baguette, but I must confess to following its progress on to the counter and a tourist's tray soon after.

Mr Engle, the general manager was fair, but firm. He would pose as a customer when he did his spot check rounds, but the pact was that whoever spotted him in the queue first was duty bound to announce his arrival loudly in the kitchen. He only ever saw us at our best and the final warning he gave me was delivered in a fair and friendly manner.

I'd been taking part in one of our regular staff competitions and was well placed to win. The challenge was to see who could get the most plates, cups and saucers on their trolley when clearing the tables. 'Yes sir,' was the answer I gave Mr Engle when he discreetly suggested I was perhaps dangerously overloaded and should return to the kitchen to unload. I was by now a skilled trolley operator, so managed to uplift a few more place settings before heading for base. The slight slope up to the dishwasher loading area was a bit of a challenge, but could be managed if you took a bit of a run at it. I never did find out who placed the upside down teaspoon at the top of the slope, which had a similar effect to the cut-out switch in our hovercraft. I hadn't quite made the finish line and Mr Engle wasn't impressed.

Clockwise from top left: Me aged 2 or 3; with Lucille (8 and 5); Scouts and Guides (14 and 11); on holiday in 1965.

Dad with my 'award-winning' train set.

Dad with one of his *loud*-speakers, 1972.

Clockwise from top left: The hovercraft, with the bike sheds behind, June 1976; me and my Honda 160 with Mickey Mouse bendy toy on the front; me and the Raleigh Runabout, before it went through the greenhouse.

Me as a sixth-former at Hampton, 1976.

Wearing the same uniform, forty-three years later.

2

OUT INTO THE
BIG WIDE WORLD
(1976 TO 1987)

PLANES, POP STARS AND A GLASS IN THE HEAD

Chris Tarrant was the breakfast show DJ on Capital Radio in the late 1990s and into the next century. He was a passenger on Concorde on a flight I piloted to New York in April 2000 and I had the opportunity to tell him how Capital Radio had played a part in me becoming a Concorde pilot.

Capital Radio Jobspot was a short advertising segment of the breakfast show each day in the mid-1970s. A jolly jingle heralded the promotion of the day's vacancies and one in particular caught my ear over breakfast. Revenue accounts clerks (with eventual promotion to Concorde pilot) were being recruited by British Airways. Well OK, I made up the bit in brackets, but British Airways was a name that conjures up thoughts of prestige, pride and patriotism. I applied straight away, not that I had any desire to work in an accounts department, but it was at the airport and I'd had enough of clearing tables at Hampton Court Palace.

My A-level results came through and despite my somewhat lazy attitude to last-minute revision, I was awarded the grades I needed to secure my place at City University in London. I had a place to study Air Transport Engineering. It was to be a sandwich course, where you spent six months at university studying, followed by six months in industry gaining practical experience.

The industrial filling in the sandwich was, for successful applicants, to be provided by British Airways, but I didn't make the grade. The university instead offered me the opportunity to embark on a full-time mechanical engineering course for three years.

I started at British Airways in revenue accounts on 9 August 1976.

It was meant to be a summer holiday job before going to university, but I stayed in the business for over forty-six years. It was a tough decision, but I didn't take that university place.

The salary was £2,227 a year. The work was dull – sticking labels on bits of paper – but I was on the ninth floor of Technical Block C (TBC), on the airport perimeter in an open-plan office, with fantastic views across the airport. I was very well placed to continue my aircraft spotting and feel connected with all the goings-on at Heathrow.

Once employed within the airline it was always easier to move around and develop your career internally. Staff Vacancy Notices (SVNs) were posted on the board each Friday and it wasn't long before I found myself moving on.

Just five months later, on 3 January 1977, I started work as, wait for it, a flight deck services assistant on a massive £3,320 a year. Based in the Queen's Building, just two floors down from where Mum and Dad used to take me to watch the planes, I was part of a team compiling the Aircraft Library – all the manuals, maps and charts that the pilots needed for their voyages. I was fitted with a smart uniform and had to take a driving test to get my airside licence.

It was shift work and the 6 a.m. starts were a bit of a challenge. I was still technically a teenager after all. Sometimes you would spend the whole shift underground compiling the library and making up a big canvas bag of documents, but the best role was being out in the field. I'd be allocated my van for the day and be responsible for collecting the bag of documents and placing each manual or chart in the allocated stowage on the aircraft.

Here I was, driving a van and going on board aircraft of all different shapes and sizes, including Concorde. I was meeting pilots, had a walkie-talkie radio, and got to flirt with stewardesses. I couldn't give that up to go to university.

I soon learned to be punctual meeting the inbound aircraft to secure my spot in the throng of other ground staff who were experienced at 'raiding the larder'. The leftovers from first class in the 747 kitchens were highly sought after and the rear galley of Concorde after it pulled onto its parking spot, J2 at Terminal 3, was so crowded it was a wonder the aircraft didn't tip on its tail.

Each time the intercontinental 707s, VC10s, 747s and Concorde returned home, all the manuals had to be removed and returned to the Aircraft Library for checking, updates and repairs. There were quite a few and they were heavy. It was good exercise lugging the heavy-duty green canvas bags up and down the stairs from the tarmac. There were performance manuals, navigation manuals, technical manuals, spare forms and, it seemed, the larger the aeroplane, the larger the books.

The first time I went on board a mighty 747 I was just blown away. Remember I'd only ever been in a Chipmunk RAF trainer before. This was something different altogether. Even once you were on board the air-craft itself, the flight deck was another flight of stairs up. A spiral staircase as well. That was tricky with several heavy canvas bags.

I had to sit down. Partly because I was out of breath after what seemed like climbing up to the third floor of a block of flats (which in fact it was), but mainly because when I entered the flight deck itself, I was just so over-whelmed. The two pilots' seats were at the front. Obviously. The flight engineer's seat was facing sideways towards an impressive panel covered in switches, dials and orange, green and red lights. I took time to look around to see if I could work out what any of it did. A few things made sense. The radios, for example, but most of what I studied was far beyond my level of comprehension. As I stretched across the co-pilot's seat to access the manual stowage at floor level alongside it, it didn't occur to me that in just over twelve years' time I'd be climbing into that very seat wearing a different uniform to actually fly the beast. A lot of water had to go under various bridges first though.

My time in the Queen's Building was fun and I was right in the midst of all the action, a vital part of the operation. I got to know a few of the pilots. The short-haul crews would fly around Europe and be found regularly in the crew report centre in the next room. The long-haul crews would have different procedures and head off to exotic, far-flung places around the globe, often away for up to three weeks.

Pete Rae and Chris Hawkes were a couple of Vanguard pilots I got to know quite well. The Vanguard was a large turboprop aircraft that had now been converted from its passenger-carrying role to cargo and been renamed the Merchantman.

Chris cleared it with his captain and invited me to go along for the ride one day in the late summer of 1977. We went across the Channel, over the Alps and into the industrial centre of Turin in Italy. As we crossed the Alps, much lower than modern jet aircraft, you could look down and see people walking in the snow. I had never seen such breathtaking views, my flying experience to date being limited to the aerobatics in the Chipmunk over Oxfordshire.

We thought we'd be stuck there for days. We couldn't fly back with a cargo door warning light glowing red on the instrument panel. Chris and the captain had checked visually that the enormous hydraulically operated door on the side of the aircraft was closed, but the cockpit indications said otherwise. Something needed adjusting, possibly just a micro switch, but the red light had to be extinguished somehow.

I had to be careful not to fall out of the cargo door as we taxied out. The pilots had started the engines and had permission to proceed slowly along the taxiway as they operated the door. It was hinged at the top. They opened it a few inches with me standing on the bottom ledge and then slammed it shut with my weight contributing to the downwards momentum. That, combined with the airframe flexing and vibrating, fixed it. The door was shut and the light extinguished.

On the way back the captain vacated his seat and let me have a go at the controls. Here I was hand flying a Vanguard over the Alps in the clear blue skies. The flight controls were quite heavy compared to the Chipmunk, but I soon got the hang of it.

These guys got paid for doing this every day. I only had three A-levels though. The intelligence and skills required were surely beyond me? In hindsight, though, this was probably a life-changing experience, the first time I ever thought realistically about becoming a pilot.

Chris and Pete rented a house together with two stewardesses just around the corner from our family home in Sunbury. We frequented the same village pubs and I'd often be back at theirs after closing time. This pilot lifestyle seemed pretty good, both on and off the aeroplane. They seemed regular guys, not supermen. Maybe I did have the ability to become an airline pilot? Oh well, maybe one day.

Growing up in the 1970s was fun. It was a good decade to be a teenager. The music was great. You had to be there to appreciate that though. Slade, The Bay City Rollers, Sweet, T-Rex, Blackfoot Sue, Mungo Jerry and so on so forth, if you liked glam rock. Led Zeppelin, Deep Purple and Black Sabbath, if your hair was long enough to like plain rock.

The clothes were great, too. You had to be there to get that as well though. I'm still hoping my flares will come back into fashion one day.

On the banks of the Thames and just a short walk (stagger) from home, the Magpie was a great pub in Lower Sunbury that Chris and Pete introduced me to. It became a regular haunt. My work in the Aircraft Library was on a shift basis, so I'd often pop in on the way home from work on my own. Closing time, officially 10.30 p.m. on weekdays, was a bit of a variable feast thanks to the relationship the landlord had with the local constabulary.

One or two nights of the week they had live music in the upstairs bar and I dashed in one night, hastily disguising my BA uniform as I went through the door, to the sound of something rather familiar. There was

Mungo Jerry belting out some great pub jug band music. Well, three-quarters of the band anyway. Not the lead singer with the big sideburns, whatever his name was, but the other three: Paul King, Colin Earl and Joe Rush. They even had a toy monkey strapped to a microphone stand with a couple of double AAs up his you know what playing the cymbals in time to the music. He had a name too – Reg. The 'four-piece' was made up with Colin Pattenden from Manfred Mann's Earth Band. I've already told you how he was fascinated by Dad's loudspeakers, and they've all been good friends of ours ever since, still belting out the big hits in various drinking establishments around Surrey.

In the late 1970s the Goat in Upper Halliford Village, Shepperton, became a fantastic venue for live music. Denny Laine from Paul McCartney's band Wings lived in the next village and would often join the others on stage.

On 16 January 1978 Laine had just finished singing 'Mull of Kintyre' – which he had written with Paul and Linda McCartney and was still at number one after being the 1977 Christmas chart-topper – as the finale to a wonderful musical evening. The lights came on and a fight broke out. 'Come on lads, break it up,' were the last words I remember saying before I was knocked to the floor and a broken beer glass sliced into my neck. Colin Pattenden's wife saved my life by keeping her thumb pressed hard on the wound until the ambulance arrived.

I felt my attacker, a known local 21-year-old hooligan, should have got more after nearly taking my life. The judge at the Old Bailey sent him away for eight months for grievous bodily harm.

They patched me up in hospital and kept me in overnight. I needed twenty stitches. When I was released the next day I felt fine, so rather than bother Mum any more, I thought I'd get the bus home. The 216 stopped right outside the hospital and again, nearly an hour later, close to home.

When conducting my research, my good friend from Scouts, Dave Miller, reminded me of that day when I flagged him down from the back seat of the 216 bus and he ended up giving me a lift the rest of the way home from the hospital, 'where they had been removing a pint glass from your skull,' he said. Don't exaggerate. It was a half-pint glass.

The atmosphere and the music never returned to the Goat after that night and it's now a fairly average carvery restaurant.

I was offered promotion from my job in the Aircraft Library, running around in a van, having lots of fun putting all the maps and books on board the aircraft. I had been to grammar school after all and was qualified to do better than that, or so the boss told me, encouraging me to be more ambitious. I became an assistant flight data officer. Impressive, eh? I was now going to learn how to calculate all the aircraft take-off and landing Aerodrome Operating Minima (AOM) and publish them in those very manuals that I'd been lugging up the aircraft steps for the last ten months. It was 14 November 1977 when I took up this new role at the former BEA headquarters, Bealine House in Ruislip, about 5 miles north of Heathrow. I wasn't sure about going back to office work though.

I wasn't quite 20 years old and was by far the youngest in the department. The next youngest, Chris Burch, was ten years older than me, and was away on his honeymoon when I started on that Monday morning. Everybody else in the small department seemed ancient. They made me welcome though. I had my own desk next to the window with six others in the office. The two managers and their secretaries were in the adjacent room with plush carpets and coffee machines. We didn't go in there very often but the highlight of my morning was when Lynne brought the mail in to us. She was rather gorgeous. She hasn't changed much in the last forty-five years.

Not only was she rather pretty but she drove a really cool car, a Triumph GT6 with a six-cylinder, 2-litre engine, and she was a girl! They didn't do that sort of thing in those days. I hesitate to admit that I drove a Morris Marina, but it was a coupe. Eventually I plucked up the courage to ask Lynne to take me for a ride in her car one lunchtime. Smooth, eh? The rest, as they say, is history.

When Chris came back from his honeymoon we hit it off straight away. We had a similar background and I soon learned that he was aspiring to be an airline pilot. He already had his private pilot licence (PPL) and at weekends he would work as a flying instructor or take friends on a pleasure flight to the Channel Islands. He was building up his hours to gain enough experience to gain a licence to fly professionally. This proved a further inspiration to me.

My role changed and evolved over the next couple of years and eventually I had the opportunity to apply for promotion to assistant aerodromes and performance officer, based in the same office. I was invited for a formal interview. That letter was dated 20 August 1979 and signed by Lynne

Norman. She was the boss's secretary, the one I had my eye on. I was successful and was to be part of a small, elite team. They were responsible for monitoring the suitability of existing airports for BA aircraft and approving any new destinations, as well as calculating all the crucial take-off and landing performance data. The pay was good, just over £5,000 a year now.

Back in November 1978 I had applied to the College of Air Training at Hamble, near Southampton. It was where British Airways sent their cadets to learn how to fly and join the airline as junior pilots. Chris and Pete, my friends from the Aircraft Library days, had been there. The competition was very tough and the selection process long and involved. There were aptitude tests, interviews, team exercises and coordination skills tests. Incredibly I got through, just, and was placed on a waiting list. I was to become a British Airways pilot, as long as I completed all the training successfully of course.

Or not.

'You should seriously consider continuing with any plans you might have for an alternative career,' the letter said that arrived on 27 September 1979. British Airways, for whatever reason, had decided that there was to be no more sponsored pilot training for the foreseeable future. This was devastating news. It looked like I was destined to spend the rest of my career crunching numbers in a prefab office in Ruislip with a bunch of ancient people and a pretty secretary.

I'd go flying with Chris whenever I could and he would let me take the controls. It was fantastic and a world away from the somewhat dull routine of Bealine House.

A month before I received that devastating letter, Chris announced he had been offered a job as an airline pilot, having qualified for his commercial pilot licence (CPL). He was leaving us. A leaving party was organised at the staff social club across the road with drinks all around. After two lager shandies I'd mustered enough confidence to get to know Lynne better. We were the last to leave the party and would have secret clandestine meetings in the weeks that followed as our love for one another developed.

Within a year we knew we wanted to spend the rest of our lives together. We needed somewhere to live. Up until then I was still living at home with my mum and dad. Crunch day was one Saturday morning when I was down at the local garage with my friends tinkering with cars and motorbikes when Clifford arrived and said, 'Hey John. There's some blonde bird sitting on your garden wall.' I went back home straight away and Lynne soon became part of our gang and my lifelong soulmate.

Chris was posted to Aberdeen. He and his wife, Jasmine, owned their own house in Ashford, Middlesex. They didn't really want to sell it as they planned to return south one day. We needed a home together so a deal was struck. We rented the three-bedroom home from them, took in two lodgers and before we knew it, were covering our costs and living rent free. We would travel to work in Ruislip together and return again each evening.

We kept in touch with Chris and Jasmine (who were by now good friends) after they went to Aberdeen for him to start his flying career on the HS 748 with Dan-Air. They rented a house up there and soon made new friends, mainly other southerners who had emigrated north to take up flying posts. We were invited up to stay with them for a few days and a perfect opportunity presented itself in early 1980 when I was off work recovering from surgery on my foot.

As part of my strange condition, which hadn't really been diagnosed by this stage, my toes had little strength nor movement. They had a mind of their own and gradually those on the right foot had become entangled and misshapen to the extent that getting comfortable footwear was becoming an issue. I was referred to an orthopaedic surgeon, who said he could relieve some of this by cutting a section out of my hideously elongated second toe and straighten it out in the process. The surgery on 18 January 1980 went well and I initially blamed the effects of the anaesthetic for what I could see as I peered down the length of the hospital bed to inspect his handiwork.

A cork, from a fine bottle of Merlot I believe, was stuck firmly on the end of my toe. It was still there after I'd rubbed my eyes, blinked a few times and shaken my head. I sought confirmation from Lynne, who had just arrived to visit the patient, and indeed, it was for real. A titanium pin with a very sharp end had been installed in my modified digit to hold the two pieces together and to stop me catching the pin on the bedclothes, or anything else for that matter, a cork had simply been stuck on the end of it. The thought of it still makes me wince even now.

Needless to say, I couldn't drive like this, so I was signed off work for a few weeks and was under strict instructions to keep my leg raised as much as possible to expedite the healing process and to use the crutches provided for getting about. After a while I got quite fidgety and the novelty of spending the day on the sofa watching TV had started to wear off. A few days away in Aberdeen would surely not do me any harm.

There's a famous pub on the outskirts of Aberdeen where aircrew tended to assemble on a Friday night, or any other night of the week for that matter. I must admit I did feel a little precarious as the bar started to fill and the beer started to flow. I was careful to keep my crutches tactfully positioned to provide a degree of protection around my right foot and caught a few people out with my cork on the end of my toe trick.

We were made most welcome and met some great people, some of whom I would still know many years later as they went on to become captains with British Airways.

It was quite late at night by the time I was tendered a wonderful invitation. I'd got chatting with a helicopter pilot. The oil business was booming in Scotland and the North Sea in the early 1980s and Aberdeen was one of the busiest airports in Europe, with hundreds of helicopter operations ferrying workers to and from the oil rigs far out in the North Sea.

It was an early start the next day, but an opportunity I wasn't going to miss. I'd never been in a helicopter before and, feeling a little delicate from the previous evening's social events, I presented myself at the arranged rendezvous point behind the hangar. In no time at all we were airborne. I sat between the two pilots in this enormous Sikorsky S-61, G-BBGS, as we thudded along with the blades slapping in time with my thumping head, at what seemed just feet above the waves breaking beneath us. We did an engine-running passenger exchange on a couple of rigs in the Forties Field and even on the back of a ship that was bobbing up and down, before landing and shutting down on another rig. I had the opportunity to disembark and tour the rig. Rather selfishly it hadn't been designed with the disabled in mind and getting around this mammoth steel construction in my condition wasn't easy. The bracing wind certainly helped clear my head though.

Fortunately, we were safely back home in Surrey by the time my boss telephoned to see how my recuperation on the sofa was progressing and he was never any the wiser. I dread to think what he would have said if he'd known I'd been hopping around on an oil rig in the middle of the North Sea.

Ironically, before going through my selection process at Hamble in early 1979, I had been successful in getting through the helicopter version

of the same and, in July 1978, been offered a place on a sponsored helicopter pilot training course that would have led me to flying Sikorsky S-61s
on the North Sea for British Airways Helicopters. I'd turned it down
though, so I could pursue my fixed-wing airline pilot dream.

You Too Can Fly

Once I was back at work I was offered a secondment back at Heathrow
for a few months doing a similar job, but for the long-haul fleets based in
Technical Block A (TBA), now a grade two listed building. Built in the
early 1950s, this was the former main base of British Overseas Airways
Corporation (BOAC), the forerunner of British Airways. There was so
much atmosphere there with over 4,000 people, mainly engineers in
white overalls, busy twenty-four hours a day. The managers' offices were
oak panelled with impressive oil paintings from a bygone era of aviation
adorning the walls. They looked out across the 'grassy knoll', as it was
known, and the duck pond beyond. The secretary had her own ante-office
where she would make you an appointment to see the boss.

I had my own room on the third floor looking directly into the main
hangar area that, while there was no daylight, afforded a wonderful
view of two or three airliners in various states of extensive overhaul.
Nicknamed 'the Kremlin', because of its ugly grey appearance, TBA had
the best canteen at Heathrow in those days, at the back on the fourth floor,
and the route there would be via the central atrium where enormous 747
undercarriage legs and engines were lined up awaiting their turn for overhaul. The building was alive and left you in no doubt you were working
for 'the World's Favourite Airline', as the billboards proclaimed. Now the
offices are boarded up, the heavy maintenance is conducted in a specialised centre in Cardiff, and the central atrium has been transformed into a
modern flight crew training centre full of multimillion-pound, three-axis,
full-motion flight simulators.

I worked alongside a lovely quiet chap who was approaching retirement, Lewis 'Lou' Blackmore. He'd spent his life working for BOAC and
had some lovely tales to share as we would eat our sandwiches together.
As a long-haired 21-year-old I was spellbound to learn that his son was
Ritchie Blackmore, a guitarist with my favourite rock band, Deep Purple.

I'd have reason to visit the senior flight managers in the corridors of power that ran across the front of the building, with views across the duck pond towards Speedbird House where Lord King, the chairman, had his office. These were the most senior pilots in British Airways who managed each fleet of pilots in both the technical and training arenas. By now the Concorde operation was well established after its inaugural flight in January 1976. I'd made the long journey, all of half a mile, from a schoolboy clinging to the chain link fence watching that first flight to the Concorde flight manager's office on the third floor. I was still quite shy and under-confident, and found the stern voice of Captain Brian Walpole quite intimidating. He sat opposite Captain David Leney, who was quiet and gentle and always made me welcome. In their very different ways they were another inspiration to me, a junior office boy with a glowing ambition inside me.

My work was interesting, but routine and dull at times too. I had a forty-year career ahead of me. I'd been accepted at Hamble, but the college really did close its doors permanently. Once planning permission was granted for a housing estate to be built on the land, its fate was sealed. The only way to gain that coveted commercial pilot licence (CPL) now was to go down the hours-building or self-improver route as Chris had done. This took a long time and was very expensive. I wasn't from a wealthy background and it was a daunting mountain to climb. Could I do it? I spent much time muttering and mumbling to Lynne.

'Stop talking about it and get on with it (or words to that effect),' Lynne said as she presented me with a booking for my first flying lesson that she had bought. The Marina and the GT6 had gone by now and we had a white MG Midget between us.

On the morning of Monday, 15 June 1981 we set off in our Midget to the British Airways Flying Club (BAFC) at Booker Airfield near High Wycombe and by 1 p.m. I was taxiing out in G-DFLY, a two-seat Piper Tomahawk painted up in the British Airways colour scheme. It was the first step on the long road to a wonderful career and if it hadn't been for Lynne, I'd still be saying, 'When I grow up I want to be a pilot.'

The BAFC had four Tomahawks with personal registrations that they used for training and when lined up in the correct order, they read, 'YOU TOO CAN FLY'. The club was open to the public, but BA staff had a significant discount on the flying rates. We were living rent free effectively, so I saved as hard as I could, helped by giving up smoking, and we pooled our savings to pay for my flying training. At £30 an hour, initially we could afford an hour or so a week and the minimum number of hours required for the CPL was 700. This was going to be a long road.

'I was watching through the binoculars and realised there was only one person in the plane,' Lynne said after my first solo on 30 August 1981. Just nine hours and twenty-five minutes of dual time had been logged, leaving the last line on the first page of my logbook free to record my fifteen-minute first solo flight. It's a very special occasion that every pilot treasures forever. I couldn't walk very well afterwards, but rather than my dodgy legs letting me down, my knees had turned to jelly. Dick Chapman was the brave instructor who sent me solo that day and he too was going down this hours-building route aspiring to be an airline pilot. We kept in touch until he retired as a 747 captain with BA.

It was normal practice to frequent the clubhouse after a lesson and today was no exception. It was after all, a very special occasion and it was 6 p.m. on a gorgeous sunny Sunday afternoon. The bar was upstairs and the balcony looked out across the airfield westwards towards the setting sun. The roar of a Rolls-Royce Merlin engine drowned out all conversation for a moment as a Second World War Spitfire roared low across the grass before pulling up into a victory roll and coming gently into land, just as I had done not long before. The landing that is, not the victory roll.

The pilot, a well-known aerobatic ace, had just returned from displaying the Spit at an air show and joined us in the bar in his flying overalls. The pilots, whether they be new students, retired jet airliner captains or aerobatic display aces, all had tales to tell and I felt I was now part of one big family. I was a pilot and for one day only the evening belonged to me. I had just done my first solo.

My day job was still an aerodromes and performance officer, back at Bealine House, now that my secondment with Ritchie Blackmore's dad had finished, and my summer evenings, weekends and annual leave were spent at Booker. We made many new friends and, like many small airfields in the UK, the place had so much history. The fuselages of the wooden Mosquito twin-engine bomber aircraft were built close by, with High Wycombe having a big furniture-making history, so an abundance of local skilled craftsmen and facilities available. The flying sequences for the 1965 film *Those Magnificent Men in their Flying Machines* had been shot there with our very own BAFC instructor, Joan Hughes, being one of the aces flying the rather flimsy-looking biplanes. Joan was to feature significantly in my log book in a few years' time. The film was set at a fictional airfield with a car racing circuit as its perimeter, based upon Brooklands in Weybridge. This was the world's first motor racing circuit, the birthplace of aviation in the UK and where much of Concorde was designed and built. Aviation is a small world and all interlinked.

If the weather wasn't good enough to fly, time wasn't wasted as there was much studying to do and classes to attend before sitting exams in subjects I couldn't even spell a few weeks earlier.

Just under a year after Lynne had kicked me up the proverbial backside and taken me for my first flying lesson, I presented myself for my driving test. In the sky. I'd completed all my training in less than the minimum forty-five hours required by the Civil Aviation Authority (CAA), so had to fly around locally just to reach that figure.

Alan Harkness, a senior and very strict Scottish examiner, who had taken me for the occasional lesson along the way, did his best to put me at ease, as all good driving test examiners do. I passed first time and once again the evening belonged to me on the balcony of the club house. After a cheque and a complex application form had been processed by the CAA, my PPL arrived through the post on 25 July 1982, a significant date in aviation history, but for all the wrong reasons.

Eighteen years later, to the day, Concorde crashed on take-off in Paris, killing all on board and four people on the ground. I was a Concorde pilot by then. Much was to happen in those eighteen years in between.

Now I Can't See Anything and I'm Married

I was now qualified to fly a single-engine, propeller-driven aircraft in daylight, in good weather, in England with passengers. Lynne was my first, of course, for a quick spin (poor choice of word in flying talk) around Buckinghamshire. Soon we ventured further afield and went to Cambridge for a picnic. The Tomahawk was only a two-seater so after a few more hours in my logbook, I did a short conversion course to qualify for the four-seat Cherokee with similar controls, which the BAFC kept aside for touring.

With our good friends Kim and Gary aboard, we ventured as far as Somerset. Henstridge is a former Royal Navy training airfield doubling as a farm. The short concrete runway was surrounded by water to permit simulated aircraft carrier landings in time gone by and the damp, long grass now provided suitable grazing opportunities. I did a low pass over the runway to shoo the cows away. Not something that BOAC pilots had to do, I'm sure.

Gary's uncle ran a hotel in the nearby village of Cerne Abbas, complete with its famous aroused chalk giant on the hillside. We stayed overnight and were, literally, the talk of the town, having flown down from London to visit. We were taking to this jet-set lifestyle.

Soon I had enough experience to start my instrument training to gain my next qualification so that I could fly in cloud. I did much of my training with my original instructors and we would venture further afield, even across the Channel to Le Touquet. We would have to clear customs each way with a quick stop at Luton International, mixing with the airliners, which was another new experience. Weight and balance had to be considered carefully as all aircraft have such limitations and we would leave Booker heavily laden with fuel. Fortunately, by the time we arrived in Le Touquet the amount of fuel used matched exactly the maximum amount of fine French wine that could be carried out of the local supermarket.

Instrument training could be conducted on fine sunny days with the student pilot wearing a hood that was carefully designed so he could only see the instrument panel in front of him and not be influenced by any external clues that you would normally take for granted, like the ground, the sky and the horizon in between. Flying without those natural clues was, at first, most disorientating, and it's a known fact that a pilot not trained to fly solely on instruments would, on average, survive for just ninety seconds if he entered cloud, before his perfectly serviceable aeroplane would exit the cloud in an ungainly manner and plummet earthwards controlled only by gravity.

Part of the syllabus was to learn how to 'recover from unusual attitudes on limited panel'. Some of the vital instruments were covered over and the instructor took control while the victim, I mean student pilot, closed his eyes. After some dramatic manoeuvres, with the engine pitch changing from high to low and the blood in your feet one moment and your head the next, the instructor would holler, 'You have control. Recover from that.'

My instructor for this particular lesson was that strict Scottish examiner, Alan Harkness, who had now been promoted to Head of Training at British Airways and was a Concorde pilot, no less. As he calmly uttered the words '… have control', the hood that I was wearing became dislodged by the high G-forces. I could see nothing, apart from the name of the company that had manufactured it, engraved upon the inside. All I could hear was Alan laughing his little socks off, bless him, as we hurtled towards the green fields several thousand feet beneath us in some kind of unusual attitude that I was now tasked with recovering from. On limited panel. It all ended well and I'm sure I'm a better pilot for Alan being strict with me and working me hard, just like Ernie throwing the board rubber all those years earlier. Like many who influenced and encouraged me along the way, I'm still in touch with Alan, who was most influential in my life. He even took me on my first supernumerary (look/see) Concorde flight in the mid-1990s.

So here I was in June 1983 with a PPL and Instrument Meteorological Conditions (IMC) rating and a total of seventy-three hours and five minutes' flying experience. Only 627 hours to go.

Two months later, Lynne and I were married. I'd proposed the previous summer in Jersey on a lovely weekend away. It was an idyllic setting. The sun was just setting as the tide was going out in Petit Port Bay on the south-west corner of the island and I prepared to pop the question.

'Oh, John.'

'What?' was how the conversation went, not for the first time, nor the last, as my wife-to-be informed me that I had sat in a nasty sticky patch of oil washed onto the rocks from a passing tanker.

The moment wasn't lost though and the wedding was set for 20 August 1983, coincidentally four years to the day that Lynne had written to me inviting me for a job interview.

By now we had bought our first home: a neo-Georgian terraced house in Sunbury-on-Thames. Our boss at Bealine House had earlier taken me aside, concerned for my well-being, and asked if I knew what I was doing? I thought at first he feared losing his secretary, but it was the fact we were taking on a mortgage of £23,500 to buy a house for £30,000, which was, in his experienced eyes, a mammoth undertaking.

Our wedding was a wonderful occasion. It was a blisteringly hot day and the ceremony was a simple affair at the local registry office, followed by a lunch reception at the Kings Manor in nearby Walton-on-Thames, which three house moves later is now our nearest pub.

We had some lovely pictures taken in our small back garden, which the previous owners had tastefully landscaped to include a pond and flowering cherry blossom. We spent our wedding night in the historic Queen Anne Suite at the seventeenth-century Great Fosters Hotel before setting off on honeymoon to Barbados.

As British Airways employees we had access to cheap standby flights, so that trip wasn't quite as extravagant as it first sounds. You would only get on if there were empty seats at the last minute, so it could be a bit stressful, and one would always keep a low profile and try and avoid the inevitable question from a fellow passenger who had paid a small fortune to sit next to you, 'So who do you work for?' You could often sense its impending arrival and soon acquired the great skill of changing the subject.

I'd taken my PPL with me on honeymoon and made a phone call to the local flying club in Barbados. After a quick training flight with the resident instructor I was cleared to fly a Cessna 152, 8P-ASM. You couldn't go far. The island is only 21 miles long and 14 miles across at its widest point and the next nearest island was 100 miles away. That's a long way over shark-infested waters on one engine, even if the water was warm. We'd met a lovely couple from Nottingham on the beach, also on honeymoon, so I was soon conducting sightseeing tours around the island. We got back from our honeymoon with only 624 hours to go.

Taking other people flying was a very pleasant way of building hours. I was also a member of a small flying club at Denham in Buckinghamshire by now and had use of their four-seat aeroplanes, a high-wing Cessna 172 and a French-built TB9 Tampico. We did some lovely trips across the Channel to Le Touquet and the Channel Islands, and I even took people from the office sightseeing over London (because you could in those days) in the lunch break.

We returned to Jersey for our first wedding anniversary in August 1984, but this time we went in style as I flew us there. The Samsonite suitcase was difficult to wheel across the grass, but we strapped it securely into the back seats and set off from Denham early in the morning. We had to clear customs at Bournemouth International Airport and with our life jackets donned, just in case, headed out across the Channel. We felt like VIPs walking into arrivals in Jersey alongside the passengers disembarking from the BA flight that had just arrived from Heathrow. We had a lovely few days and I was very careful not to sit in any oil when we returned to our favourite bay. You learn from your mistakes.

It had taken me two years to clock up my first seventy hours, so at this rate I'd be about 83 by the time I had enough for my commercial licence and would have spent a fortune. The way around this was to become a part-time flying instructor, who were all most patient and skilful individuals. As an instructor you logged the flying hours as a pilot in command (PIC) while your student was credited with pilot under training (PUT) time. The student paid, of course. The instructor was paid a small flying hour rate payment, a pittance, so most had to hold down a proper job to pay the bills.

'I'll let the dog out of the car for a quick tinkle whilst you go and get the aircraft ready old boy.'

Joan Hughes was only 5ft tall and walked out to join me in the right-hand seat of the BAFC Tomahawk with a cushion under her arm. I'd completed the pre-flight checks and off we went on my Flying Instructors' Training Course. I spent the spring of 1985 flying with Joan and it was one of the most honourable periods of my flying career.

There is a famous picture of Joan standing alongside the wheel of a Second World War Short Stirling, a four-engined bomber that she had just flown ... solo. The tyre is as tall as she is. Joan was born in London in 1918 just as the First World War ended. She and her brother started flying training when they were just 15 years old. At 17, Joan became the youngest qualified female pilot ever in the UK and when the Second World War broke out she was one of the first eight women to join the Air Transport Auxiliary based at White Waltham. She and her female colleagues were given nothing more than a book of notes and a map and left to ferry aircraft, large and small, around the country, often in appalling weather conditions. Alone. Joan was the youngest pilot to join the ATA and the only one to be qualified to instruct on every aircraft type that the RAF had in service at the time. Here she was teaching me to be a flying instructor. After the dog had taken his tinkle.

I've been instructing for many years since then and, like any good school teacher, you learn to adjust your style of training to suit the student. Some lack confidence and need to be built up gently. Others are too sure of themselves and need to be brought down a peg or two. Joan had a unique style that I saw put into practice, not with me, I hasten to add. If you didn't get it right first time she would shout at you. After a second unsatisfactory attempt, you'd get whacked round the back of the head with a rolled up copy of the *Daily Mail* of the day. That sort of thing was becoming rather non-PC by the mid-1980s, and Ernie's board rubber back at Hampton was being used solely for cleaning the board by then. I was groomed to join the modern band of friendly, patient teachers.

I was Joan's last ever student. I hope I wasn't the cause of her retirement and that stories of her shaking her head in exasperation as she left the school after her last day with me are wild exaggerations. Joan succumbed to cancer at home in Taunton in 1993. I was most privileged to have learned so much from this heroine of a bygone era.

BANG – MAKE OUT LIKE A SWAN AND TEACHING OTHERS

By June 1985 I was a flying instructor at the weekends, albeit with the word 'assistant' as a prefix for a probationary period, and an aerodromes and performance officer, Monday to Friday.

The performance bit of that job, I've already touched upon. It was number crunching in an office. The aerodromes part of the role was a little more glamorous. The department was responsible for checking out any new airport that BA was going to fly to and ensure our strict criteria were met. We would get involved in negotiations with airport authorities around the world if they were planning to resurface their single runway to ensure that there was sufficient length left available for our services not to be disrupted. I managed to smile at the right people and pick up most of the work in the Caribbean. The fact that Lynne was the boss's secretary was just pure coincidence.

I represented British Airways on an international mission around the Caribbean with other airlines who operated to the region, including the late Pan Am. Some of the airports and runways were in need of repairs and modernisation, particularly now airlines, including BA, were flying jumbo jets with 400 seats into these destinations, which were designed for much smaller machines. On this mission, in December 1982, we started off in Barbados, where the runway needed resurfacing. We were the only transatlantic operator at the time so needed the most runway length to get back to the UK non-stop. I played a vital part in planning the works to secure that availability.

In Port of Spain, Trinidad, we were approved to go out in a truck to inspect the runway for potholes and cracks. It was in a bad state, nearly as bad as the roads in Surrey. It was a quiet time of day and no scheduled flights were due to land for another half an hour or so. Fortunately, it was me who happened to look up at the right moment and spotted an aircraft on final approach.

'Run, run, run!' I shouted as loud as I could. We then dived into the long grass as a BWIA DC-9 on a training flight touched down.

They had another go at killing me ten years later. I'll come to that.

Lynne was with me on this trip, a glamorous jaunt away from her desk in Bealine House, even if she did have carpets and a coffee machine. There must have been six of us who went out for dinner in Port of Spain that night. Dick Garner from IATA, a lovely English chap from Byfleet with a wonderful dry sense of humour, was leading the mission. He'd been to Trinidad several times and said he knew where to go for dinner. We didn't take him seriously when he told us the place we had chosen only served curried goat and it was awful. They did and it was.

Back at Bealine House I'd write up my reports and Lynne would type them up, missing out the bits about the dive into the long grass and the curried goat. As air traffic increased in the Caribbean region, parking spaces came at a premium, and still are to this day. Schedules were planned so you didn't have too many wide-bodied aircraft on the ground at any one time. I redesigned the parking layouts at Antigua and St Lucia to use the limited space more efficiently and make sure nobody got boxed in. I allowed myself a quiet, proud smile when I first flew a 747 into Antigua at the end of 1989 and parked up on the apron that I'd designed.

I started instructing at Booker on 9 June 1985. I was assigned six students that day, all at different stages of their training.

As I was having a well-earned lunch break, I spotted a rather nervous-looking chap in his 50s approaching the reception desk. His name was

Douglas Smith. He was there for his first flying lesson, just like I had been four years previously. He didn't aspire to be an airline pilot, but was a civil servant who had always wanted to learn to fly, his passion for aviation dating back to the early 1930s when he was enthralled by the Air Pageants at RAF Hendon.

Douglas was assigned me as his instructor. It was quite a while before he knew that it was my first day as an instructor. Douglas is 95 now, lives with his wife, Jane, in Bournemouth, and has only fairly recently stopped playing tennis, but under my tuition, fulfilled his ambition. We met for our annual lunch recently, when he always admits 'he wasn't a natural'. He took twice as long as average to meet the required standard, but I remain particularly proud of Douglas for achieving his ambition and gaining his PPL. He and Jane were waving vigorously from the crowd when I took Concorde into Bournemouth fifteen years after his first flying lesson.

The Piper PA-38 Tomahawk was a great little training aircraft. It had two seats up front, so the student and instructor (me) sat side by side, which hadn't always been the case. Earlier military trainers, like the Chipmunk that I'd had my first flying experience in and the even earlier Tiger Moth biplane, had a tandem arrangement, where you sat behind one another in your own separate cockpit. I guess with the instructor sitting behind the student it was easier to whack them round the head with a rolled-up copy of the *Daily Mail* (or any other well-known tabloid that came to hand), whereas the side-by-side arrangement of modern civilian trainers lent themselves to a more friendly environment.

As my instructional skills developed I learned to 'read the student' more, looking for signs of nervousness, like white knuckles from gripping the control column too tightly, or beads of sweat on the forehead. To get the best out of a student it was important to put them at ease as much as possible, so my body language and verbal behaviour were important. I never sat there, for example, with my arms folded. They'd be resting on my legs or I might even have one arm resting nonchalantly on the side window frame. Even if the student was scaring the wits out of me at the time. I learned to speak slowly and calmly. I learned when to speak and when to remain quiet so they could concentrate. It was important, as an instructor, that even when the workload got high, or something untoward happened, you maintained that consistent aura of calmness. Rather like a swan on a fast-flowing river, a constant majestic, smooth profile while paddling like fury out of sight under the surface.

So when the engine went 'Bang!', the whole aircraft started shaking violently and the windscreen, which up until now, only had a few bug splatters typical for the time of year, adopted a nasty shade of oil, it was important I made out like a swan.

It didn't help that the aircraft had about 60 degrees of bank on at the time and full power. It did help though, that we were quite high, about 4,000ft I think. There's an old saying that the two most useless things in aviation are 'runway behind you' (on take-off) and 'sky above you'. So we had quite a lot of air beneath us, which meant we had time to deal with this rather troubling matter.

The student, a lovely chap, was flying the aeroplane from the left-hand seat and today's lesson was steep turns. The clue is in the title and it's a great way of developing precise aircraft handling. When you turn an aeroplane, as I'm sure you know, you lower one wing, in the desired direction and, all being well, the one on the other side goes up by the same amount. The radius of the turn is governed by two factors, the speed of the aircraft and the amount by which you've lowered the inboard wing. A normal turn is anything up to 30 degrees of bank. In fact, modern airliners have inbuilt protective systems, separate from the automatic pilot, that kick in and override the pilot should you be daft enough to try and turn much steeper than that.

The laws of physics dictate that when an aircraft turns, the nose tends to drop. The steeper the turn, the greater that tendency, so the pilot must pull back on the control column more and more in direct proportion to the angle of bank. If he or she neglected to do so, the nose would keep dropping and a spiral dive would develop. That's not good and things would likely get spilt in the cabin around this time.

So here we are then, out over Oxfordshire somewhere, about 20 miles to the north-west of Booker Airfield and the other side of the Chiltern Hills, with a most diligent student, flying a very nice example of a steep turn. He'd wound on 60 degrees of bank, had pulled the control column back into his chest with his left hand and, to counter the increased drag from such a manoeuvre, had progressively applied full power by easing the throttle fully forward with his right hand. We'd already flown a very nice turn, through a full 360 degrees, to the right and now we were going back the other way. The point of the exercise was to not lose or gain any height during the manoeuvre, so he had his eyes pinned to the spinner, the pointy bit in front of the propeller, and kept it nailed to the horizon. That is until he couldn't see it any longer because the oil was blocking his view.

I took control at this stage, levelled the wings and reduced the power on the engine, which, rather fortunately, was still running. It was shaking around though and was clearly in poor condition. I'm not an engineer, but I knew enough about engines to know that something, somewhere, was broken. As long as it was producing power though and we could keep air flowing over the wings, so a speed of 70mph or so, we had a flying machine that was still capable of flying.

Part of the training course was to cover practice forced landings (PFLs), whereby a simulated total engine failure is introduced by the instructor, simply by closing the throttle, and the student learns to glide at the most efficient speed, choose a suitable field and go and land in it. Simple really. In theory anyway, but you only needed a small ditch or rut of some sort to spoil your day and tip you upside down.

I felt it was important to involve my student as much as possible in the management of the whole situation. After all, two heads are generally better than one and I didn't want him just sitting there with time on his hands to think too much about our predicament. Similarly, I didn't see any pressing need to turn this into a forced landing – that's a PFL without the practice – and possibly damage the aeroplane further and leave us with a long walk home. If, that is, we could still walk after said forced landing.

I gave him back control of the aircraft and asked him to use a low engine power setting, maintain a speed of just over 70mph and turn in the general direction of Booker. That gave me the capacity to think about things and manage the operation. I didn't know it at the time, but a few years from now, I would learn that's exactly what the big boys do. In airline operations, when anything untoward happens, the co-pilot would be tasked with flying the plane while the captain manages and communicates.

We kept our workload evenly balanced, again just like in the airlines, and regularly shared our mental models. We were flying over open countryside most of the way back so we always had a field lined up just in case the motor up front suddenly stopped motoring altogether. She seemed to be fairly comfortable at about 1,700 to 1,800rpm or so, rather than the normal 2,300rpm for a cruise. The vibration was bearable and the oil was just spitting onto the front screen periodically. Our instruments told us that we still had some oil inside the engine and it was doing what oil is designed to do. So, on we pressed, descending gently as we made progress towards home. I'd made various radio calls including that word you'd normally only hear in the movies: Mayday. This was doubtless, a serious situation with a loss of life possible.

We reached the Chiltern Hills and we could see Booker by now, about 10 miles ahead. There was a westerly wind blowing so a landing on Runway 25 was appropriate, but (and that's a BIG but) the final approach was over a housing estate and the small matter of the M40 motorway. If the engine failed completely at that stage, we'd not be the only ones unable to walk home. I came up with a cunning plan.

My student had done a wonderful job of getting us back this far and I took over for the rather crucial final approach. I came in much, much higher than would be normal. Twice as high, if not more, so that if the engine failed suddenly I'd be sure of gliding the rest of the way to the airfield. As luck would have it, the engine kept going, but now, of course, as I approached the M40 just before the runway, I was far too high. Even with the engine back at idle power (tick over) we'd be touching down a long way down the runway and likely run off the end into the grass and maybe the trees beyond.

Now I'd thought about this in advance and had briefed accordingly that once I knew we'd clear the houses and motorway without any power, I'd execute a thing called a forward slip manoeuvre. This isn't something we taught students and I'd had little or no practise at it myself. Indeed, it isn't even approved on many aircraft. I had to do three things at the same time, which isn't easy for me at the best of times. I lowered the left wing in the normal manner with the ailerons. To counteract the left turn that would bring about, I progressively applied virtually full opposite rudder so the nose of the aeroplane was pointing well to the right of the runway, but its path over the ground was still taking us towards it. A weird picture indeed, and at the same time I had to lower the nose significantly to maintain a safe flying speed, knowing that the airspeed indicator was now giving a false reading because the input to the static sensor was affected by the fact we were technically flying sideways. That's an explanation for another day.

All this brought about the desired result. The aeroplane descended like the proverbial brick. Clearly not a suitable rate of descent to reach ground level though – that would have hurt – so I had to judge it just right and ease out of the sideslip and return to a normal descent and flare for the final touchdown, which was actually one of my better ones. We were surrounded by lots of blue flashing lights on the top of bright-red vehicles – all very colourful, but thankfully, not needed.

We were back in one piece with an aircraft that needed a bit of attention but was likely repairable rather than being up to its axles, or worse, in a field in Oxfordshire. And we were back early as the lesson had actually been cut short. Normally the instructor would have just fifteen minutes in between lessons but they managed to get someone else for my next student, so we could have a nice cup of tea and review what had just happened.

I flew the rest of the afternoon and my student went home quite unfazed by all the excitement and went on to gain his pilot's licence. The next day the engineers told me a valve had dropped out of the cylinder head and gone through one of the pistons. Nothing trivial then.

Soon I was racking up the hours at a tremendous rate and had 400 by the end of 1985. I loved my instructing days and it was the start of something special, a big part of my life. I've been teaching pilots on all sorts of aeroplanes, from many different backgrounds, for the last thirty-five years and I look back fondly at those days at Booker with Alan laughing upside down, Joan's dog having a tinkle, and Douglas's quiet determination to achieve something quite special.

By the end of 1986 I had flown 700 hours. Well technically anyway, as my students had flown most of them and rarely further than 20 miles from Booker. All I needed now was to pass some really complex exams, again in subjects that I couldn't spell, like meteorology and navigation (so I can spell them really) but the knowledge had to be to a much greater depth. It was to the equivalent of degree standard, they told me, but I wouldn't know, having bypassed that university stage that most pilots went through. I studied at home, often late into the night, with a desk rigged up in the spare bedroom so I wasn't distracted by the TV. Déjà vu.

THE TOUGHEST FLYING TEST IN THE WORLD

The next part of my flying course was called an instrument rating (IR), and above is exactly how it had been described to me. It had to be completed on a twin-engine aircraft. The lessons were very expensive, with the hourly rate proportional to the number of engines, so at least twice that of PPL training. I undertook my training at Leavesden Airport in Hertfordshire, now a massive film studios and the home of many James Bond and Harry Potter films.

The CAA examiners at Stansted had a variable reputation, with one in particular notoriously strict, intimidating and unfriendly. I presented myself for test at Stansted on 12 March 1987. Mike Stow had been my IR instructor at Leavesden and he came with me on the short flight to Stansted in G-TWIN, a Piper Seminole, somewhat larger than the Cherokees and Tomahawks I'd been used to. He did his best to settle my nerves. He drank coffee, smoked a cigarette or two, paced around the room clockwise and then again anticlockwise. Conversation was short and muted. He reassured me that, as long as I didn't have Captain XXX, I'd be fine, just before the said gentleman marched into the room.

The 3-mile, or so it felt, walk out to the aeroplane was conducted with the minimum of interaction. The flying test that was ahead of me was the toughest any pilot would undertake, his initial instrument rating test. The flight was to be conducted under instrument flying conditions without the aid of an autopilot with approaches in simulated cloud (under the hood) down to 200ft with one of the engines shut down. Holding patterns had to be flown accurately and non-precision approaches flown, which involved following a meandering needle on a dial tuned to a radio beacon on the ground.

When the examiner removed the cord from around the waist of his anorak after circumnavigating the sleeping flying machine, I became even more unsettled. He had to be admired for his skills at improvisation as he used this cord, some 6ft in length, to measure each of the propeller blades. Back and forth he went several times without muttering a word. I could see Mike pacing backwards and forwards quite clearly 3 miles away, or so it still seemed, wondering what on earth was going on.

When asked why the propellers were different, I was unable to explain. While being the same length, according to the well-known international scale of the anorak cord, it couldn't be denied that one had a slightly more rounded tip than the other. The 3-mile walk back to the waiting room took a good five minutes or so. I had paid vastly to fly the aeroplane to Stansted, an exorbitant landing fee, a CAA exam fee and an hourly rate for Mike to pace up and down as if his wife was in labour and it now looked as if we weren't even going to get airborne.

After a couple of hours (I'm not exaggerating) the examiner was finally satisfied. Paperwork and maintenance schedules had been consulted and the local garage where the servicing was carried out, or aviation equivalent thereof, had been spoken to and finally my new friend from the CAA was happy that the aeroplane was safe to fly and that the propellers were genuine Piper-approved parts. I was exhausted as we walked 3 miles back to the aircraft and we hadn't even started.

At 3.40 p.m., two hours behind schedule, we finally set off on the pre-planned route. Most of those plans had gone out of the window though as a weather front had come through and my calculations to allow for the forecast winds aloft were now well out of date. The examiner said very little as the flight progressed, just appraising me of the next challenge periodically, without indicating if the previous event had been demonstrated to his satisfaction. The en route phase of the trip should have been the most straightforward. I had to use the instruments to fly from one ground-based radio beacon in Kent towards another in Hertfordshire. In a hangover from a bygone era, each radio beacon transmits a three-letter identification in Morse code and it was essential you identified the correct beacon, and therefore confirmed you were following the right needle, before you blindly latched onto it. Even in the 1980s you had to learn Morse code as part of your training.

I had taught myself Morse code by sitting in my car with a cassette tape produced just for this. There were easy ways to remember each letter and self-assessment tests every now and again. I'd sit in the staff car park at Hatton Cross during my lunch break, right next to the runway, listening to all these dots and dashes. In my other ear I'd have my air band radio tuned to the Heathrow control tower frequency and would be following the comings and goings of all the airliners just like I had done on the box my dad had made me twenty-five years earlier. As well as breaking the monotony of learning Morse, it helped me become more familiar with the discipline and professionalism of air-to-ground communications. Aircraft of all shapes and sizes would taxi past, some going to small airports in the UK, others heading off across the world somewhere.

A monster of a Boeing 747 jumbo jet, a double-decker, 200ft long with 400 seats, in Pan American livery, was following a thirty-seat Shorts 330 in British Midland colours out to the runway. The 330, by any sense of the imagination, was an ugly looking flying machine. Its nickname, 'the Shed', even used in air traffic control instructions (e.g. 'After the Shed in front of you line up Runway 28 left'), was most appropriate. I choked on my ham sandwich when a deep southern American drawl came over the airwaves from the 747 Flight deck towering above us, 'Hey buddy did you build that yourself?'

Back to my airborne exam, I was tracking from Detling beacon towards Daventry with my friendly examiner doing nothing apart from making the occasional note on his knee pad. The three-letter codes for the beacons were 'DET', which was behind me, and 'DTY', which was ahead. The trap is they both have a 'D' and a 'T' in them. I hoped upon my wallet, apart from anything else, that Captain whatever his name was hadn't spotted my error. I'd been navigating most accurately towards DTY but with the dots and dashes of DET repeating their tune in our earpieces. Eric Morecombe once said something about playing all the right notes but not necessarily in the right order. Technically, I had been navigating using a radio beacon that I hadn't yet correctly identified.

We landed back at Stansted at 5.20 p.m. It was nearly dark. As we walked silently back towards the office I could see Mike still pacing up and down eager to know how I'd got on. As we got nearer, with the examiner walking on my right, I discreetly gave Mike a thumb down indication. This was going to be a serious expense to come back and do all this again just because I'd got DET and DTY in Morse code mixed up. I also feared that my flying had deteriorated once I'd recognised and been distracted by this error.

The atmosphere in the briefing room was cold and frosty, rather like the forecast for the night ahead. The stern-faced examiner produced a collection of pens and much paperwork from his historic briefcase that had clearly flown some miles. He still hadn't spoken but then I spotted his lip start to move.

'That was a very expensive mistake wasn't it Mr Tye?' were his exact words. I remember them like it was yesterday. They say that comedy is all in the timing and his was. The timing, that is, but there wasn't much comedy. He paused just long enough before continuing, 'You won't make that mistake again will you, Mr Tye?'

'No sir,' I muttered as I looked across the desk and saw him write 'pass' on his paperwork. I've never misidentified a radio beacon since and, because of my diligence and attention to detail, have never got lost, well not by too much anyway.

My commercial pilot licence with instrument rating was issued on 26 March 1987, almost six years since Lynne drove me to Booker and said, 'Stop talking about it and get on with it.'

All I needed now was a job.

1987 WAS A SIGNIFICANT AND VERY SPECIAL YEAR

Earlier on today, apparently, a woman rang the BBC and said she heard there was a hurricane on the way. Well, if you're watching, don't worry, there isn't.

Michael Fish, BBC weather forecaster,
15 October 1987

British Airways is recruiting Direct Entry Pilots with a minimum of 1,200 hours.

Advert in *Flight International*

We've never done this before, but we'd like to use you as a guinea pig.

Alison from HR at Dan-Air

Are you sitting down? I've got some good news.

Lynne

The baby was due in November 1987.

I was a massive 500 hours short of BA's minimum requirements. This new opening was for pilots who were already qualified to fly commercially, perhaps ending a career in the Royal Air Force or keen to move up from a charter airline in the UK. While I didn't have the minimum hours needed, I did have eleven years' experience in BA in flight operations. Surely that was worth something?

I worked with many of the senior management pilots by now who had encouraged and inspired me along the way. Despite their support, though, the captain who was head of pilot recruitment peered over his glasses, adjusted his rather pompous bow tie and gave me his 'best advice'.

Lynne's pregnancy was going well. She enjoyed time at home as her bump grew, but carried on working until September. We were now in our second home in Upper Halliford village in Shepperton. It was a quiet cul-de-sac and there was a lovely family-run nursery school in the village just a few yards away from that wonderful pub, the Goat. You know, the one where I had a pint glass embedded in my neck? Half a pint actually.

Anyway, back to the BA pilot recruitment manager. His best advice went like this: 'This company, young man, will never recruit a direct entry pilot with less than 1,200 hours. The best advice I can give you, is to leave and get some experience elsewhere. We'd be glad to consider you once you've got 1,200 hours.' Words I will never forget. It was like being hit with a sledgehammer for a second time after Hamble had closed its doors in my face eight years earlier.

Once more, Lynne picked me up, dusted me down and kicked me up the backside. I started writing. I wrote to every airline in the country, executive jet operators, too. Knowing that some of them would be losing their pilots to BA in this recruitment campaign, surely they would need me. Many didn't even reply. Some responded courteously saying they had no opportunities currently but would keep my details on file.

I got my big break that summer when I opened a letter from Horley in Sussex. I was expecting another 'keep your details on file' response but it was an invitation for an interview next Wednesday. That went well, as did the group exercises and aptitude tests, and I went back for a simulator assessment the following week. I had to fly an airliner for the first time. They marked me on my flying accuracy and ability to fly holding patterns and instrument approaches, just like I had done in my instrument rating test with the examiner who improvised with his anorak cord.

Bealine House in Ruislip had closed down by now, to be replaced by a supermarket, and we, and other departments based there, had been relocated to Aerad House, a low prefab building in the Hatton Cross complex, in the shadow of the ten-storey TBC, where I'd started in the accounts department eleven years earlier.

I was at my desk in the aerodromes and performance office, in Aerad House, the following week, when Alison Beadie, the personnel officer I'd met at Dan-Air headquarters when I went for my interview, telephoned.

'We'd like to offer you a job,' were the best words ever, 'But there's a catch,' followed and prompted me to politely excuse myself from the eavesdropping surroundings of the small office.

I didn't really need to be discreet because all my colleagues, including my boss and his new secretary, were most supportive and were keen to see me achieve my ambition of becoming an airline pilot.

'We normally put all our new recruits on to the HS 748 turboprop aircraft to start with,' continued Alison once I was in more private surroundings, 'We've never done this before. We'd like to use you as a guinea pig.'

Dan-Air offered me a job straight into a 159-seat jet airliner, the Boeing 727. I'd never flown anything bigger than a Piper Cherokee (apart from the Piper Seminole for my instrument rating) and never been further than Le Touquet. This was going to be quite a challenge. I asked what would happen if I didn't get through the challenging training course and Alison reassured me that I'd transfer to the HS 748, so there really was nothing to lose.

This was a fantastic opportunity and if I was successful, would be a tremendous achievement. I accepted immediately and handed in my notice at BA. Gulp!

'British Airways is recruiting Direct Entry Pilots with a minimum of 750 hours,' read the next advert in *Flight International*. Just weeks after the recruitment manager had told me, 'This company, young man, will never … 1,200 hours …' they had just dropped it to 750!

What a dilemma. I had a fantastic job opportunity with Dan-Air starting in September. The pay on the 727 fleet meant that we could afford for Lynne to stop working. Had I joined Dan-Air on the HS 748, I would have been taking a pay cut and things would have been very difficult for us with the baby coming along. I was leaving BA in less than a month. I could knock out the fifty hours' shortfall in a very short time if I needed to. The BA selection process, though, would take a few weeks and if I didn't get through I'd be right back to square one, having let a fantastic opportunity pass me by.

I went to see Captain Barnes, the Director of Flight Ops, the Chief Pilot at British Airways. I knew him well and he understood my predicament and how special the Dan-Air offer was. He seemed genuinely keen to keep me in BA and I found myself recalling this meeting when we shared a pint at a Concorde flight crew dinner at the RAF Club, thirty or so years later.

'Young man,' which I should have taken as a compliment really, because I was nearly 30 years old, boomed the recruitment manager. 'I've been told to give you a rapid selection process, the result of which you will know before you are due to leave,' he added, after telling me off for going over his head. I respectfully reminded him of his statements and best advice from just a few weeks ago and how I had nothing to lose. As always, it seems, there was a catch. I was told, in no uncertain terms, that I'd only be considered for the HS 748 based in Aberdeen and I'd be there for a minimum of five years.

The advantage was I'd be able to keep continuous service in British Airways and my career would have more opportunities in the long term. Dan-Air, after all, only operated charter flights to the Mediterranean in the summer and the ski resorts in the winter. The logistics of moving or commuting to the north of Scotland with a new baby, though, were quite an issue. It was a real dilemma.

Lynne, soon after we met, with a necklace I made her.

The pink car, all the way from the USA.

You couldn't do this nowadays, July 1982. The MG Midget was fast enough, let alone that thing behind it.

On the same spot in July 1985. I was collecting the PA-38 from Heathrow after it had been repainted in the new BA livery.

3

Dan-Air
(1987 to 1989)

BOEINGS, BERLIN, BRAKES AND BRANIFF

I started at Dan-Air in September 1987.

I was made most welcome and everyone was very friendly. Compared to the enormity of British Airways, this was a whole different world. There were six of us on our training course, but I stuck out like a sore thumb when it came to comparing previous experience. There were pilots from other airlines, an executive jet captain, a former Royal Navy helicopter pilot and a fast jet pilot from the Royal Air Force. I was a senior aerodromes and performance officer and part-time flying instructor on Piper Tomahawks.

The stunned silence didn't last long though and we all got along very well. There was classroom work initially and then some heavy simulator sessions learning how to handle the B727 in both normal and abnormal situations. It was an old simulator, so unlike the modern-day equivalents that have visual effects to equal a small child's video game, you saw nothing out of the window at all. Bizarre as it may seem, this wasn't a problem. You could learn how to fly the aeroplane very well on instruments with various technical failures. It was just the take-offs and landings that couldn't be taught.

Base training is therefore the final stage of the type rating training before being let loose on the public to Corfu, Malaga, or wherever else there was an abundance of brightly coloured stuffed donkeys. It was an expensive but necessary conclusion to follow the ground-based training. We took an empty Boeing 727 out of service and a team of training captains and engineers would take us trainees to Shannon on the west coast of Ireland for a couple of days. The plan was to fly circuits and bumps, touch and goes, for as long as it took (within reason) until you could achieve safe and consistent landings without any training input.

That was the plan anyway.

Lynne was very large and uncomfortable by now. We had separately survived the great storm of 1987 when the weather forecaster, Michael Fish, had reassured everybody the night before that, despite a concerned viewer phoning in, we weren't going to have a hurricane overnight. He was wrong. The Great Storm of 1987 came through on the night of 15 October. Winds blew at 86mph, with gusts up to 134mph in southern England. It was the worst storm in over 300 years. Fatalities would have, undoubtedly, been much greater if the population hadn't been tucked up in bed. We awoke to devastation, me in a hotel near the simulator in Horley and Lynne with a tree across the front of the house in Shepperton.

The baby was due when we were scheduled to go base training in Shannon. Dan-Air were fantastic. They didn't want me to be distracted, nor to miss the birth, so they told me to stay at home and call in when our family was half the size again that it was now.

Jennifer Katherine Tye entered the world on 17 November 1987. As any parent understands, there are no words good enough to describe that feeling. It had been a long labour for Lynne, culminating in an emergency caesarean birth. I checked her feet and legs straight away (Jen's not Lynne's) though, to make sure she hadn't inherited my feet and leg deformities. She was perfect.

Six days later, I was introduced to the delights of Durty Nelly's, one of Ireland's landmark Irish pubs in Shannon.

Dan-Air took another 727 out of service just for me and we went to Shannon for two days to train me up on flying the aeroplane for real. It was a big day, taking off from Gatwick at 150mph and with a lot more power than the little Pipers I'd been used to. To be fair, there was another trainee along. The ex-Navy helicopter pilot had had some problems adjusting from putting a Wessex onto a helipad on a ship, so they gave him some extra training on my session and thankfully got him up to standard.

With me duly passed to fly the 727, the next two years were fantastic. It was wonderful to have Jen in our lives. Before long she was crawling, walking, running and talking, not necessarily in that order. She slept through the night from an early age and it all seemed rather straightforward. I was never away for long, as Dan-Air flights were normally 'there and backs', perhaps an overnight occasionally in Tenerife or Harlow, north London.

Dan-Air had an operation from Stansted Airport, north-east of London. While they had cabin crew based there who lived locally, it was more practical to use us pilots from Gatwick. To cover the early morning flights to Palma and Ibiza, we would go up the night before in a taxi and stay the night in a lovely old pub in Harlow just twenty minutes or so from Stansted. We would sometimes stay a few days and that would be known as a 'Stansted tour', all very glamorous, you understand.

There would be the occasional ad-hoc charter operation laid on at the last minute and I recall being assigned one of those from Stansted. The

Boeing 727 had a crew of three on the flight deck. I was the first officer and flew the aircraft from the right-hand seat. The more experienced and distinguished captain, who had more stripes and a bigger pay packet associated with the increased responsibility, was in the left-hand seat.

We also had a flight engineer who would look after all the aircraft systems, the hydraulics, the electrics and pressurisation, manage the fuel balancing and generally keep an eye on what us pilots were doing. I'd enjoy the banter and the fun of working with flight engineers for the next thirteen years. They always knew where the best beer was served and the cheapest breakfast, sometimes at the same time.

The three of us were called from standby late on a Saturday afternoon to cover the early flight from Stansted the following morning. On this occasion there were no rooms available in our usual haunt in Harlow so we were to be accommodated in a rather magnificent country house hotel somewhere in the locality. We took some smart clothes so we could dine in style that evening and fly off to Palma and back in the morning. Remembering to pack all the items of uniform was often a bit of a challenge. Mum always used to pack my bag for me when I went off on school trips.

Flight crew have an inbuilt ability for sniffing out a good party from a great distance. That night was no exception. We mingled quite happily at the wedding reception being held there, dancing along to all the latest hits from the live band and consuming vast amounts of fancy vol-au-vents and sausages on sticks. No alcohol, sadly, as the hotel wake-up call was booked for some ungodly hour dangerously close to 6 a.m. I was puzzled when I awoke naturally and it was light outside. My bleary eyes took a while to open properly before I could read the note that had been slipped under my door quietly to explain that the flight had been cancelled and to let the operations people know when we had finished breakfast and needed the limousine to collect us for the run back to Gatwick. We had enjoyed a great night out and hadn't even seen an aeroplane, let alone flown one.

The Berlin Wall had been hastily erected in 1961 and it physically separated West Berlin from the communist lands that surrounded it, including the eastern part of the same city. Before this, not long after the Second World War, the Soviet Union set up blockades preventing essential supplies from reaching Berlin overland. The Berlin Airlift was a huge multinational operation to supply the city by air in the summer of 1948. It started when the city was down to just thirty-six days of food remaining. Dan-Air started in 1953 and inherited DC-3 aircraft and a contract for a second airlift from Southend to Berlin.

During my time at Dan-Air, the West German national airline, Lufthansa, was prohibited from operating from West Berlin so contracts were held by other European airlines, including Dan-Air, which served the city uninterruptedly throughout the airline's history. Three air corridors, each just 20 miles wide, with a maximum altitude of 10,000ft, linked Berlin with West Germany. Accurate flying was essential to remain within this closely monitored airspace to avoid an international incident, but it was fun keeping the Russians on their toes by entering the corridor inbound at 9,900ft at nearly 400mph.

Berlin postings had been a feature of a Dan-Air pilot's career in earlier days, with many months based there, but by the late 1980s, a week at a time was the longest we spent there, often less. That suited me with a young family at home. It was quite lucrative and the flying was fun. Long day trips to the Canary Islands and back were common, taking the West Berliners to the sun loungers of Tenerife or Fuerteventura. We flew with bilingual German cabin crew, based in Berlin, so there were no language issues with the passengers.

We would often get back quite late but the Irish bar didn't close until 2 a.m. and we would have the next day off, time to spend visiting the famous Berlin Zoo or the surrounding neighbourhood. It was an eerie experience to visit the wall close to the Brandenburg Gate or Checkpoint Charlie and read the tributes to those poor souls who, often quite young and in recent times, had been shot dead trying to escape from the East into the bright lights of West Berlin.

One of the locally based engineers took us out for the day and into the countryside on the edge of the city near the lakes. Steinstücken was a small village that, for whatever reason, should have been included inside the wall when it was hastily erected in 1961. An arrangement had been in place for many years whereby American helicopter pilots would fly daily shuttles over the wall, between the village and West Berlin, a journey of just half a mile or so, to ferry their troops and supplies back and forth.

Eventually an agreement was reached whereby a hole was cut in the wall and a short corridor created linking the village to the West as a small annex. The village had several large detached houses with lovely gardens and our guide took us to a secluded vantage point where we could see across the railway track into one of the gardens. A child, perhaps 4 years old, was swinging back and forth on her garden swing. It was late afternoon on one of those perfect autumn days. The leaves were turning to gold and a misty evening lay ahead. The rays from the late sun were picking up the early traces of such. It was a beautiful picture of innocence. Until, that is, you looked to the right and there was one of the many watchtowers along the wall, which was on the edge of this lovely home. Standing in full military uniform was one of 'the goons', as they were known, with his rifle slung casually across his body, watching us, watching the peace and tranquillity. If I had been an artist, I would have captured that scene on canvas in oils.

I enjoyed my time in Berlin. It's a beautiful city and when I last went there with Dan-Air in the summer of 1989 there were no signs that the wall would be torn down inside a year, Germany would be reunified and the goons and their watchtowers confined to history.

Our boss on the Boeing 727 fleet was Captain Vaughan Dow. A wonderful gentleman, it was he who had approved me staying at home until Jen was born and laid on a separate base training session just for me. He spent much of his time in the office managing the day-to-day running of the fleet and only flew occasionally to keep current. I was invited to go with him on a trip to Berlin to conduct a test flight on an aeroplane that had been stuck there badly damaged for several months and was now ready to return to service.

The brake accumulator on a Boeing 727 held in reserve enough brake pressure for about three applications of the brakes, the pressure dissipating slightly with each push of the pedals. In normal operation the accumulator was kept pressurised by engine-driven hydraulic pumps, therefore providing an unlimited supply of brake pressure. As long as they are switched on.

On the day the aircraft had been damaged the fully laden Boeing 727-200 had taxied out at Berlin, full of Germans keen to get their towels on the sun loungers in Tenerife. A warning light indicated a possible technical problem that needed to be checked out before take-off, so they returned to the gate and deplaned. The engineers got to work straight away, fixed the fault and taxied the plane away to do an engine run on the other side of the airfield. In those days, engineers were qualified to taxi aircraft for such purposes, but not now. The holidaymakers looked pleased as they pushed their noses up against the glass in the terminal building watching their aircraft taxi back on to the gate, knowing it wouldn't be long now before they were off to the sunshine.

Or not.

On the fourth application of the brake pedals, there was no resistance nor reassuring nod of the nose as the shiny 727 closed in upon the jet bridge, which, a moment later, smashed into the top left hand corner of the flight deck, just shortly before its supporting tower arrested the aircraft's passage by burying itself in the left wing. And fuel tank. Thankfully, there was no fire but the ensuing massive fuel leak brought about a closure of the airport until the situation had been brought under control. It was like a scene from that iconic 1980 movie *Airplane*.

Vaughan and I, along with a team of engineers, were tasked with flying the aeroplane for the first time since the accident. We were there for a few days so I was able to let Vaughan drag me, kicking and screaming, to the Irish bar on at least one evening. I waited until he had just the right amount of beer inside him before raising the subject of a delivery flight that was rumoured to be coming up shortly.

Braniff was a medium-sized airline based in Dallas, Texas, that operated Boeing 727s and they had one for sale that Dan-Air had secured. This was going to be a wonderful opportunity, clearly very sought after by more experienced and senior pilots, but I knew that Vaughan would be the captain to bring it home to Gatwick. 'Yes it'll be very good experience for you John,' he replied when I pitched to be his co-pilot on this adventure, as I topped up his Guinness one more time before I left the Irish bar for what would turn out to be the last time in my Dan-Air career.

THAT LOOKS ABOUT RIGHT …

What an adventure it turned out to be, and he was right, very good experience for me, as a fresh new airline pilot who had never been further than Tenerife.

In mid-January 1989 we flew business class with British Airways from Gatwick to Dallas in a DC-10. The crew spoiled us rotten, especially when they learned that we were fellow crew and that Vaughan and I had a mutual appreciation for Drambuie after a fine lunch had been served. The pilots welcomed us into the flight deck, as they could in those days. They were ex-British Caledonian and had just adopted their new uniforms having recently merged with British Airways.

Vaughan was a large chap, about 6ft 3in, so towered above me. He hired a large American car, bought a Stetson hat and a pack of cigars and looked right at home in Texas very quickly. We visited the Southfork ranch, home of J.R. Ewing and family from the hit TV show *Dallas*, and went on a few other cultural expeditions while the aeroplane was prepared for handover and the long trip home.

We left Dallas, Love Field, rather than the better-known DFW International Airport, at 4.26 p.m. local time, so 10.26 p.m. in London, on 17 January 1989 for our four-hour, thirty-six-minute flight north to Gander, our only planned stop on the long journey home. Our newly acquired aircraft now wore a British registration, G-BPNS.

We arrived in Gander at 11.30 p.m. local time (bizarrely, they are three and a half hours behind the UK) and booked into a local hotel. It was very cold but the locals were friendly and we made the most of the local hospitality for the forty-eight hours we were there before preparing for the tricky bit, the long transatlantic flight with very little navigation equipment.

Gander Airport was in a time warp. Before Boeing 707s and later 747s, along with the great British VC10, were able to cross the Atlantic non-stop to and from major American cities, a refuelling stop in Gander was routine for transatlantic airliners. Come the end of the 1960s, the stopover there was required less frequently, perhaps only for craft destined for the west coast airports like San Francisco, so the place became virtually deserted and is preserved as a tribute to the vital role Gander played as long-haul travel prospered.

Crossing the Atlantic nowadays is commonplace, with airliners equipped with state-of-the-art satellite navigation and communications equipment. The Boeing 727 is a short-to-mid-haul aircraft and standard navigation equipment was typically VORs and NDBs. These are simple radio beacons on the ground that transmit on prescribed frequencies, just like pre-digital radio stations. The on-board aircraft equipment could be tuned to the relevant frequency and a needle on the instrument panel would point to the beacon. A VOR normally had a DME (distance measuring equipment) associated with it. With this, a second signal transmitted, was received by the aeroplane and bounced back to the ground. That signal travelled at a known speed, so a clever bit of maths built into the aircraft could convert the time taken for that return trip into a distance and display it on your instrument panel. Now you knew where you were in relation to the radio beacon and how far you were from it, so you could plot your position on a map. This was all very good flying overland, or at least within range, 150 miles or so, of the ground beacon, but over the ocean you were lost. Literally.

We left Gander around midnight local time on 19 January. All was going really well for the first 30 seconds or so. When I raised the undercarriage the needle on the hydraulics quantity gauge started to unwind anticlockwise. That's not a good thing. Thankfully, it stopped when the wheels were tucked safely away and we had two main hydraulic systems, plus a standby, so we pressed on.

The needle on the ADF (automatic direction finding) instrument was soon pointing reassuringly to the powerful beacon on the bottom of Greenland. The plan was to head towards that initially and then hang a right to route towards Scotland. We were going to pass about 100 miles south of Iceland, so we should be able to get a bearing and a distance read out from the VOR/DME beacon there. We had filled the fuel tanks but needed a pre-calculated amount of tailwind to help us along and reach our intended destination, Southend, on the east coast of England. The aircraft was due to be repainted in Dan-Air livery there before going into service.

We had no fancy equipment to tell us how much tailwind we actually had. All we could do was to take a bearing and distance from the Reykjavik radio beacon every two minutes (using the stopwatch from my £14.99 Casio watch) and plot it on the map. We could measure how far we had travelled in that time, and using a £9.99 pocket calculator, convert that into a ground speed.

It would be 'left a bit' or 'right a bit' every two minutes until the radar station in Scotland picked us up. We had done pretty well really and weren't far off course. Aviation is full of acronyms. We had just crossed the Atlantic using a sophisticated navigation procedure called TLAR – 'That Looks About Right'.

It was clear we hadn't benefited from as much tailwind as planned, so fuel was getting a bit tight for Southend. The latest weather report there helped our decision-making process. The early morning fog had been slow to clear and, even though it was nearly midday, the visibility wasn't good enough for us to land there. We diverted to Manchester.

The customs people in Manchester were always known to be very thorough. It was a training station for the officers, so everything was by the book. We had turned up unannounced and unexpected in an American aeroplane with all the paperwork and documents set up for it to be imported into the UK via Southend. There was much head shaking and tutting, and suggestions that the aeroplane might have to be impounded until this was all resolved.

One of the more senior officers came a little closer to me each time his authority needed exerting a little more strongly, but he took one step too far. As he invaded my personal space I noticed a smell of alcohol on his breath. At my suggestion, he and I adjourned to a quiet corner of the room, where a fairly short conversation took place. An agreement was quickly reached whereby he kept his job and we kept our aeroplane and off we went to Southend now the fog had cleared and we'd topped up the fuel.

After a few days off, it was back to the normal way of life, perhaps three early morning flights there and back to a popular European holiday destination, followed by a few late shifts and wrapping the block of work up with a return night flight to Tel Aviv. That was a long night.

The staff car park at Gatwick was behind the Hilton Hotel and was quite a long walk to and from our operations room. It was a walk I did several times a week. As I got more tired towards the end of a block of work, I found I was frequently tripping – over nothing – catching the front of my right foot on the ground and having to consciously lift it with each step. This, in hindsight, was the first sign that something was seriously wrong.

'British Airways is recruiting Direct Entry Pilots with a minimum of 750 hours,' read the advert in *Flight International*. Yet again.

It was late summer 1989. I certainly had the experience now, but I was loving my time at Dan-Air. I could be a captain within a couple of years. What a dilemma.

Had it not been for that passenger flight out to Dallas earlier in the year, I might not have been tempted, but that had given me a stark reminder of what the British Airways service was all about and it would certainly be a more prestigious uniform to wear. There was no point losing sleep over it. There was no decision to make at that stage, but I might as well apply and then weigh up the pros and cons should I make it through the strict selection process. Lynne helped me decide to apply by stating what is generally known as 'the bleeding obvious'. 'You've always wanted to fly Concorde and you're certainly not going to do that in Dan-Air.'

Dan-Air was a great airline to work for and they had been so good to me, given me my big break straight on to jets, bent over backwards so I didn't miss Jenny's birth and given me the delivery flight opportunity, so my loyalty was strong. It was small and friendly. You weren't 'just a number'.

The boss was most understanding and supportive. I was dreading going to see Vaughan and tell him I'd been offered a job at British Airways. He told me I was doing the right thing and that he would do the same in my shoes. Neither of us could have predicted that Dan-Air would collapse a year later and be bought by BA. They only kept on pilots who were qualified to fly the Boeing 737, so I would have been unemployed had I stayed. Phew!

I WAS ONLY AN ORDINARY PERSON

The flying on the B727 at Dan-Air was very seasonal. The summer was busy flying tourists to the sun spots of Europe but that market died in the winter months. There was the odd trip to Geneva and back with people who were intent on sending themselves down mountains in the snow with various contraptions strapped to their feet.

Much of our income was what we called variable pay. On top of a basic salary we earned flying pay and meal allowances, so things got a bit tougher in the winter months when that wasn't coming in. While it was nice to be at home with Lynne and Jenny, I needed something to keep me busy.

'Ever thought of doing some modelling?' a friend asked.

'What? Certainly not. Tell me more though.'

I signed up with an agency called Ordinary People. The clue is in the title. In no time at all, I was going into London regularly to sit in front of cameras in various studios. Typically, I'd appear on those leaflets you find in the racks in banks promoting mortgages and other financial products. I'd always been interested in photography. It was fun and paid well.

I carried on doing this into the 1990s even after I'd moved on from Dan-Air and our second daughter, Natalie, had been born. One shoot called for a family scene. I was to play a businessman coming home from a busy day at work with his jacket slung over his shoulder. My wife (played by another model) and children (my real ones) were in the front garden and briefed to express delight at Daddy coming home from work as the cameras rolled. Jenny was old enough to understand what was required, but Natalie was only a toddler, so the only way we could get her to come crawling towards Daddy was for a camera assistant to throw her favourite chocolate on to the grass in front of me, just out of shot. It was the kind of trickery used to get animals to perform for the camera.

Modelling for Ordinary People was great fun for a few years but I had to give it up when I found myself working full time again. Who knows. Perhaps I should go back to it in retirement?

Opposite page, top to bottom: On the snow-cleared ramp in Gander; over the Atlantic, TLAR, 19 January 1989; we all had the same hats from Gander.

Ready to leave Dallas, 17 January 1989.

At Southend eventually. Note the Vulcan bomber behind.

Ask Midland
for
<u>free</u> advice.

Would you buy a pension from this man?

4

British Airways
(Subsonic)
(1989 to 1998)

AROUND THE WORLD IN TEN DAYS

I re-joined British Airways in November 1989.

Just over two years after leaving BA as an aerodromes and performance officer, I was back. As a 747 pilot on a starting basic salary of £15,641.

It was all in the timing. Initially, I was to be posted to the BAC 1-11 fleet and fly the BA domestic and European routes in this rather noisy British-built twin jet, but at the last minute some vacancies cropped up on the mighty 747 jumbo jet. They were based at Heathrow and Gatwick and the choice was mine. I preferred the idea of Gatwick because it was a small friendly base even though I lived closer to Heathrow. Some thought I was bonkers. The Gatwick aircraft only flew to the Caribbean and the crews at Heathrow earned much more money as they were paid supplements for doing the ultra-long routes to the Far East and beyond.

The 747 training course was not too much of a struggle, to be honest. I now had Boeing experience and the aircraft systems, which had to be understood in depth, were a step up from the older-generation 727s that I'd been flying with Dan-Air. The main difference was the sheer size of the beast. It could carry 400 passengers, was 70m long with a wingspan of 60m and weighed up to 372 tonnes, so more than twice what I'd been used to. It had first flown in 1969, the same year as Concorde, and had transformed civil aviation, heralding the arrival of affordable air travel for the masses.

There were four pilots on our course. Ozzie and Bernie were like me, newcomers to BA. They had been flying fast jets in the RAF, so had many stories to tell over refreshments in the evening. Noj had been in BA for the best part of twenty years. He'd flown several aircraft types including Concorde and was now transferring to the 747 but gaining his command at the same time. Apparently, John or Jon is a common name for pilots so, to minimise confusion, this particular Jon always spelt his name backwards. Noj and I became good friends and would go on to fly together on the 747 several times as he too was destined for the base at Gatwick. I didn't know at that time that we'd end up taking a supersonic airliner low level over his village on the south coast. It was, after all, only a minor deviation from our planned route from Heathrow to Bournemouth and was surely good PR.

After the classroom work and a couple of days back at Shannon getting the landings sorted out, I was off. Still under training, despite being destined for a Gatwick base and the holiday routes, I was given a taste of the Heathrow route structure.

After a quick trip to Washington and back, I then spent ten days, literally, going around the world. Apart from my single transatlantic delivery flight from Dallas, I'd never been further than Tenerife. The training captain was a lovely chap, very tall and bearded with a most jolly persona. We went to Moscow, Tokyo, Osaka, Anchorage and back to Heathrow, with forty-eight hours off in most of the stopovers.

I slept right through my alarm. We had arrived in Moscow the evening before and been driven to the only hotel suitable for Western airline crews, which was quite a shock. It was dreadful. The room was brown and smelly. A 'dragon lady' issued you with your allocation of toilet paper in the corridor and a bar of soap if you were lucky. It certainly wasn't the glamour I was expecting now I was a British Airways pilot. The crew met for dinner in the hotel restaurant on the top floor. This looked a bit more like it. There were waiters, tablecloths and chandeliers. The menu was extensive, even though we couldn't understand a word of it. We soon learned you could choose anything you wanted, as long as it was Chicken Kiev. Bottled water was available but very expensive. The local vodka was a fraction of the price, so it was vodka all round.

That might have been why I slept right through, but when I did awake, I was cross with myself that I'd missed the agreed rendezvous for a trip to visit Red Square and the other famous sights of this fascinating city. There was nothing else for it. I'd have to go alone.

We didn't have Google Maps or the internet, so armed with a folded map from the helpful concierge, I set off for the local train station. I'd struggled with French at Hampton but scraped through the O-level. German was less successful and Russian certainly off my radar. The letters aren't even like ours. Here I was setting off alone behind the Iron Curtain with very little life experience. What could possibly go wrong?

I made it on the first train journey OK, alighting at the main terminus just a short walk from Red Square. With any luck I'd bump into the rest of my crew so I'd be safe then. The station was underground and absolutely wonderful. The architecture was a sight to behold. There were large chandeliers hanging gracefully from the summit of each archway and it had a real atmosphere to capture. I was smart enough to note which platform I had arrived at and assumed that the adjacent one would be a likely place to commence the return journey. I was wrong.

Red Square was fascinating and I explored freely without being challenged or accused of spying. GUM is the Russian version of Harrods and its shop front borders Red Square. Window shopping alone was a fascinating experience. Poverty was clearly still an issue in the Soviet Union as the display windows were virtually bare. It was another time warp, with a reel-to-reel tape recorder, the sort of thing that we had outgrown in the UK ten years earlier, attracting much attention and drooling.

It was time to face the return journey. With my folded map clutched firmly in my hand, I set off back down the ornate steps and counted my way back to the adjacent platform. The look of horror on my face as the train came in from the wrong direction must have been plain for all to see. A very helpful businessman standing close by was about to board but took pity upon me. His English was about as good as my Russian, but it was clear that he was trying to help me. I was able to point to my intended destination on my rather creased, and slightly moist, map. 'Follow me,' he said, or words to that effect, as he set off back up the stairs. He led me to the correct platform and waited with me until my train pulled in and saw me safely on board. What a gent. All I had to do now was not lose count. The station names were unintelligible but I knew it was six stops. It was my one and only time in Moscow, so I'm glad I made the effort.

The Japanese struck me as polite, courteous and gentle people, and they all seemed tiny compared to Captain Mike, who was at least 8ft 4in, or so it seemed as they craned their necks skywards to take in his full nautical bushy beard.

Just forty-eight hours after leaving Moscow, we were now in a park on the outskirts of Osaka. This long-haul lifestyle was very different from doing a quick Palma and back and home in time for tea. It was early 1990 and Europeans were clearly a rare sight in the park. The locals were discreetly nudging one another, pointing and giggling, all very politely. It was all very sweet really. There was just the three of us flight crew. The 747 also carried a flight engineer in those days, whose main responsibility was still to keep us pilots out of trouble.

Again the language, both verbal and written, was a real challenge. I never had this problem in the Irish bar in Berlin, but it was all part of the fun. Captain Mike spotted a kiosk and set off at a brisk pace to treat us all to a soft drink and snacks. The drink was in a fairly conventional can with a ring pull, but goodness knows what it was, some kind of orange fizz that was quite refreshing in the humidity. This was another culture shock, being on the other side of the world, with an eight-hour time change and it was hot and humid, very different from the early summer weather we had left behind in England.

The snacks were disgusting. There is no other word for it. I didn't want to be ungrateful nor impolite, so I popped another handful of these things into my mouth, albeit a slightly smaller handful, and swiftly washed them down with the mysterious orange fizz.

The locals were now positively laughing out loud and pointing at us with all discretion abandoned. It took us a while to figure out what was causing them so much merriment. Eventually the penny dropped. It's no wonder the snacks were so unpalatable. They weren't intended for human consumption. They were packets of deer food and as these majestic creatures with fine antlers started homing in on us, we realised Captain Mike had kindly treated us to a pack of deer food each. Oh, how we laughed.

Flying in these different regions was, for me, an education. English is thankfully the official language used globally by air traffic control, but getting used to all the different accents was a challenge, with 'what did he say?' becoming one of my most used phrases. My listening skills were fine-tuned somewhat when a forfeit of a beer was attached to each of my misunderstandings.

Anchorage was wonderful. Again, it was my one and only visit. The most amazing thing was that it never got dark. It was mid-June, a pleasant climate, but it felt like we were on the edge of the Arctic Circle. There were floatplanes on the lake and it clearly got very cold here in the winter. Vacating a fine restaurant at midnight and finding it was still daylight was most peculiar.

It was a strange feeling arriving back home after such a long time away. We had circumnavigated the globe in ten days. We had experienced different cultures, languages, climates and taken in so much. We had carried hundreds of passengers on their global travels and done our best to give them the very best of British Airways. We were a family by now, but all went our separate ways back to the real world, never to meet again.

In Dan-Air I often flew with the same crew members several times, simply because it was a much smaller operation. Unlike office work, where you knew you were going to be with the same people every day, each duty as a pilot is with a completely different team each time you arrive at work. You would typically meet in a crew briefing room just over an hour before departure and meet the rest of your crew for the first time. If you ever flew with somebody again it was just by pure coincidence. The captain is not just there to fly the aeroplane, but is the leader of that team from that first meeting until you get back to base at the end of the trip, whether it be a quick Paris there and back, or a ten-day global adventure.

It still amazes me that you can put ten to twenty people together in a room, who have never met before, and after a short introduction and briefing, they can all work together like a well-oiled and professional team in an aluminium tube, 7 miles above the Earth. It works very well, a credit to selection and training procedures.

There are over 4,000 pilots in British Airways and something like 20,000 cabin crew, so even after all these years, it's rare I see a familiar face when I go into that briefing to lead and motivate my crew.

The Caribbean is Fun, but Dangerous

After a couple of trips from Heathrow I was ready to be introduced to Gatwick operations and the delights of the Caribbean.

Mount Gay rum is one of my favourites and it didn't take long to become reacquainted with its sweet taste after I returned to Barbados for the first time at the controls of a 747. In the years since our honeymoon we had longed to return, and now, here I was, flying the big bird down the picturesque west coast past the exclusive hotels and catching glimpses of our majestic shadow on the turquoise water beneath us in the late afternoon sunshine. I sat on the beach with my first rum punch and had to pinch myself. Until three years previously, I had paid a lot of money to fly aeroplanes and saved hard to be able to afford a trip to a budget resort in Barbados. Now I was being paid to do the flying and to sit on the beach of the four-star Hilton Hotel.

I spent the next nine years as a first officer (add the prefix senior and a third stripe on each shoulder after four years) and loved every minute of it.

In those days, flying big jets into small Caribbean airports was quite a challenge at times. The air traffic control wasn't quite up to Heathrow standards and they didn't have radar or other instrument landing systems that we were used to at major international airports. The weather was generally good, though, and it was never that busy. It was often 'back to basics': no autopilot, just look out of the window and fly it like a big Piper Cherokee. The views were fantastic. There is something very special about flying a big jet, the biggest in fact, past the Pitons on the west coast of St Lucia in the late afternoon sunshine. I've never tired of this kind of flying and my career has gone full circle since those days in the early 1990s, as I now operate those routes in the B777 just as often as I can.

BA typically serve two of the major Caribbean islands on one flight, perhaps touching down in Antigua to discharge half the customers before carrying on to Grenada, 'the Spice Island', or the idyllic Tobago, for example. Aircrew are limited legally in the number of hours they can fly in a day, so by the time you touched down at the first stop, you had probably done a ten-hour working day, and carrying on to the next island was pushing it a bit, even though some of them were only a forty-minute hop.

A typical crew rotation, therefore, was to get off in Antigua, or wherever that first stop was, rest up for twenty-four hours and then pick up the service the next day to shuttle, as we called it, down to Grenada, etc. and back again. Depending on the schedules, it was quite common for the service not to operate on a daily basis, so we'd have two or three days off sometimes in these exotic locations, being put up in top-class hotels. It was a tough job but somebody had to do it. I always meant to ask the tax man if I could claim for sun cream under the 'allowable expenses to do the job' column.

The flying was the safe bit. It was on the ground where it got dangerous. For a few months BA were conducting a trial to save some money whereby the flight crew (two pilots and a flight engineer) would operate two sectors from Gatwick to St Lucia via Barbados. It could just about be flown within the legal maximum hours, but a significant delay would send the operation to the wall and cause major disruption. The cabin crew took no part in this, so were disembarked in Barbados and a fresh crew joined us and would fly a shuttle trip to St Lucia and back.

St Lucia is beautiful, lush undergrowth with a full tropical rainforest on the slopes of the hills. The roads were poor and meandering, and with most of the hotels at the opposite end of the island to the airport, the journey was long and windy and not suitable for anyone prone to travel sickness.

It was on the way to the airport in St Lucia to operate the long night flight home to Gatwick via Barbados that the accident happened.

The three of us had plenty of room and had stretched out on a bench seat each in this small minibus, the type with the sliding door on the left side, often found in the Caribbean travelling at great speed with loud reggae music helping it along. We were sitting quietly enjoying the scenery and thinking about the night ahead when the driver did something, well, rather silly, to put it politely.

There was a large flat-bed truck struggling up the hill and we came up rapidly behind it. Our driver decided he could overtake it well before the top of the hill. We simultaneously sensed that might be somewhat ambitious and sat upright in unison to watch the accident in slow motion. The inevitable happened. A similar bus to our own came hurtling over the top of the hill towards us. Our progress was fair but not fair enough. We were halfway alongside this enormous truck but it was clear we weren't going to be safely in front of it before the oncoming vehicle joined the party.

Now at this stage, you or I would have admitted defeat, taken our foot off the gas pedal and dropped back behind the truck. No. Mr Gonzales had a different plan. He put his foot to the floor in an attempt to squeeze a bit more out of this old bus, but all that was squeezed out of it was a lot more black smoke from the rear end. He soon realised that wasn't going to work, so tucked himself in tight alongside the truck in the hope there was room for three of us across the width of this mountainous road. At this stage, it became obvious that he hadn't taken into consideration the fact that this truck was carrying something: a large bulldozer that was wider than the truck itself.

As we tucked up alongside and slowed down, the blade of this bright-yellow machine joined us inside the bus through the side window and, aided by the slight difference in speed between the two vehicles, sliced its way forward down the left-hand side. Then we hit the vehicle coming the other way head-on for good measure, albeit slowly.

Incredibly, nobody was hurt. Our driver leapt out and ran away. That was handy. We were now trapped in the mangled metal with the main exit unusable. I kicked a window out and we were soon standing, somewhat shaken, on the side of the street with our luggage. The flight was due to depart in an hour and a half. This wasn't good. The rules were such that we had to have a medical check-up before flying after an incident like this, so the local airport manager made arrangements for us to be seen urgently at a local hospital that wasn't far from the airport.

Our hours limitations can be extended by a thing called captain's discretion. It's an authorised procedure whereby we can operate up to two hours over the limit if we all agree and feel fit and well rested. It's used occasionally in the event of long technical delays, for instance, but this was unusual. We did the sums between us and set a limit by which time we had to be out of the hospital. The captain and engineer were seen swiftly, so it looked as if our 400 passengers would suffer no more than a short delay to their flight home.

However, a lady was then rushed in through the waiting room, right past me and into the doctor's room. She was going into premature labour. The whole operation was about to fall apart because a lady was going to have a baby. You couldn't make this up. There were no spare hotel rooms in St Lucia or Barbados, so people were going to have to spend the night in the terminal or on board the aircraft if we couldn't solve this.

Eventually, another doctor was found and I got the all-clear, so the mission was saved. We decided there was no need to tell the passengers that the delay was caused by the flight crew having just been released from hospital after a serious road traffic accident.

The other close call I had, and I mean *close call*, was at 3.50 p.m. (local time) on 8 July 1992 in Barbados.

I was the co-pilot on the scheduled BA255 from Antigua (ANU) to Barbados (BGI). Another crew had brought the aeroplane, a B747-200, registration G-BDXJ, across the Atlantic from Gatwick and we had left the hotel in Antigua late morning to do a quick shuttle. We would leave our luggage and jackets behind at the hotel, jump on the bus and then the plane and fly a quick hop to another Caribbean island. Yes, there's a lot of jumping and hopping involved. The passengers would deplane and we'd have lunch while the cleaners cleaned and then another quick hop back again, all being well, back at the hotel in time for the typical Caribbean happy hour. Normally a nice easy day out. Today was different though.

Whenever I do such trips nowadays I always brief my crew on our way to the airport along the lines of, 'Now, it's easy to shake the sand out of our ears, don our uniforms and think that this is just a quick shuttle, but please don't be complacent. The worst incident I've ever had in over thirty years of flying was on a quick shuttle.'

Bryan Sweet was the captain, a lovely chap with not long to go to retirement, at 55 in those days of course, and the flight engineer was Malcolm Norris. I'd been flying to the Caribbean for three years now so I was fairly au fait with the nuances of the operation but Bryan and Malcolm were old hands. We had 160 passengers on board. A few had joined the flight in Antigua but most had come all the way through from the UK. We left Antigua seven minutes early.

Bryan taxied the aeroplane out of the tight parking apron, the one I'd designed way back in my previous life as an aerodromes and performance officer, and we backtracked Runway 07 to make a 180-degree turn at the far end ready for take-off. Airports in the Caribbean rarely have taxiways that take you directly to the runway ends, so it's quite common to have to backtrack and turn. Quite a crucial manoeuvre in itself with little margin for error. While we were doing this, the cabin crew checked all the passengers were strapped in, tables were stowed and cigarettes were extinguished. Actually, to be fair, smoking had been banned on aircraft just two years earlier. Then we got two 'dings' from the cabin ready indicator and we were all set to go.

It was a typical lovely afternoon in the Caribbean, with a temperature around 28°C and a steady breeze from the east. The aeroplane was fairly light with a fuel load of some 20 tonnes, about a fifth of that required for an oceanic crossing. She went up quickly and at 500ft Bryan commenced a gentle right turn on to a southerly heading towards Barbados. Our route took us down past Guadeloupe, Dominica, Martinique and St Lucia, all clearly visible out of my right-hand window. The flight time was planned at just over an hour, so not much time in the cruise. The cabin service was minimal, just afternoon snacks and a quick drinks round. The steward up front had popped in to take our lunch orders so they could be ready by the time we were on the ground.

In no time at all, Bryan was flying a lovely visual approach into BGI. The skies were still clear and as usual, Runway 09 was in use, so landing towards the east. Barbados is a pear-shaped island, 21 miles long and 14 miles across the bottom. Grantley Adams Airport is on the south coast and the capital, Bridgetown, is on the south-west corner. There are no significant hills and, unusual in the region, they have radar and an instrument landing system (ILS).

We were No. 1 to land and had been cleared for a visual approach. Bryan had disengaged the autopilot and was hand flying the 747 down the west coast at 2,000ft and 280 knots, about 300mph. When I'd started my 747 training I'd been told it was like flying a block of flats by looking out of the letterbox.

The throttles were closed and the aircraft was gradually decelerating in level flight as the gorgeous beaches and premium hotels passed by down the left, affording many of our passengers a glance of where they would be shortly sipping cocktails watching the sunset.

We were heading due south and just before we got to Bridgetown where we would start a left turn to line up with the runway, the approach controller came on the radio on frequency 129.35. In the subsequent investigation I learned his name was Alan.

'BWIA [pronounced Bee-Wee] 426 maintain 3,000ft and reduce to minimum clean speed.' Just from that statement I could put a picture together. Situational awareness, they call it.

BWIA stood for British West Indian Airways. Based in Trinidad, they flew jet aircraft, including McDonnell Douglas MD83s, around the Caribbean and to the USA and Europe. They had tried to kill me ten years previously when I nearly got run over by one of their DC-9s in Trinidad.

As Barbados is the eastern most of the islands, BWIA 426 was likely inbound from the west and as he'd been told to slow down, was probably faster than us and converging. I looked out of my window to the right, towards the west, hoping to spot them. Nothing. And no reply to the radio call, which was slightly disconcerting.

At the same time, Bryan called for 'Flap 5', which was my cue to move the lever alongside my left thigh one more click rearward, having first acknowledged the instruction and silently checked that was a safe course of action. The indication on the panel in front of me confirmed that the enormous 747 wing some 100ft/30m behind us and out of sight from the flight deck, was changing shape as the flaps extended further rearward to enlarge the wing area and provide extra lift for our reduced approach speed.

'BWIA 426 orbit right,' was the next instruction from controller Alan, a minute or so later. The cockpit voice recorder (CVR) on our 747 picked up me saying, 'He's fucked that up and got us too close together,' as I pictured this other airliner with up to 130 passengers on board closing in on us rapidly from behind.

Our left wing dipped gently as Bryan rolled on 20 degrees of bank and took X-Ray Juliet south of Bridgetown and Carlisle Bay, past the Hilton Hotel, where we would stay if we were slipping overnight in Barbados, and then levelled the wings as he lined up with the runway visually some 7 miles ahead. 'Gear down, Flap 20,' followed right on cue as we approached the final descent point to commence our final approach down the 3 degree glide slope.

Bryan was a few feet left of the extended runway centreline but correcting gently. That was a life-saving fact. A fact that saved some 300 lives.

At 1949.52(Z), so 1549.52 local time, as recorded on the black box (that's the big red thing strapped securely in the tail section), the controller announced most assertively, 'BWIA 426 turn right *immediately. Turn right immediately.*'

I looked to the right and there he was. Nose high, no wheels or flaps extended and right alongside us. His left wing lifted and he turned away to the right. His nose-high attitude meant that the pilots wouldn't have seen us ahead of them. We were a few feet left of the centreline and they a few feet right. Had that not been the case, they would have flown straight into the back of us.

I met up with Alan a little later and he told me his radar screen worked in 100m increments. He'd seen us merge on his screen and didn't expect a response. He thought we'd all gone into the sea just off the coast in full view of all the beaches in the Rockley and St Lawrence Gap areas.

There was no panic. We don't do that. Part of our training and professionalism I suppose, but I calmly advised, 'Don't turn right. Carry on. He's turning away.'

We landed safely a few minutes later. When we'd shut down, completed our checks and our passengers were disembarking, Bryan asked me how close he had been. He couldn't see the other aircraft from his seat. 'See where he is now, parked on the next gate? That's how close he was in the air.' That brought home the realisation of how close a call that had been.

TCAS stands for traffic collision avoidance system. It was a mandatory modification for all airliners from 1 July 1992, a week before our incident. It was unserviceable on our aircraft and a dispensation had been granted. TCAS is now a factory-fitted piece of equipment that ensures mid-air collisions are a thing of the past. It's even been adapted for use in small private aircraft.

The standard turnaround on this 'quick shuttle' operation was two hours. We, of course, now had reports to write, phone calls to make and a lunch to eat. The shock of what had just happened, or more accurately, what hadn't happened, but very nearly had, crept over us. As I was carrying out my pre-flight checks ready for the return flight, I realised I was not concentrating. I asked Bryan and Malcolm how they were feeling. We told the ground staff not to board our passengers. We had to take time to seriously reflect and decide if we were mentally fit enough to fly again that evening. Nowadays, it would be out of the question. Anyone involved in a serious incident would be suspended from duty immediately. Not by way of apportioning any blame, but recognising that shock and distraction are powerful physiological influences.

We did fly back but it took some effort to remain focused. Lynne had come with me on this trip and had spent the afternoon by the pool in Antigua while we did our quick shuttle.

'Did you have a nice day at work darling?' she asked upon my return.

'I'll tell you over a beer,' I replied, ripping my uniform shirt off. 'Several large ones.'

There was, of course, a full inquiry but I was astonished to learn that no action was taken against the BWIA captain. He had ignored at least three specific instructions from air traffic control. Politics!

X-Ray Juliet always held a place in my heart after that day. She carried on flying safely on the Caribbean routes for another ten years until she was retired from BA after 9/11. Then she embarked on a movie career, being fitted with dummy engines and starring in the 2006 James Bond film *Casino Royale*. She's the one you'll see in the background of any *Top Gear* episode filmed at Dunsfold Aerodrome in Surrey. And to think she came so close to becoming a wreck on the seabed in the Caribbean.

'I DON'T LIKE THE FOOD AND AEROPLANES STINK'

We genuinely thought this could be the start of World War Three. It was 2 August 1990 and two very significant events happened that day.

Saddam Hussein and his merry men decided they didn't have enough oil in their home country of Iraq and thought it would be a jolly good idea to march into their next-door neighbour's land and have some of theirs. The invasion of Kuwait was the headline news story as we awoke that morning. The missiles were lighting up the sky and the convoy of tanks crossing the border were all there in glorious Technicolor on the TV.

Speculation was rife about how this could escalate and soon the oil fields were burning fiercely. The Gulf War, as it became known, soon dragged the American and British armed services into the conflict and it took six months to politely persuade Mr Hussain that he really ought to leave these folk next door alone and return to his side of the garden fence. History would tell, of course, that wasn't to be the end of the matter and there's much written in the history books about the Second Gulf War and the weapons of mass destruction that turned out to never actually exist.

Any major military conflict, or other significant global event, as we are finding right now with Coronavirus, has a significant detrimental effect on the aviation industry. The Gulf wars did exactly that; not too bad at first, unless you were the BA 747 crew who had landed in Kuwait just hours before the Iraqi invasion and found themselves being held as hostages, but by the time the Second Gulf War was in full swing the public had cut back on flying quite a bit. People still took holidays though, so life on 'the Beach Fleet' carried on in full swing.

The second event of 2 August 1990 was even more significant. For me anyway. Natalie Charlotte Tye was born. She opened her eyes and looked up at us for the first time completely oblivious to the atrocities that were unfolding in the Middle East. She was beautiful and Jenny was delighted to have a little sister to play with. Our family was now complete. We even had a pet cat as well.

Lynne and I had adjusted to the new lifestyle fairly well. It had been hard work as her second pregnancy had progressed, but Mum and Dad were close by and helped out enormously. Jenny was at nursery school in the village, so Lynne had some time to rest during the day, while I was sunning myself in the Caribbean.

I'd typically be away for five days or so, but would then have the best part of a week at home before heading west again. It worked out well and I think I probably had more quality time with the girls while they were growing up than other dads who were catching the 7.42 train every morning into their office in London. Time at home during the week was a bonus. Unlike many dads, I would be a familiar face on the school run, always able to attend sports days and the Christmas play.

We had a bidding system so you could apply for certain days off and express a preference for your favourite trips. Some pilots might favour the golf courses of Jamaica, while others liked the long layovers in the Seychelles. Those with young children wanted the shorter trips and school holidays at home. There was something for everyone.

When I was deliberating over whether to plump for the big bucks of a Heathrow base when I joined, or the somewhat repetitive and less-varied route structure at the small Gatwick base, I sought advice from others who had more experience. The pale-skinned, tired Heathrow pilots spoke about how much they earned in long-range premium payments and the smiling, suntanned Gatwick pilots had tales to tell of a lifestyle much more suited to my character. Howard was a pilot of high regard at LGW (Gatwick) and he described the bidding system thus: 'It's like this John. Every month BA send you a holiday brochure and you just tick off where you'd like to go.' There's more to life than money and there's not much point in being the richest corpse in the graveyard.

By the time the girls were 6 and 3, the logistics of taking the family away with me on the longer trips were quite manageable. We did it quite a lot and once they were at school, most school holidays included a trip to the Caribbean with Daddy. It was sometimes a bit of a gamble that there would be three empty seats. I was guaranteed mine. It was at the front on the right with a really good view, but Lynne and the girls had to take whatever was left over after all the passengers had boarded. We would choose the trips carefully and often only commit to them coming at the last minute when a study of the bookings would give us an indication as to how things would work out. Normally they got decent seats but once or twice I'd make up a bed in the back of the flight deck for the girls to sleep on while Lynne sat on a spare crew seat. It wasn't all glamour, and out of the question nowadays of course, with bulletproof and locked flight deck doors. It was a very different world pre-9/11, with passengers actively encouraged to visit us on the flight deck and even join us for landing sometimes.

I've written earlier about how I picked up Dad's clever way of turning the simplest things into something educational, particularly if it involved sums of some sort. Nowadays, airliners have complex computer support and accurate weather information to help you manage the flight in the most efficient manner to minimise fuel burn and emissions. In those days, it was all very simple, so simple in fact that a 6-year-old could do it. Literally.

Jenny quickly learned that to calculate your top of descent point, the point at which you would leave cruising altitude of say 33,000ft and glide down to your destination, was simple maths. Pilots will tell you that you have to be good at mathematics but all you really need to know is your three times table. Going out to Barbados, Jenny was sitting in the flight deck, her school homework tucked firmly away in her backpack. We had promised the teacher that she would have it done by the time she got back and that there was an educational benefit to going to work with Daddy, even if it was to Barbados for a few days.

She soon understood, at 6 years old, that you take your altitude, knock off the zeros and multiply it by three, then add 10 miles to slow down. It's not rocket science. Well, I suppose it was in a way. I'd taught her what the instruments were for and where the DME readout was. Remember, that's the distance from a radio beacon on the ground. She did the sums quietly, confirmed her answer with me and (from 33,000ft) when the DME read 110 miles, she tapped me on the shoulder, woke me up, and told me we needed to start the descent. Every day's a school day.

The girls learned to swim in the magnificent hotel pool in Montego Bay, Jamaica. They put their armbands on and swam with the turtles in Barbados. In February. They developed their social skills, meeting and mixing with all the cabin crew, even joining in with the early evening room parties that got everybody together and in the mood for a good night out. In hindsight, they missed out on the sort of things I treasured from my childhood, like sailing my model yacht in the boating lake with Dad, or huddled in a cosy beach hut sheltering from the horizontal rain on a Devonshire seafront, but they had seen more of the world than most youngsters.

It inspired Jenny to pursue a career in aviation, but when asked, Natalie was adamant, 'I don't like the food and aeroplanes stink.' Wise words out of the mouths of babes.

A Barbie Jeep and the Ganja Express

Orlando was one of the few destinations that didn't actually have a beach. Well, it did if you were prepared to hire a convertible Mustang as we often did and head out to Coco Beach on the east coast.

The exchange rate was more favourable in the 1990s so shopping was most attractive. Our hotel was actually an integral part of an enormous mall, one of the largest in the country at the time. There were some real bargains to be had and most of us did all our clothes shopping there. Steaks from the local supermarket were also far better than anything you could get in England and importing them was OK in those days. There was a particularly cold part of the 747 at the top of the spiral staircase by the emergency exit that would serve as an excellent fridge for the eight-hour flight home.

I was lucky that the flight engineer was in the shop at the same time as me when I spotted the must-have item for Christmas for the girls. It was enormous. A two-seat, electric, bright-pink Barbie jeep weighing, well, quite a lot, was going to be a challenge to get home. But we liked challenges, didn't we? Some pilots used to bring ride-on lawnmowers and big American BBQs home, so this was nothing by comparison. You just didn't see these sort of things in the UK.

We managed between us to carry the bulky cardboard box out to the taxi rank and hailed a minibus. That was the first bit done. The crew bus was large enough, so we made it to the airport OK. There were some funny looks from passengers as we presented this thing at the check-in desk, but a warm, friendly smile seemed to reassure them that they were in safe hands, even if we were behaving a bit strangely. The staff at the counter were used to pilots turning up with all sorts of strange things to slip in the boot of the 747, so this was no different.

Red tape, or any other colour for that matter, was minimal at airports then, so the crew bus at Gatwick would meet us at the aircraft steps and drive us straight to the crew car park, immigration and customs just being a paperwork exercise for crew. Literally. The kind bus driver pulled up right behind my car, which, thankfully, was a large one. Between us we managed to wedge the box in the boot, well, half of it anyway, the rest was sticking 3 or 4ft out of the back. I drove home carefully and quietly backed the car into the drive. It was about 6 a.m. and still dark, so the world was yet to come to life properly. I manoeuvred the jeep, still well packed and protected, into the garage and covered it over with some old bed sheets. Mission accomplished. That was Christmas sorted. I felt very pleased with myself. That was the moment I realised I'd left my suitcase sitting in the middle of the car park at the airport 30 miles away. That wiped the smile off my face. Nowadays the bomb squad would have been called and it would have been blown to smithereens.

An hour later, when I got back to the car park, it was still there. And no sign of the bomb squad.

The Barbie jeep was a great success though. Natalie took to driving it better than Jenny and was quite comfortable travelling at the higher of the two forward speeds. She soon mastered reverse too and three-point turns, and she was only 3. They would drive round to the local garden centre with me struggling to keep up behind, pull up outside the cafe, open the side doors and we would go for an ice cream. Heads would certainly turn. It lasted for many years. In the end, only one of them could fit in at a time and it was grossly overloaded with the wheels buckled out somewhat. You can buy them in the UK now of course, but in the mid-1990s this was akin to something from another world. The USA.

Jamaica was one of our favourite trips. The flight only went twice a week, so it meant you had a few days off there. We would touch down in Montego Bay first of all, the north coast having some of the finest holiday resorts, golden beaches and top-class hotels. We would charter a minibus and go to Ocho Rios to climb the Dunn's River waterfalls or head west to Rick's Cafe for lunch. The locals were familiar with our schedules and knew which day of the week to compete for our custom with their jet-skis or catamaran boat trips with open bars.

After two or three days the big blue bird would come in from London and we would shake the sand out of our ears, get all dolled up again and be there to meet her and swap over with the inbound crew. We had a heavy day's work ahead of us. All of nineteen minutes, as we would shoot up over the mountains and touch down in Kingston, the capital, on the south coast. This flight was probably the shortest 747 sector in the world and nicknamed 'the Ganja Express'.

Kingston was a whole different world from the tourist scene in Montego Bay. There were warnings about safety and strong advice against going out alone at night. The hotel was in the centre of town, a good forty-minute drive from the airport, which was on a long spit of land surrounded by the sea and close to the historic Port Royal, formerly the largest city in the Caribbean until it was demolished by a massive earth-quake in June 1692.

Keen to get the second part of our paid holiday under way quickly, I'd dart off the plane through the tiny arrivals hall and turn right to the little rum shack on the edge of the car park. My uniform hat made a great ice bucket and, as each crew member boarded the bus after their hard day's work, they were presented with a refreshing rum and coke. Mr Black was the driver, a lovely friendly Jamaican, who knew the routine well. As the bus pulled gently away, so as not to spill anything, I'd lean forward and push play on his cassette player in the dashboard and my UB40 tape would blare out 'Kingston Town'. The party started there.

The next day Mr Black would pick us all up again about 10 a.m. and after a quick stop for supplies at the supermarket, we would head back out to the airport. And drive right past it. Half a mile further along the road we would meet up with Conrad, who had the boat ready. This was a rather special boat that he would charter for the day, and one might refer to it perhaps as a gin palace. It had a couple of decks and plenty of space for twenty or so of us. There were often a few family members along on the trip with us, known affectionately as 'Clingons'.

Conrad would weigh anchor just off the beach at Lime Cay (pro-nounced 'key') and we would wade ashore, taking care not to tread on the sea urchins. It was generally a weekday and we would have this gorgeous little desert island to ourselves for the day. You could walk around it in twenty minutes and then spend the day swimming, reading, snoozing or joining in some of the organised games that normally involved drinking rum. The boat crew would set up the BBQ, catch the fish and serve a won-derful lunch. We all thought the world of them until about 5 p.m., when they had to round us all up, look for the missing flip-flops and shirts and help us (some more than others) back on to the gin palace for the journey back. Mr Black had to put up with some dreadful singing on the way back into town but he was handsomely tipped for his trouble. Plans were normally made to meet for dinner in the hotel, but rarely materialised by the time the after-sun lotion had been applied and weariness overcame us.

I went back to Kingston in June 2017 for the first time in nearly twenty years. Mr Black was by now a supervisor, leaving the driving to his younger staff, and I found Conrad lounging under the same tree at the port with more grey hair than the last time I saw him. It was great to spend some time reminiscing and they remembered 'Mr John' straight away, which was a bit of a worry.

It was quite a long flight to the Seychelles, but worth it when you got there. It was one of the few destinations where we headed south from Gatwick, crossing over Europe, much of Africa and out into the Indian Ocean. The early morning arrival was spectacular, with the runway nestled up against the side of the steep hills in a bay, which meant a careful curved approach had to be flown around the bay, lining up with the runway at the last minute. It was one of just a handful of airports that required specialised training, which we could accomplish in the simulator, the visual effects being so realistic by now that it was just like the real thing.

Rather like Jamaica, it was a two-centre holiday with three days spent in two different top-class hotels. We would hire Mini Mokes and tour the main island of Mahé, stopping off to swim in the unspoilt bay at Anse Intendance, rumoured to be the film location for the Bounty Bar adverts.

Lynne came with me on one of these ten-day trips and we took a plane ride out to Bird Island, where we stayed in a lovely log cabin for a couple of nights. It was great. Apart from all the bloody birds. I didn't realise these particular terns didn't sleep at night. It was a nature reserve, a tiny island with just a few lodges with no electricity, just candles to light your way to the sumptuous BBQ and buffet in the evening. The sunsets were amazing and, with no light pollution, a night sky that was just peppered with millions of bright twinkling stars.

It was on a later trip to the Seychelles in 1994 that my flight engineer was to change my life forever.

A Movie Star in a Slum and Karting with a Princess

The route structure at Gatwick started to expand and soon we were going to places that didn't have beaches. Dubai, Delhi and Hong Kong were some of my favourites; all very different and it was actually quite nice to have some variety now.

It's been demolished now and turned into a cruise ship terminal, but the old airport at Hong Kong, Kai Tak, was something very special. And challenging. Special training and certification was required before you could take a 747 down the approach among the skyscrapers, and I can still remember it now: at precisely 680ft above the ground you would roll on 15 degrees of bank, adjusted slightly for any crosswind, and turn this 200-tonne monster still travelling at 150mph through 47 degrees, levelling the wings just seconds before all sixteen wheels touched the concrete. It wasn't over then. You had to get it stopped pretty quick as the sea, which had claimed several unsuspecting victims in large aeroplanes over the years, was beckoning you at the far end.

We all loved Hong Kong. It was great for cheap shopping in those days: made-to-measure suits from Sam's or, my favourite, silk Chinese pyjamas for my girls from Stanley Market after a spectacular bus ride through the hills. The night life, live music and restaurants were also most popular, and with an eight-hour time change, it was easy to turn nocturnal.

A friend of mine, another 747 pilot, had been visiting Delhi for many years and had taken two boys from the slum under his wing. Joe had taken Manoj and Raju for meetings at schools and even with Delhi's Director of Education at government level. His plan was to get them educated so they could put something back into their poor community. Joe was now changing aircraft type and wouldn't be visiting India any longer. I was honoured to be able to take over from him and pick up on the relationship.

The stench was absolutely appalling. There were dead dogs, rats and excrement along the sides of the unmade lanes that led between the corrugated tin and heavy-duty blankets that were the makeshift homes for hundreds of people on the outskirts of Delhi. It was shocking. They were people, though, people who had pearly white teeth, beautiful complexions and warm, friendly eyes. Mothers cradled their babies in their arms and boys played mischievously among the rubbish. Mr John was made to feel very welcome.

I'd visit regularly, once a month or more, and take a spare suitcase with children's clothes that I'd accumulated from the girls' school back home in Surrey. Families donated much that their own children had outgrown and it was all gratefully received in the slum. My arrival was heralded as families appeared from all directions and followed eagerly behind me as I wheeled my bulging Delsey full-size case down the lane to the little hut that Manoj and Raju would welcome me to. It was a bit of a bun fight, sometimes with each mother eager to acquire something suitable for their children, so I'd leave the case unopened until things had died down a little. One day, I said I'd leave the case with the boys and suggested they could share things out as they saw fit once I had gone. I went back the next day and Manoj said, 'I'm sure you didn't mean to give this away Mr John.' My casual watch was in the side pocket of the case and they were wise and honest enough to make sure it wasn't given away.

Raju was a beautiful boy. There is no other way to describe him. He was small, had enormous deep-brown 'chocolate button' eyes and wonderful thick hair. His teeth shone brightly against his unblemished dark skin. He was like something out of a photograph from the cover of *National Geographic*. He stood out from the crowd. He was clean and dressed with more care than the other children. His favourite outfit was a bright-blue shell suit, a hand-me-down from a child in England somewhere and delivered in another visitor's Delsey. 'Raju's been in a movie,' his friends told me, which I took with a pinch of salt as the Indian film industry is enormous and half the population have probably been extras as some point or another. It was only when I took a bunch of them out for the day that I realised there was more to this statement than I'd first thought.

After we had left the slum and were making our way back to my five-star hotel, I noticed people were pointing at Raju and wanted to talk to or touch him. We caused quite a stir in the hotel coffee shop and I wasn't convinced it was going to end well as I tried to control six or so of these excited little street urchins who had never seen a knife, fork, cup or saucer before. They knew how to devour the cream cakes I bought for them pretty well though. I asked Raju about his movie experience.

'Do you know Mr Eddie Murphy, Mr John?'

'Well I know who he is, a famous American actor. Why?'

'Well, I've been to his big house in America, Mr John. Do you know Mr Keanu Reeves, Mr John?'

'Well, I know who he is, Raju. Why?'

'I've just made a big movie with Mr Keanu Reeves, Mr John.'

I went back home and Joe and I, with our wives, went to the cinema in the West End of London to see Raju starring in *Little Buddha* with Reeves. Raju was Little Buddha. The population of India then was about 500 million and here we were in the cinema watching our little boy starring in a big movie. It was a *Slumdog Millionaire* story years before *Slumdog* was made.

A double-page newspaper article the next day told the story of how the film director had been searching India for his star and knew he had found him when he came across Raju begging in Connaught Circus in the middle of Delhi. I went back a week later and took the paper to show Raju.

'Why do you still live here?' I enquired. 'Surely you were well paid.'

'Why would I want to live anywhere else?' Raju explained. 'Everybody I know and love are here. This is my home.'

I fully understood. These people in the slum had nothing. Nothing material, that is, but they had love for one another and friendship with a community spirit like no other. They were some of the happiest, kindest and most genuine people I have ever met in over thirty years of travelling.

Raju was well paid. The money was placed in trust for him and he had treated himself to a video recorder so he could watch movies and develop his acting skills further. I eventually stopped going to Delhi but I'd telephone occasionally to check on the boys' well-being. There were no phones in the slum, of course, but I'd call the small shop on the corner and they would send a boy down to the hut to get Manoj and Raju, who were eagerly awaiting my return call a few minutes later. I think of them often. They will be grown men by now and Joe kept in touch with Manoj, even setting him up in a flat in Delhi where, when I last enquired, he was living happily with his wife and several children of his own. Wonderful people in a wonderful place.

Many years later, I was to visit the Dharavi slum in Mumbai, the largest slum in Asia at the time, with a million people, from umpteen different religions, all living happily together in a square mile. Again, the happiest, kindest people you could hope to meet living in absolute poverty.

My friend Joe, who had introduced me to Manoj and Raju, called me in November 1993. It was lovely to hear from him as it was a while since we had last spoken. In the course of the conversation he threw another rather wonderful opportunity my way. It was top secret, so I wasn't allowed to tell anyone, but it's thirty years ago, so I'm sure it's OK to talk about now.

Now Joe knew I liked go-karting and wasn't too bad at it. In fact, I'm still racing now to a fairly good standard. I was a bit worried that I'd be one of those with 'all the gear and no idea' when Lynne bought me my own professional race suit and helmet for my 60th birthday. Sixty-year-olds don't do that sort of thing. Well, this one does. And he still gets on the podium occasionally.

Joe invited me to be part of a small team he was putting together representing British Airways to race against the Royal Protection Squad. Joe's old pal from school was Princess Diana's bodyguard. It was top secret because the princess herself was coming along to join in the fun. What fun it was too. All jeans and T-shirts, no formalities, but no cameras either, and we all met at an indoor karting centre in a converted warehouse in Uxbridge, London, on 2 December 1993. Out of the public eye, Diana was able to relax and enjoy it as much as we all did. It was a fundraiser for one of her supported charities, the Red Cross, and she sent us all a lovely personal letter of thanks and a certificate afterwards.

A STOLEN CAR, A ROCKING HORSE AND A SPY

It was a long walk to the beach in Islamabad, Pakistan.

Even though we were still known as 'the Beach Fleet', this became another of our favourite trips. The BA118 would route from Gatwick to Manchester, pick up remaining passengers there and then fly across Scandinavia, the former Soviet Union, Afghanistan and into Islamabad. The airfield there was quite challenging, sitting in a bowl surrounded by mountains, and early morning fog and tailwinds were the common hazards. It was too long a day for one crew to operate all the way through from LGW, so we would do the thirty-minute hop to Manchester and get off, continuing on with the next service twenty-four hours later.

Bizarrely, Manchester was one of our favourite destinations on the long-haul route network. No time change, no nasty diseases nor extremes of climate. Marks and Spencer's was well stocked and you could get a decent curry. What else did you need? We would stay overnight in the lovely boutique V & A Hotel right opposite the Granada TV studios, so it was commonplace to mix in the hotel bar with faces you recognised from one of the long-running soap operas or comedy shows. This became one of my favourite trips after a while and you'll understand why when I get you as far as the United Nations Social club in Islamabad. First, though, we've got to survive a night out in Manchester.

The bar in the V & A became my local and Simon, the young barman, was always good at taking care of us crew. I'm sure the fact we normally had quite a few pretty ladies among our team had nothing to do with it. When he finished work, we would often go on somewhere upon his recommendation, knowing that we could lie in the next day as the onward flight to Pakistan didn't leave until early evening. Simon's friend, Dave, drove us one night. He didn't touch alcohol, so was quite happy to squeeze a few of us in to his ageing Ford Escort. It was his first car and his pride and joy. He was slowly doing it up and had just fitted a replacement boot as the original was damaged. The new one had come from a breaker's yard and was a different colour from the rest of the car but that didn't seem to bother him.

We hadn't stayed out long but we came out of a bar somewhere in Manchester and were laughing and joking as we turned the corner to where Dave had parked his wonderful machine. I walked right into him as he stopped dead in his tracks. There was an empty space where his car had been just an hour earlier. We all offered moral support as we walked a short distance to the police station, where they took down all the details.

We could fully understand Dave's look of horror once he confessed to the fact that it wasn't even insured. The last thing this young kid needed from me was a fatherly talk about driving without insurance, but he got one anyway.

After a wander around the shops the next day, we set off for Islamabad, a packed aeroplane with quite demanding passengers, so quite hard work for the cabin crew. They would pop up the spiral staircase to grab some peace and quiet on the flight deck every now and again until eventually the passengers settled down to sleep.

The hotel in Islamabad was another magnificent wonder. It was a dry establishment though, so not really suitable for us. We had an honorary membership of both the British Club, which was perfect for a game of pool and a few pints of bitter, or the rather exquisite UN Club, where we would enjoy fine dining at a long table on the terrace with candles and fine linen tablecloths. The ladies would dress in their fine little black numbers and heels, and the flight crew would put on a clean polo shirt and deck shoes, which they all seemed to wear. I still had a bit of a rebellious streak and would wear something loud, colourful and patterned. The women would normally outnumber us fellas by quite a large majority, which again, made us most welcome at these sort of places, with the ex-pats keen to join in with our gang.

A round of after-dinner liqueurs arrived, served by the waiter in his white gloves, with the compliments of Mr Denham. This sort of thing wasn't unusual and was often in proportion to the number of women on our crew and in inverse proportion to the length of their dresses. A while later, a second round appeared, so I thought I'd better show our appreciation and went to locate Mr Denham to pass on our thanks. That was the start of a friendship that lasted a few years.

Denham, of course, was his Christian name, just like I'm 'Mr John' in India, Jamaica and various other parts of the Commonwealth. He was a quiet chap, an American, who just enjoyed seeing us all having fun. He didn't drink himself and laughed his little socks off when I set fire to the tablecloth.

I'd never experienced the delights of a flaming sambuca before, served in a small shot glass with a coffee bean gently roasting atop the clear aniseed-smelling liquid. Apparently you had to knock it back in one, a trick that Sharon opposite demonstrated with aplomb, with spontaneous applause to follow. What could possibly go wrong? Nothing, unless like me you lost your nerve just as the glass reached your pursed lips and the flaming liquid continued on its trajectory as the glass stopped dead. Instantly my loud, patterned shirt was ablaze, quickly followed by the fine linen tablecloth. Oops! Instead of applause, the air was filled with shrieks of laughter. No lasting damage though.

Denham invited us all back to his house after dinner. Mad fool. It was a wonderful home that he shared with his colleague, Walter. He discreetly moved the centrepiece gladioli to a safer location as he gave the crew a free run of his drinks cabinet. The music got going and the drinks started to flow while I sat quietly on the stairs chatting with Denham. He didn't talk much about his work apart from the fact he worked for UNICEF. He kept switching the conversation back to me and flying, seemingly fascinated about all things to do with aviation.

'I wouldn't touch that John, if I was you. I got it in China and we call it Snake Juice,' warned Denham as a mysterious bottle with a rather ornate shape was making its way around the room, its contents slowly disappearing. That is until they reached such a level that the snake's head became visible in the bottom.

An evening with Denham and Walter became a regular event for me, and whoever was on my crew each time was welcome to come along. As I got to know him better he started to open up a bit and got some of his toys out one night. Remembering this was the early 1990s when we didn't all have the latest smartphone sticking out of our back pockets, we were amazed at a small briefcase that was produced one night. The lid popped up and one of the crew used this sat-phone to call her mum back in the UK. It was like something out of a James Bond film and there-in, I think, was a clue, reinforced by various other clever bits of kit that I was privy to glimpse along with an invitation to pop into China in the King Air when I was next in town.

Islamabad was a wonderful place to buy all sorts of things at very reasonable prices. Old-fashioned gramophones, ethnic clothes, all sorts of pots and vases, silk shirts, curtains for the lounge and rocking horses were popular. There were many furniture shops and the local speciality was dark rosewood with brass inlays. I'd brought home a coffee table and matching side tables on two successive trips. This was easy compared to a bright-pink, two-seat Barbie jeep, so when I spotted the matching rocking horse, I was a man on a mission. It was big and solid, beautifully carved out of solid rosewood with real horse hair for the mane and a leather saddle. It sat on the old-style long, curved rockers and would make a wonderful feature in our lounge. I shipped it home OK on our flight and we had a big 4×4 SUV by now, so I could get it home OK. Lynne's face was a picture though when she opened the door to greet me.

We kept it for years. It survived the forthcoming house move to Walton-on-Thames in 2001, but the rooms here were much smaller and it didn't really work any longer. It had to go and was snapped up by a very happy family on eBay.

We had recently completed some major building work on the house and, with our passion for nice cars still a factor, I wanted a double garage as part of this project. We couldn't extend the existing one sideways as we were already on the boundary, nor lengthways due to blocking light for next door, so I had one of those rare events: a bright idea. We would go up. We had the garage roof reshaped and installed a car lift so my Jaguar XK could sit up top as it only came out on rare sunny days. The rocking horse sat at the front of the garage waiting for its new owners to come and collect it. I had a quick look round to check all was clear before bringing the lift down, but failed to appreciate that the front of the Jag was actually sticking out from the front of the platform. I also discovered that a solid rosewood rocking horse is far more sturdy than the plastic underside of a Jaguar as the ears of the horse disappeared inside the bottom of the car. The front grille was also slightly bent, but I decided to live with it, feeling somewhat of a fool. Nobody would ever know. Apart from you, dear reader.

The long flight back from Islamabad took us over the most spectacular scenery of Afghanistan and Iran with the spectacular Mount Ararat, described in the Bible as the resting place of Noah's Ark, marking the entry into Turkish airspace. This was one of our rare daylight flights home and, again, routed via Manchester so we had a night there before the final hop home.

Back in the bar of the V & A Hotel, Simon had some good news. While we had been away, Dave had been out and about and spotted his car, stolen a few days earlier. He had the keys with him, so stole it right back again. He was delighted to get it back, but even happier when he spotted the thief had sprayed the boot lid the correct colour to match the rest of the car and installed a decent sound system. That could only happen in Manchester.

The Sunset of the Beach Fleet

I did my last 747 flight from Gatwick on 12 April 1998, Easter weekend, and shortly after that the magic of the Beach Fleet came to an end. We had enjoyed our own little airline down at Gatwick with our fleet of just ten or so 747 Classics, as they became known; the ones with the spiral staircase that led to the upper deck. There used to be a bar up there originally, for the passengers, that is, not the crew, but that didn't last long once the airlines realised they could get another twenty or so seats up there. We'd started off in BA way back in 1970 with the old -100 series aeroplanes with Pratt and Whitney engines. They weren't that efficient and were soon supplemented by the -200 series with more powerful Rolls-Royce RB211s. And bunk beds for the flight crew. That was a great leap forward. The beds that is. The engines were much better too and paved the way for longer routes to be flown.

It was the 747-200s that we had based at Gatwick (or LGW, as opposed to LHR, which was Heathrow) but BA had an expanding fleet of the even more efficient B747-400 based at LHR. They had an even greater range, even better bunk beds and the aircraft systems were simplified and automated such that there was no requirement any longer for a flight engineer to manage the hydraulics, fuel balancing, pressurisation and then lead us to the cheapest breakfast in town.

It was the end of an era. The 747-200s were transferred from LGW to LHR, where the fleet continued in operation, mainly to the east coast of the USA, until they were grounded virtually overnight after the atrocities of 9/11 and the associated collapse of the air travel industry.

Caribbean operations continued from Gatwick but were operated by the 747-400s for a while, with pilots flying from both London airports. Our little family operation, where we all knew one another, was sadly broken up. We were transferred to LHR, along with the aeroplanes, where we were absorbed into the enormous workforce and became just another number.

It had been a wonderful nine years for me. Great flying, great fun and I'd made lots of friends along the way. I had developed my management skills, too.

Whether it was organising another beach barbecue in Barbados, a catamaran cruise in Antigua or a coach trip to the waterfalls in Jamaica, there were always logistical challenges to overcome.

There had to be one last party before it all folded up, so with a little help from my friends, I organised a big bash at a hotel close to Gatwick. We called it 'the Sunset of the Beach Fleet'. There were grass skirts and bikini tops made out of coconut shells in abundance. And that was just the training captains. We had the finest steel band in the country, normally headlining at the Notting Hill Carnival. We had a raffle, with funds being raised for Dreamflight, a wonderful charity I'll tell you about shortly. The prizes were most sought after, things like a bag of sand from Antigua, a bottle of Mount Gay Rum from Barbados or a case of Red Stripe beer from Jamaica. It was a wonderful night, and by pure coincidence, earlier that evening my good pal Nick Eades and crew, flew the last ever 747-200 out of Gatwick. They parked it at Heathrow, jumped in a cab and came straight back to join in the party.

I spent the next five months flying the Classic from Heathrow before my next life-changing opportunity came along. Flying from Heathrow on the vast route structure, with so many people, was very different. The trips were much shorter, perhaps just twenty-four hours in New York or Chicago. The cabin crew tended to be, shall we say, more experienced, and had been flying a lot longer, so they had been there and done that many times before. It was quite normal to arrive in a hotel somewhere after a long flight and everyone would disappear to their individual rooms to watch TV.

Now I knew why LHR was Heathrow and LGW was Gatwick. One stood for 'Let's Have Room Service' and the other for 'Let's Go Wild'.

PLAYING WITH SOMERSET – IN A HARRIER JUMP JET

During my time flying 747s I flew with several captains who were ex-military. Most had been in the RAF before joining British Airways, some flying fast jets including the Red Arrows and some flying transport aircraft like the C-130 Hercules. Whatever their background, they often had interesting or amusing tales to tell.

When I was back in the CCF RAF section at school, I did ponder over the idea of pursuing a career in the RAF, but didn't really think it was for me. I'd applied for a flying scholarship when I was 17, a most sought-after opportunity to have quite a few hours' free flying training in a light aircraft and be sponsored well on your way to a Private Pilot Licence. There was no commitment to join the RAF, but the idea was that it gave you a good taste of what flying was like, such that you might consider joining up.

I failed the medical and was told I'd probably never fly an aeroplane in my life. That was at the RAF selection centre at Biggin Hill in Kent and it was simply that I had a bit of a cold that was diagnosed as blocked sinuses.

They probably did me a favour because I didn't really think I was cut out for life in the military. All that marching about with people shouting at you wasn't for me. Once I started meeting pilots though, who had enjoyed much fun and adventure in 'Her Majesty's Flying Club', I did wonder if I might have perhaps enjoyed it.

I got another little taste of what that might have been like on 15 May 1997 when I got let loose in a Harrier jump jet. Another fantastic British invention, the Harrier always stole the show at air displays with its fast manoeuvres initially, but then coming to a complete standstill 50ft up in the air, twisting on its own axis and then nodding to the crowd, who would be absolutely captivated. The Harrier was used by the RAF for landing in cuttings in the forest and by the Royal Navy and the Fleet Air Arm for operation from aircraft carriers. In such a role, it played a significant part in the success of the Falklands War in 1982.

It was as a guest of 899 Squadron of the Fleet Air Arm at Yeovilton that I was most privileged to experience this amazing aeroplane. It's rare that civilians are granted access to this highly sophisticated war machine.

A good friend of mine, who I had known for many years, held a senior position in British Airways and had been invited down to Yeovilton one Friday for some meetings about pilots transferring from the military to BA at a time to suit both organisations mutually. Geoff had just gained his PPL through the BA flying club at High Wycombe and thought he might fly himself down in one of their Piper Warriors. As this was quite a long trip for him, with the ink still wet on his licence, he asked me to join him, particularly as the invitation was to stay overnight and return the next day when the weather was forecast to deteriorate somewhat. Geoff explained that the team at Yeovilton were sure to take good care of us. They certainly did that. The first thing on the agenda was the Harrier ride. A fine banquet was to follow.

ZD992 was a two-seat training version of this vertical take-off jet that, once its nozzles had been swivelled back to the conventional flight position, was capable of 735mph. It was first introduced to the Fleet Air Arm in 1979 and would remain in service for twenty-seven years, the same as Concorde.

It took quite a while to get fitted up with our parachutes and bone domes and to undergo the rigorous safety and ejection training, all of which left me feeling excited, but also slightly nervous.

Geoff went first and I was there to greet him when he came down the steps from the cockpit forty-five minutes later, grinning from ear to ear. 'How was that compared to a 747?' asked the instructor. 'No it's John who flies 747s,' explained Geoff. 'I've only just got my PPL.' Oops! They'd got airborne and Geoff had been handed control of this high-powered military jet immediately, the instructor thinking he had thousands of hours of flying experience. He had us the wrong way round.

My turn was next. I soon learned why Geoff had been grinning when he returned. I hauled myself up the metal ladder to the front cockpit and the ground crew helped strap me in. There were heavy-duty straps coming from every direction and all meeting in an even heavier-duty buckle in the centre of my stomach. This was all rather different from the spacious 747 flight deck to which I had become accustomed. No wardrobes and certainly nowhere to rest a china mug full of tea.

After the rocket under my seat had been armed and I'd been reminded which handle not to pull (the one labelled EJECT in large letters), the canopy was slammed shut and secured from the outside with a friendly, firm pat of the hand to indicate to Bill, my instructor, that we were all ready here.

Seconds later, the single Pegasus engine roared into life and in no time at all we were taxiing out to the runway. The take-off was conventional, in that we went forwards horizontally, rather than vertically, but was rapid and the ground run very short. The acceleration was phenomenal, like nothing I'd experienced before, and the glass bubble that was all around me affording a tremendous view. The rubber mask, similar to but more sophisticated than the one I'd had to wear in the Chipmunk all those years ago, was fitted tightly across my mouth and nose. It was an unpleasant feeling at first but I quickly got used to it and communication with Bill in the rear cockpit was unhindered.

The words 'you have control' were loud and clear through that intercom and I didn't need telling twice. I took the stick and quickly found how light the controls were. Just the lightest touch was all that was required to change the flight path in any direction. I loved the low flying the most. Such fun. I couldn't work out why the sheep and cattle weren't falling over. I guess all the noise was behind us and by now, they were probably used to low-flying noisy jets tearing across their pastures at 500mph. Bill took over to show me some aerobatics and we were, literally, playing with Somerset for forty-five minutes, including beating up the holiday camp at Minehead on the north coast, where we used to take our family holidays. Apart from the aeros, I flew most of the sortie, handing control back to the instructor when we arrived back at Yeovilton. He slowed the aircraft down as we approached the runway just like any conventional aeroplane. And then stopped. We hovered above the runway before landing vertically, an incredible experience.

We were supposed to meet in the officers' mess right afterwards, but I needed some time to settle down. I never had been very good with aerobatics. We were guests at the evening banquet with black ties and glasses of fine port in abundance, which was a wonderful experience. The after-dinner speech from the admiral brought the house down and much fun was had by all.

Next day, the weather had deteriorated as expected, so I earned my free dinner and Harrier ride by helping Geoff fly the little Warrior safely back to High Wycombe on instruments in cloud. No aerobatics and it seemed so slow.

Geoff and I still reminisce about this wonderful experience and how he was mistaken for an experienced airline pilot and given control of a high-performance jet. It made me think that I would have enjoyed flying in the RAF, but my legs would probably have let me down earlier than in civvie street. You don't see officers limping around a parade ground when they should be marching or jogging, and standing still on parade was out of the question for me. Too painful.

During my time flying the 747 I became a training co-pilot, which meant I spent time in the flight simulators training and checking the other pilots. It was rewarding and a natural development of the instructional skills I'd learned with Joan and Alan back at Booker all those years earlier. Training added another dimension to the job, kept you at the top of your game, and gave much satisfaction while helping others improve their skills or knowledge. It was a role I carried with me on to other aircraft fleets as my career progressed.

DREAMFLIGHT – CHANGING LIVES

It was in the beach bar in the Seychelles in March 1994 that my next life-changing event occurred. The flight engineer whose company I was enjoying, Derek Pereira, had an MBE after his name. He was quieter than many flight engineers and we sat on adjacent stools during the late-afternoon happy hour. I was keen to learn more about Dreamflight, a wonderful children's charity that Derek had founded with his former partner, Patricia Pearce, also MBE. I was captivated, sometimes laughing, sometimes crying, but overwhelmed and inspired by the stories of the sick and disabled children whose lives had been changed, who had been inspired to achieve great things by Dreamflight.

Each October Dreamflight charters a B747 jumbo jet from British Airways and takes 192 seriously ill and disabled children on a ten-day trip of a lifetime to the theme parks of central Florida. Their parents stay at home. The 747 is flown by a carefully selected volunteer crew. I volunteered that late afternoon as the sun was setting close to the equator in the Indian Ocean.

Three years later, I got the call. Was I still interested? I was introduced to Patricia, a former British Airways trolley dollie, as she calls herself. Pat has devoted her life to Dreamflight, from its initial conception with Derek back in the early 1980s right through to the 2020s and likely beyond. She treats every child as if they were her own and there have been well over 6,000 of them so far.

I was honoured to be invited to be one of the pilots on Dreamflight 1997, and again in 1998, in what turned out to be almost my last flight on the 747.

The United Kingdom is divided into twelve regions, each named after a favourite children's character. This is purely for Dreamflight purposes, you understand, and not a reform of local government, although that's not a bad idea. Sixteen children are selected from each area aged between 8 and 14. They are disabled or seriously ill, and for them this is just a jolly good holiday that they couldn't otherwise have.

The children have often spent much time in hospital and never been away from home before. Dreamflight gives them the opportunity to spread their wings and fly for the first time, often literally.

Once selected (that's a tough job for the charity's medical director, a professor in children's oncology from Newcastle), the group will meet up in late summer for some initial bonding time before they all come to a hotel close to Heathrow on a Saturday in mid-October. The party starts there with the latest hits from the kids' pop parade, or whatever it's called nowadays, being played by the volunteer DJ, with well-known celebrities and stars from sports and TV dropping in to wish the children well and put a smile on their faces and a signature in their autograph books as well as the 'must-have selfie'.

The next morning a fleet of buses, driven by volunteers, ferries the children out to the waiting 747, which has been prepared and loaded by volunteer engineers, loaders, cleaners and caterers. Yes, this whole mammoth operation is run by volunteers. The flight itself is like no other: a non-stop party but with time to sleep and take in a movie so they are well rested for the VIP arrival in the late-afternoon Florida sunshine.

An arrival like no other awaits these VIPs, or VICs as we call them. The water cannons from the Orlando Fire Department provide an arch over the aeroplane as a squadron of police Harley-Davidson motorcycles circle around with lights and sirens ablaze. There is no queuing at immigration nor fingerprints to be taken as the relevant formalities have been carried out quietly behind the scenes. These children and their escorts are disembarked straight into a fleet of buses, one for each group, before the motorcycle cavalcade escorts them along the 15 miles of roads to the hotel, closing off junctions and highways along the way, just as they do for the president.

The next eight days are spent at different theme parks. There's much more to it than giving kids rides on roller coasters in the sunshine though. The children are like flowers coming into bloom. They come out of their shells. They gain confidence day by day. They don't have people staring at them, taking in their funny walks, their missing limbs or their badly burnt faces. For the first time in their lives they feel normal.

There is a tremendous team of medically qualified and 'non-medic' volunteers who have travelled with the children and they are boosted by American helpers who give up their time to push wheelchairs or help anywhere they are needed. The BA crew, used to five-star hotels and cocktails on the terrace, find it a very different trip. Their time off isn't time off at all. They act as pool attendants by the hotel pool each morning and evening and are assigned to one of the groups as a helper, often finding themselves cleaning up an unmentionable mess somewhere that means it's not worth applying the usual lip gloss and nail varnish. And that's just the pilots.

When I first went along in 1997 we didn't have digital cameras nor smartphones, so there wasn't much to capture all these magical moments. What we did have was a team of three professionals from the TV industry, there as volunteers, who would film, edit and produce a forty-minute TV-quality film of the whole trip that each child would receive in the form of a VHS cassette. Remember those? It was a wonderful production, fit for broadcast, but with 400 people (children and adults) appearing, each child only featured briefly. It was also too long for promotional purposes.

When I was in the sixth form at Hampton grammar back in the 1970s, I had visited the school careers office, filled out various forms and read many brochures to help me decide what I might be most suited for. The careers master sat me down and had a chat and recommended I might consider a career as a TV cameraman. I went on to become an airline pilot!

He must have spotted something though, because by the time Dreamflight ran again the following year, I'd set up a team of volunteers from the TV industry to come on the trip to film each group and, between us, edit and produce twelve different ninety-minute feature films with every child a star. We were lent professional cameras and editing software was donated.

The project quickly evolved and reached the stage where each February we would borrow a cinema in the centre of each region and the children and their families would reunite for the film premiere and the opportunity to put the long winter behind them and relive the Dreamflight adventure from the previous October. They would go home smiling again, happy to be reunited with special friends and with a DVD to treasure for the rest of their lives, however long or short they may be.

Dreamflight had its own song written and recorded many years ago. I'd perfected my editing skills after a couple of years and put film clips to this three-minute, most moving composition. I covered the whole of the Dreamflight trip, from the hotel at Heathrow to the tearful reunion with parents ten days later, in three minutes, with each clip in time with the music and the tempo and changing mood of the song. We would play it before auctions at fundraising events and there wouldn't be a dry eye in the house and it would encourage supporters to dig deeper into their pockets.

We decided upon a longer version that we could send out to interested sponsors, so I used the three-minute *Glimpse of Dreamflight*, or *The Glimpse*, as it was now known, and asked Sir Cliff Richard to narrate it. Cliff had been a patron of the charity and a tremendous supporter since the beginning, and was pleased to help. We met at a mutual friend's house in Surrey. I'd written a script for him, deliberately leaving out facts and figures that would quickly go out of date, and we shot it in one take. Almost. The closing sentence was a rather cheesy 'It's a real one-off Summer Holiday', a take on one of Cliff's biggest-selling records. I wanted a slightly stronger attenuation and a big pause for effect, so we shot it again. Here I was, an airline pilot directing Sir Cliff Richard in a movie. Whatever next?

I had quite a shock in 2010. I was most honoured to receive the prestigious and occasional Mike Baldock Award from the Guild of Television Professionals, as it's now called. It was for my production of *The Glimpse* and for creating an opportunity for TV professionals, cameramen and women, editors, sound recordists and all the other individual trades, to develop and expand their own personal skills in a charitable environment.

Now, I've never been to any of these award dinners, but I've seen plenty on the TV, so I knew what to say in my gushing acceptance speech. Well it was all a bit less 'darling' in reality, because the room was mainly full of burly cameramen. The chap sitting next to me, for example, was to be recognised for his work on the most recent David Attenborough nature series. I opened up thus: 'My careers master at school suggested I might pursue a career as a TV cameramen, but I ended up as an airline pilot. How did that happen? And now I'm standing here being recognised in the honourable company of the Guild of TV Cameramen.'*

A complete book could be written about Dreamflight but before I move on, I'll recount one story that explains how the charity changes lives and how important the role of the film crew is.

Toby was in the Peter Pan group, which covers Dorset and all counties west. He was a lovely quiet lad who walked with a slight limp and, unlike most of the others, always wore long trousers, even though it was baking hot. He gradually came out of his shell as the week went on and was popular with the other children. His smiles became more frequent and his inhibitions weaker.

One evening, rather than the usual mayhem in the hotel dining room, the children have a pyjama party on their hotel corridor with pizza delivery being the staple diet of the evening. Pillow fights, hide and seek and any other games that come naturally are encouraged and the film crew pop up to catch a glimpse of all these going on. It's part of the story after all. I was the cameraman for the group and had my tape rolling just in time to

* *That's what the guild was called in 2010, the word 'Professionals' being introduced more recently.*

see Toby coming charging down the corridor noisily chasing somebody or other. This was wonderful to see but caught me out because Toby was about 18in shorter than he had been earlier. I'd been with him and his group for several days and hadn't appreciated he had artificial legs. Hence the long trousers and the limp. That evening was Toby's life-changing event. A pyjama/pizza party. He overcame everything.

The next day I was on hand with the camera as he wore shorts out in public for the first time in his life. All inhibitions gone forever, I was there to capture him come off a particularly wet ride in Universal Studios grinning from ear to ear and soaked to the skin. He stood proudly in front of the long queue for the ride, took one leg off and poured the water out and then did the same with the other. A few days later in the wave pool of a well-known water park I noticed the other children were calling Toby 'Bob'. Why I enquired, fearing I'd had his name wrong all week? Chuckling, he explained 'It's my new nickname, because without my legs on, all I do is 'Bob about!' Children eh!' That's what Dreamflight is all about. Changing lives forever. In over thirty-five years of operation, Dreamflight has changed more than 6,000 lives, each with a story like Toby's.

I went on to join the board of trustees of Dreamflight, working with Pat, the co-founder, and the rest of the wonderful management team quietly shaping the charity for the long-term future.

The Dreamflight trip itself takes place each October. Well before then, soon after the Christmas decorations are taken down in fact, there is much planning and drawing up of contracts with hotels, bus companies, theme parks and other support organisations. Each year it gets finely tuned, building upon the experience of, and lessons learned from, the previous year's trip. In April or May each year, Pat and somebody from the Dreamflight office would travel to Florida to meet with the management of all the theme parks and the hotel on what we called a set-up trip. It was all this attention to detail that made everything run so smoothly the following October.

In 2004 things were different. Pat herself had been diagnosed with cancer in March and spent the year experiencing first-hand what many of those Dreamflight children had been through. She was forced to step back from her full hands-on role at the helm and let the rest of us manage the operation for that year. I was her nominated deputy and she handed over her 'bible', as she called it – a little black book full of contacts, from every nurse who helped change dressings to the Chairman of British Airways. I wouldn't have been surprised to have found Walt Disney's mobile phone number in there.

'If we could only bottle this John, we'd have a fantastic airline,' Mike Street, Director of Operations, said to me as we stood at the top of the aircraft steps watching volunteer baggage loaders on their days off, running with bags and equipment from our broken 747 to the replacement aircraft next door.

Pat was in hospital, making good progress with her treatment. It was the usual Sunday lunchtime departure for Dreamflight in that eventful year, 2004, from the engineering base at Heathrow and this was the first Dreamflight that Pat was going to miss. It was as if the specially prepared chartered 747 didn't want to go without her. An oil pump had failed on the No. 3 engine, manifesting itself after the first two engines had been started and we were all set to go. As Pat's nominated deputy, I was trip director and now faced with an unprecedented situation in Dreamflight.

The aircraft had to be swapped for another, which, thankfully, wasn't needed by BA that day and was parked up close by. The logistics of an aircraft change in the normal airline world are significant, but with 192 seriously ill and disabled children with all their special medications, special meals, 100 wheelchairs and much medical support equipment, this was a challenge we hoped we would never have to face.

Mike Street got the message from Ops Control as he was tucking into his Sunday lunch at home. He dashed back to the airport to oversee this mammoth task and rolled his sleeves up and got stuck in himself. Thankfully, I'd already sent Pat a text message saying we were all closed up and on our way, before the oil pump failed. I decided it best to keep the latest development from her. She had enough on her plate after all.

We entertained the children with movies and games while everything was transferred across. We gave them lunch and cleared all that away and finally we were ready to transfer our VIP passengers and get under way.

I overheard two memorable conversations between pairs of children as they disembarked the stricken jet. Many of them had never flown before of course, so they had no idea what to expect. 'I thought it would be warmer than this,' one young lad said to his friend, clearly under the impression we had actually touched down in Florida. Another asked his pal if his ears had popped along the way. The whole complex procedure had taken six hours, even with the team of volunteers working flat out.

Instead of the usual 4 p.m. local time arrival in Orlando with water cannons and a fleet of police Harley-Davidson motorcycles to meet us, it was dark and subdued. The local team of volunteers were there to help us unload and transfer to the hotel, but we were all absolutely shattered by the time we had the children tucked up in bed. Our wonderful team of doctors, nurses, physiotherapists, and non-medic volunteers had been on the go since 6 a.m. and it was now 10 p.m. local time, 4 a.m. in the UK.

The original plan was that a fleet of twelve buses would depart the hotel at 9 a.m. the next morning for a day at Magic Kingdom. Getting 192 children fed and dressed at the best of times takes a while, but with medication and physio treatments to factor in as well, the day starts at 6 a.m. for some. I was asked what Plan B was, given our late arrival and the need for sleep. There wasn't one, I declared. The children only get one shot at this. We were all tired but they were full of beans and raring to go.

We had many challenges on that trip, medical and logistical. It always seemed to run smoothly when Pat was in charge. Thankfully, she made a full recovery and took back the reins the following year. We had all missed her.

Before Pat's return to full power though, Val Wright, another trustee, and I went on the 2005 set-up trip. I hired a convertible Jaguar XK8, my dream car, and at my expense I hasten to add, so we could cruise from one meeting to another in style. It broke down on day one. The hire company were great though and we weren't left standing on the hard shoulder for long. It was swiftly replaced with another in a different colour and off we went.

On the Wednesday morning we met with Bill and his team at SeaWorld to discuss entrance and catering arrangements for our party of 400 and review anything that was going to be different that year. It was a fairly straightforward meeting but as we approached the end, I asked Bill to tell me more about their new theme park that had opened recently.

Discovery Cove, he told me, was a small specialised park, much different from any other. It was quiet, peaceful, limited to only 1,000 guests a day and very expensive. There were man-made beaches in abundance but he really didn't think it would be suitable for Dreamflight. My attitude was that we wouldn't know until we tried, and Dreamflight was, after all, about overcoming hurdles in life. I took the idea back to our trustees' meeting the following week and they all agreed. Let's give it a go. The SeaWorld team worked hard to overcome some of the physical hurdles. They invested in a fleet of special wheelchairs with wheels and tyres like a 1970s beach buggy. They bought the entire stock of decking, or so it seemed, from the local Home Depot DIY store. They helped us enormously to make this work. The money was significant though. It was going to cost around £20,000.

Ian Poulter, the well-known Ryder Cup golfer, and his family live in Orlando, and for twenty years have been tremendous supporters of Dreamflight, raising the charity's profile, as well as organising their own fundraising events. When Ian learned of our plan to include Discovery Cove as a trial but saw our apprehension about the cost, he offered to pay for that first year.

Discovery Cove was a great success in October 2005, and is now the highlight of the trip each year, where each child gets to swim with a dolphin, one-on-one. It is just the most emotional experience imaginable to see a severely disabled child being lifted out of their special beach-buggy wheelchair and see their face light up as they wrap their weak hands around the fin of the dolphin for their gentle ride on its back in the warm waters of Discovery Cove. Priceless close-up footage to be captured by the Dreamflight film crew and featured in slow motion in the blockbuster movie to be released a few months later.

I stepped down as a trustee at the end of 2011 when my own leg issues had reached the stage where I couldn't get around the theme parks any longer. The film crew has continued to evolve, now being managed by the young cameraman I took on as a 21-year-old, twenty years or so ago.

Dreamflight will forever be a big part of my life and those of Lynne and our girls.

Dreamflight: www.dreamflight.org.

THE 'FUNNY WALK' EXPLAINED

It was April 1995 when I was first properly diagnosed by one of the world's leading experts in neuromuscular neurology. Professor Anita Harding saw me upon referral at the Institute of Neurology in London. I was still flying 747s around the world from Gatwick; Barbados one week, Antigua the next and loving every minute of it. By now though, my right foot drop was significant and virtually constant rather than just intermittent after walking a fair distance.

Not for the first time, I baffled the medical profession. I'd seen orthopaedic specialists as a child about my strange legs, but nobody really knew if it was a muscular problem or something neurological. Various theories, including polio, thalidomide and my birth mother taking something in a failed attempt to abort me, were tabled as possibilities in the first five years of my life.

As I went into adulthood I understood there was nothing that could be done to fix it, so why waste anybody's time, including mine, attending umpteen clinics only to be told to get on with life. That's exactly what I had been doing, and enjoying it too.

By 1995 my walking was getting worse as the foot drop had progressively worsened. I'd actually used my disability to create much merriment with my children. I'd often fake that false trip that comedian Norman Wisdom had perfected, even after he knelt before the queen to be knighted, which amused her greatly. I was, however, tripping regularly and an increasing number of my falls were genuine, such that the girls didn't know whether to laugh or cry. I was clearing the table after dinner one evening and fell backwards. The door to the dishwasher was open and they all smiled as this was a rather spectacular stunt. Their smiles turned to a look of shock, though, when I got back up and a fork was hanging out of my arm! We've loaded the dishwasher sharp ends down ever since.

I was going to have to get some support for my leg and by now feared my flying licence might be at risk when I went for my annual CAA medical. Professor Harding sent me for all sorts of tests, including rather uncomfortable EMG studies. Sensors were placed on my head and what felt like a knitting needle pushed deeply into selected muscles connected to some machine with cables all over the place. As if the knitting needle wasn't painful enough, I then had to tense my muscle as hard as I could and hold it for what felt like an hour. Various wiggly lines appeared on a screen with associated beeps and whistles when I tensed really hard. A look of puzzlement came over the scientist conducting these tests, who clearly had something against me for some reason as he made me do each several times.

Professor Harding wrote to me that summer and advised that her research into my condition wasn't complete but that she was pretty sure it was a form of asymmetrical spinal muscular atrophy. There was no cure and further muscle wastage was likely, albeit slowly. I learned how this was a genetic condition and that anterior horn cells in my spine were not doing their job properly so that the signals from my brain weren't reaching the muscles as they should. That's what the EMG tests were all about. I went back for more in 2015 and again four years later for ongoing assessment of the condition.

Sadly, Professor Harding died suddenly in September 1995 before her research with me was complete but other eminent neurologists have since supported her initial diagnosis. On 25 July 2019, Professor Modarres wrote, 'The significant longstanding wasting of his right lower leg is most likely related to distal segmental spinal muscular atrophy as previously …'

I was very fortunate. SMA is a wicked disease in its full form. I'd come across it through Dreamflight and learned how children can suffer terribly and have significantly reduced life expectancy. It's a form of motor neurone disease, so if all I had to put up with was the occasional tumble into the dishwasher and not being able to walk and run properly, I could cope with that and live life to the full.

I was fixed up with an ankle/foot orthotic, a splint, for my right leg. It was a plastic device moulded for my foot that fitted under the foot and up the back of my leg, secured with Velcro. It stopped the foot from dropping and was a fantastic simple, but effective, device. The CAA needed to be updated now, though, as a condition of my pilot's licence, and I feared they were likely to pull my medical ticket and end my career with a stroke of a pen.

I made an appointment to see the head of British Airways medical services, Professor Mike Bagshaw, who has always been held in the highest regard in aviation and medical circles. Mike was fantastic, pragmatic and reassuring. They were only concerned, he explained, with conditions that were likely to render a pilot incapacitated suddenly. My condition was never likely to change rapidly. Once he was happy that I could still push the brake pedals and work the rudders, Mike had no hesitation in reissuing my medical certificate. I was 38 years old. Compulsory retirement age was then 55. My target was to make it to that and enjoy every minute of my flying. At the time of writing I'm approaching 65 and still the holder of a Class One Medical, so am very much into 'bonus territory'. That is the absolute limit though for any form of professional flying.

I've had my medical suspended and reinstated three times since then though. Nothing trivial. Just a carotid artery dissection (2004), an irregular heartbeat (2012) and a benign tumour in my neck (2020), but I'll come on to those shortly.

My muscle wastage has continued slowly, just as predicted, and I have orthotics on both legs. They are much more sophisticated now though. I am the proud wearer of two Silicone Ankle Foot Orthotics (SAFOs), developed by Dorset Orthopaedic in Ringwood, Hampshire. They are fantastic. My 'rubber feet', as I call them, are moulded to each foot and are just ankle-boot high, so neatly concealed within a wide pair of normal boots. Rather like wearing high heels all day – not that I've tried! – it's always a delight to peel them off, though, after a long flight to somewhere hot and humid.

The only sport I can do, believe it or not, is waterskiing. I have to remove my SAFOs, so walking down to the boat is the hardest part of the mission, but then I drop into the water with a single mono ski strapped to my strongest leg, the left one, with my right, lifeless foot shoved in an ungainly manner into the rear binding. The boat roars off up the lake at JB Ski in Thorpe, or Jodi's Ski School when I'm on a layover in Orlando, and out of the water I pop with a big grin on my face. I'm never going to win any medals but, to be honest, I'm rather proud that in my mid-60s, with virtually no active muscles now below my knees, I can still mono-ski. I'm going to keep it up as long as I can, even though I promised Lynne I'd never ski again after a bad fall on a lake dissected my carotid artery on 19 August 2004. I think I mentioned earlier how patient and understanding my wife is.

I've also got the only ankle foot orthotic in the world that has travelled at twice the speed of sound!

Before the terrorist atrocities of 11 September 2001, when hijacked aircraft were deliberately flown into the Twin Towers in New York and the

Pentagon, airport security wasn't anything like it is today. You certainly didn't have to take your shoes off. No passengers, or fellow crew for that matter, ever saw the flesh-coloured plastic splint I had strapped to my right leg.

By the time security was stepped up, I was the proud owner of these two SAFOs, so taking shoes off at security wasn't a problem or an embarrassment. They were no higher than the top of my socks, so all very discreet. They had to go in for a service once though and I had to manage without them for a week or so. Rather than stumble around without any support, I found a temporary solution to my instability.

I still had my original plastic AFO, the splint. Two, in fact, but both shaped for my right foot because that's the only one that needed support originally. They were moulded to the shape of the underside of my foot. With a bit of heat and a decent hammer though, I managed to reshape one so it was virtually flat and usable on my left foot. The Velcro straps to go round my leg just below my knee needed replacing, but it wasn't too long before I was all ready to go again. Now, these things were flesh coloured and I needed to wear them with my black uniform shoes and socks, so I managed to do something clever with black enamel paint to disguise them effectively. Well, I simply sprayed them black, so not that clever really.

I hadn't figured on airport security being an issue but it was. Most places have a separate crew channel and rarely do they require the removal of footwear but I came a cropper in St Lucia, of all places. Now, the Caribbean is normally considered to be a fairly laid back, relaxed sort of place, but they had recently had an FAA audit on their security procedures and had been picked up on a couple of things, so boy were they strict. We shared the same channel as the passengers and when I was met with a rather officious 'shoes', I was rather taken aback. Not a 'please' or a 'thank you, captain' (because I was one by the time of this incident) in sight, just 'shoes'. I tried to ask if I might comply with their polite request in a more discreet environment, knowing that my passengers were all around me, but was just presented with another 'shoes'. Oh well.

The lady behind me nearly passed out when it looked initially as if this British Airways captain had removed not just one, but two, artificial legs. These plastic splints, with their gleaming black enamel paint, were fixed firmly in my equally gleaming black uniform shoes and had to come off with them. I think the security guard was a little embarrassed, but not as much as me. Thankfully, my 'rubber feet' were back from overhaul by the time I got home so this somewhat humiliating experience was a one-off.

I Felt As Though I was Living on a Time Bomb

I always thought waterskiing was a safe sport until it nearly killed me.

It was Thursday, 19 August 2004, a lovely summer's afternoon. Al, a jolly Kiwi coach, was driving and I was really going for it. I took a massive tumble and must have hit the water at 50mph as I shot diagonally across the wake of the boat. I shook myself up a bit, but retrieved my ski, which had been ripped from my feet in the fall, and carried on with my session, albeit somewhat gingerly. I remember the look of horror on Al's face, though, and he told me later he didn't expect me to come up. He described it, with his southern hemisphere twang, as a 'serious wipe out'. At that stage though, I didn't realise how serious.

At about 4 the next morning I awoke with the most unbelievable headache imaginable. I put it down to the wine we'd had with dinner, but we had been quite restrained as I was flying the next day. I felt better after an hour or so and managed to get back to sleep, waking later with just a nagging ache, which I thought I'd better try and work off before going to work. I took my ski gear and uniform and went for a ski on my way to the airport. I took it gently and the exercise left me feeling fine. I'd never fly feeling under the weather and there are always spare pilots on standby, so I'd have called in sick if I had any doubts about my fitness. I flew G-EUUC, an Airbus A320, to the Portuguese capital and back, landing at Heathrow just after 9 p.m.

On the Saturday morning, nearly forty-eight hours after the accident, I felt unwell again and summoned a doctor to the house, by which time my face was a bit strange (or stranger than usual) on the right-hand side, the same side I'd had the headache. It felt a bit droopy and I feared I'd had a stroke, but I was reassured by the doctor's diagnosis of a probable infection from the dirty water. The relief was short-lived though.

My right eye went droopy the next day, so I went to hospital. It took several scans and a few days to establish that I'd dissected my right carotid artery in the fall. It hadn't happened immediately, but the theory was that the impact caused me to wrench my neck and create a small rupture in the lining of the artery, which broke away at 4 a.m., blocking it completely and stopping all blood flow through the right carotid. I'd lost 40 per cent of the blood flow to my brain. The scan was quite clear. To say it was shocking is an understatement. I was extremely lucky that I hadn't suffered a massive, and likely fatal, stroke. The risk of me suffering such a stroke was reducing each day. Surgery was not possible and it felt I was living on a time bomb that was gradually losing its potential as each day passed. The advice was to take it easy and come back in six months to see if it had healed up naturally. The symptoms went away and I felt fine physically. Needless to say, that was the end of my flying career, possibly forever.

I went back for the second scan six months later. It was just as clear. The injury had healed and the blood was flowing freely again. The medical experts at the CAA were wonderful. They had never been faced with one of these in a pilot before, so were fascinated. They conducted much research into carotid artery dissections and, as rare as they are, concluded that the risk of reoccurrence was less than 1 per cent, so cleared me fit for flying again.

Incredibly, this injury was within a centimetre of where my life-threatening 'glassing at the Goat' incident had occurred twenty-five years earlier. Even more incredibly, a third serious event in 2020 grounded me for five months after urgent and delicate surgery was required to remove a 2cm tumour from my saliva gland within a centimetre of the other two injuries. We will never know if anything linked them, but for me, it's too much of a coincidence.

I promised Lynne I'd never ski again after the accident in 2004, but the call was too great and it was, after all, a freak event. I ski gently and cautiously now, letting the handle go at the slightest wobble and rarely even get my hair wet. What little hair I have left, that is.

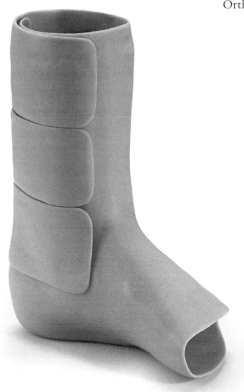

I haven't fallen into the dishwasher once since I've had a pair of these. (Courtesy of Dorset Orthopaedic)

Lynne and Jenny, with Natalie imminent, 2 August 1990.

Summer 1991.

Take your daughter to work day, with Jenny, March 1991.

Another take your daughter to work day, this time with Natalie, April 1993.

Me with Raju in the Delhi slum.

5

TO THE
EDGE OF SPACE
(1998 TO 2000)

INITIAL TRAINING

Back to October 1998. The Dreamflight trip that year was my last flying the mighty Boeing 747. Bar one.

After a few days recovering from a most rewarding but tiring ten days with the sick and disabled children in Florida, I set off on my last 747 flight to Cairo. We had a day and a half off in Egypt, so plenty of time to venture out to visit the pyramids. A few days after riding roller coasters in Florida, I found myself riding camels in Egypt. This really was a very special career with amazing opportunities presenting themselves.

After a tiring day out in the dust and heat, I was exhausted when I got back to our luxury hotel on the other side of the city. I went straight to bed as we had a very early start the next morning. Smelling of camel. I slept right through my alarm and was shaken from my dreams by a phone call from the hotel lobby, where the rest of the crew were ready to board the bus to the airport. I ran around the room like a headless chicken a few times, leapt in the shower, threw on my uniform, stuffed everything into my suitcase and, somewhat embarrassed, joined them on the bus.

After nine wonderful years flying the 747 I was presented with a leaving present, an alarm clock!

I'd been stopped in the corridor in September 1998 by Captain Mike Bannister, chief Concorde pilot. He told me that my name had cropped up that morning at the Concorde management meeting. They were considering running another training course and Mike was asked if he thought I was suitable. 'What did you tell them?' I said. 'I'll let them know when your cheque's cleared,' he joked, holding out his hand.

Every June a pilot has the opportunity to bid (apply) for a change of fleet or position (first officer to captain). Once you've changed seats though, you can't move again for another five years. Every year I had submitted a bid for Concorde. Seniority is the main deciding factor. When you join the airline as a pilot your name is added to the bottom of the Seniority List. As people retire you work your way up. It's as simple as that. It had taken nine years for me reach a position such that I could even be considered for Concorde. Before commencing a Concorde training course though, one had to be deemed to be suitable.

Pilots, quite understandably, are the most checked profession out there. Every six months flight crew undergo a two-day check in the flight simulator, where they are tested on their ability to manage abnormal situations – a reassuring message for every nervous passenger. Line checks are also part of the audit process, whereby a training captain will ride on the spare flight deck seat monitoring a crew in a normal flight situation. Intertwined with these mandatory regular checks, which are pass/fail situations, there are ongoing recurrent training sessions to complete the package to keep everyone at the top of their game. Reports are written so every pilot has a training file, a record of all his or her training, testing and check results. Before being considered for a Concorde course, it was essential a pilot had an above average track record. It was the toughest training course in aviation, so if you'd had a borderline record on conventional aeroplanes, you were unlikely to meet the required standard on a unique supersonic jet.

There was also the fact that the role of Concorde pilot was very much a high-profile one, something I was destined to learn for myself in Seville in February 1999. It wasn't just a case of being able to count backwards from three.

After a review of my training file, and my hypothetical cheque having cleared, I was offered a place on Concorde Training Course No. 28. There really had only been twenty-seven courses before mine in twenty-two years of operation. To put that in perspective, at peak times, it's not unusual for training courses to start on conventional aeroplanes every day.

There are four different stages to any aeroplane-type conversion course:

1. Ground school – A period of classroom or computer-based training to learn, and be examined upon, all the technical aspects of the particular aeroplane. The hydraulic system, the electrical and pneumatic plumbing along with the flight controls and fuel systems, all had to be understood. Some were more complex than others.

2. Flight simulator training – Not your home PC type of game, but large, multimillion-pound, hi-tech training modules where the flight deck is an exact replica of the real aeroplane, such that all the instruments, controls and even seats are interchangeable with the real thing. Simulators are large boxes that move in three axes to create acceleration and turning G forces. They are supported by banks of computers and technicians and instructor panels from where a touch of a button can introduce any fault, fire or emergency that a pilot could ever be faced with in real life.

3. Base training – Simulators are good. Very good, such that they are often cleared by the authorities for 'zero flight time'. A pilot completing his take-off and landing training on a ZFT simulator would

be exempt from base training. The first time they would fly the real aeroplane would be on a scheduled passenger-carrying flight, albeit alongside a very experienced training captain. ZFT simulators are a good investment because base training is very expensive. Especially on Concorde. Base training is where an empty aeroplane is taken out of commercial service and the trainees are flown somewhere quiet, sometimes for a few days, to practise take-offs and landings until they reach the required standard. Sometimes that took quite a while.

4. Line training – By the time you've completed your ZFT or base training, you are now qualified to fly your new aircraft type and the Civil Aviation Authority will have amended your pilot's licence accordingly to reflect your new qualification. Line, or route training, as it's also called, is the final phase, whereby you learn to operate the aeroplane in the commercial world. You'll be familiarised with a selection of different airports and introduced to the intricacies of flying over Africa or the Atlantic. And with Concorde, learn what it's like to fly at 1,350mph, Mach 2, at 60,000ft.

On any conventional airliner the whole training package would last about two months from start to finish. The Concorde course was six months long, with potential to fail at any point along the way. So not to be underestimated.

British Airways has a multimillion-pound, hi-tech training centre in Technical Block A at Heathrow with two or three simulators for each type of aircraft in its fleet. Although Concorde was manufactured at many different locations, the final assembly lines were at Filton near Bristol and Toulouse in France. Flight crew training centres were set up at both airfields and the simulators were based there, one at each. They remained in situ for twenty-seven years, being deemed too delicate and expensive to relocate to the BA and Air France training centres.

THE GROUND SCHOOL

The ground school for a typical subsonic aircraft, like the Boeing 777, would take about ten days with much self-teaching from computer-based training aids that you could run at your own pace and rewind as necessary.

Concorde ground school took six weeks and was what we call 'chalk and talk'. A core group of teachers, ground school instructors, would run classroom sessions with good old-fashioned chalk and blackboards, just like school days in the 1970s. They had mock-ups of the hydraulics and fuel systems that they could wheel in and out as necessary.

I felt like quitting on day one, when the instructor explained that Concorde had thirteen fuel tanks. And they were numbered one to eleven! Thankfully, that mystery was soon solved with the explanation that there was a 5A and 7A in each wingtip, added later in the design phase after all the others had been numbered. Phew. I'll stick it out a bit longer, thought I.

For six weeks we took the long journey to Filton on a Sunday evening, knowing that we had to switch off from absolutely everything else in life until the journey back home the following Friday.

The instructors made it fun. There was so much to take in but they all had a sense of humour and could do great things with a piece of chalk and a blackboard. Roland even had a party piece of being able to write in mirror writing. Take a close look at the picture at the end.

The flight deck crew of Concorde was made up of three people: a captain, first officer and flight engineer. Course No. 28 had two of each, so two complete crews. Ron Weidner was my captain and Mike Hollyer the flight engineer. The other crew was Captain Richard Westray, First Officer Peter Benn, and Flight Engineer Liam Cooper. We all got on well, and again became good friends.

Each evening we would have homework and revision to prepare for an exam at the end of the week. It was just like being back at school. Lunch was taken in the management dining room but we soon learned to decline the wine on offer and not to eat too much if we wanted to stand any chance of soaking up the afternoon's syllabus.

We had been plagued by fire alarms two or three times a week in our hotel in Bristol as we studied alone in our rooms. The ritual of packing everything up and making our way outside to the rendezvous point was becoming a bit tiresome. The routine was becoming quite familiar. The fire engines would arrive, the fire-fighters would check everything out and within half an hour or so we would get the all clear to return to our work. Except, that was, on the last night before our final exam.

I was completing some practice test papers against the clock in final preparation for our big four-hour exam that was to decide if you continued to the simulator phase of the course. I took my time gathering everything up as this was surely yet another false alarm. Only it wasn't this time. The flames were leaping out of the roof of the wing where some of us were staying. We sure weren't going back there that night, so I was on the phone pretty quickly to find some alternative accommodation.

The fire was quite severe, caused much damage and I even made the evening news being interviewed about our lucky escape. Despite all this drama, the final exam went well and we all passed and set off eastwards along the M4 again for a few days off before moving on to the simulator training.

That was fun. But hard work. A typical day was a two-hour briefing session before four hours 'in the box'. There were nineteen sessions as a minimum, twice the number a B747 pilot would need to convert to a similar subsonic aeroplane like the B777. We learned how to put into practice all the technical information we had absorbed over the last six weeks. We soon knew what every switch, button, dial, lever and instrument was for. The pilots had to understand the flight engineer's panel and vice versa. We learned how to take off, how to land, how to climb, descend and go through the sound barrier. All without leaving a converted hangar in a suburb of Bristol.

We went on to cover abnormal situations, hydraulic failures, engine failures, fuel leaks. We practised landing in crosswinds and thick fog. We ran virtual flights with passengers and crew to develop our flight management skills.

The last simulator session was light at the end of the long tunnel, a session spent with no emergencies nor abnormalities, but concentrating on flying take-offs, landings and circuits, preparing us for flying the real aeroplane for the first time on base training. This was where the fun started for real.

Before we get on to that, though, let me show you around the office. Let me give you a short tour of the world's only supersonic airliner. You're all probably fairly familiar with what Concorde looks like from the outside. She's long (almost as long as a 747, funnily enough), thin and streamlined with, even now, a futuristic look about her. The unique and amazing delta wing has twists and turns built into it. From whichever angle you look at her, Concorde is beautiful.

You might not have seen so much of the inside though. Turning right from the main entry door near the front on the left, you'd first go through a short corridor with a toilet on your left and a wardrobe on your right, into the passenger cabin. Concorde had 100 passenger seats, two each side of the aisle, so twenty-five rows altogether. It was all one class, Concorde class, with fares generally slightly higher than those a first-class passenger might pay on a subsonic flight. There were two cabins separated by another small crew area, with our most valued customers being served by just six highly trained and experienced cabin crew.

Turn left going in that front door instead, and you'd have to duck your head significantly as you made your way down a narrow corridor with banks of computers and circuit breakers hidden behind the panels either side of you. Then you'd emerge into the most amazing flight deck ever produced for a civilian airliner. It was narrow and cramped with dials and switches everywhere, but with room for four crew in reasonable comfort plus a fifth fold-down jump seat in the entranceway.

The first person you'd come across was the flight engineer. There were only ever fifty-seven flight engineers who flew Concorde for British Airways throughout the twenty-seven years she was in service. Often underappreciated, he (and I can say that because we never had any females in the role) would sit sideways facing his panel with his left shoulder towards the front. His panel contained all the switches, valves, lights, gauges and dials to manage all the aircraft systems. The hydraulics, pressurisation, fuel, anti-icing, electrics, pneumatics, engine intakes and so on and so forth were all managed by this one professional, who sadly had the worst view out of everyone on board. He was nowhere near a window, but even if he had been, he wouldn't have had much time to look out of it. The flight engineer was always busy. I'll take you round his panel shortly.

The two seats at the front were for the two pilots. The captain, by tradition, always sat on the left, the same as any multicrew aeroplane. His seat would come rearwards quite a bit to permit easy access. The first officer sat on the right and his or her (yes the wonderful Barbara Harmer was our only ever lady Concorde pilot in the UK) seat didn't come back far at all because the flight engineer's panel was in the way. It was a tricky manoeuvre to get in and out of there. I could say something about young, slim and fit first officers compared to the shape, size and flexibility of captains, but I'd probably better not go there.

Take a look at the picture of the flight deck below. This is a recent picture of Concorde G-BOAD sitting on the pier next to the Intrepid Air, Sea and Space Museum in New York, where she is on display to the public. That really is the Manhattan skyline you can see through the flight deck windows and the visor beyond in the raised position.

Now I appreciate the next bit might not be of interest to everyone, so feel free to jump ahead if this gets boring.

Ignore the white cable you can see on the left. That powers a lamp used to illuminate the instrument panels for display purposes. Let's start on the roof panels and work our way down.

At the top of the picture, above the window, there are switches for the alternative way to power the flight controls and then, in the next row, switches for anti-ice systems (rarely used) and landing lights and then a bank of warning lights below them, orange or red depending on the severity of the fault.

On the glare shield just below the front window are all the autopilot and autothrottle controls with a radio box at each end for tuning navigation beacons and the instrument landing system (ILS).

Concorde pilot's instrument panel.

The instruments in front of the captain on the left are pretty much the same as those in front of the co-pilot, so the aeroplane can be flown just as easily from either seat. Looking at the captain's panel, the main instrument is the big round one (circled), the top half of which is blue and the bottom half black. The line between the two colours represents the position of the natural horizon, so this is known commonly as the artificial horizon (AH), although the correct term is attitude indicator. It's essential for flying in cloud as it represents what you would see outside. If you ever saw it the other way round, with the blue at the bottom, then we were all in trouble.

To the left of the AH is the airspeed indicator (ASI), the 'speedo'. It reads from 60 up to 570 knots, even though at altitude the actual speed would be more than twice that, but that's a subject for another day. Underneath the AH is a rather sophisticated compass, and to the left of that, underneath the ASI, the Machmeter. That tells us how fast we are relative to the speed of sound. It peaks at just over Mach 2.

To the right of the AH is a strip instrument also with blue at the top and black in the lower half. That's a vertical speed indicator (VSI) to tell us if we're climbing or descending. There's actually another version of this as well, slightly further right and a bit lower, a black square LCD display. That was retrofitted in 1992, after Concorde had been in service for sixteen years, to comply with a new requirement to be able to display other aircraft close by as part of a traffic collision avoidance system (TCAS).

To the right of the original VSI, the strip instrument, is a radio altimeter (RA), which measures very accurately the exact height above the ground directly underneath the aeroplane. It only reads below 2,500ft, is used for judging landings more than anything and it is even wired up to the autoland system.

There are a few standby instruments close by but let's move to the central panel. You'll see four columns of instruments with five in each. These are for each of the four engines and to the right of those you'll see the angle of attack indicator with the lever to operate the movable nose section and visor just above that in a black square box. You won't find one of those in a 747.

In the centre console, at around knee height, are two boxes with buttons. They are two inertial navigation computers (INSs). There's a third out of shot at the back of the console. The big round instrument behind the co-pilot's INS is a temperature gauge and shows the crucial temperature on the nose of the aircraft. That mustn't exceed 127°C. The outside air temperature is also displayed, typically -60°C.

There's an empty box in the middle at the front of the centre console. That is where the all-important performance and navigation manuals would be stowed, the ones I would carefully put there before flight when I worked in the Aircraft Library back in the late 1970s.

To the outside of each pilot you'll find a black handle connected to a tiller, which is used to steer the aircraft on the ground by turning the nose wheel, located 37ft behind the pilot. In front of that there's the all-important cup holders. Perhaps that's a good excuse for a tea break now, before we go on to the flight engineer's panel?

Here you can see the back of the co-pilot's, or first officer's, seat on the left and then how the panel is vertical in front of the engineer and then slopes backwards to follow the roof contours. I'll just point out some of the features.

On the left at head height are the controls for the engine intakes, controlled by the first digital computers to be used in aviation. There's a row of secondary engine instruments to the right and above that the controls for the cabin pressurisation system.

Concorde Flight Engineer's panel.

Concorde fuel panel.

Right in front of the seat, starting halfway up the upper panel and going down to the fuel shut-off switches (circled), is the mammoth fuel control system, shown in more detail above.

At the far right are the hydraulic controls (top) and the electrical system management panel beneath.

The fuel system was a most complex and crucial part of the aeroplane. If you look carefully, you can see the thirteen fuel gauges and in the middle the vertical centre of gravity indicator with the associated computer controls to its right. The LED indicators at the bottom tell us how much fuel each engine has used so far on this flight.

So there we are – ready for the exam?

BASE TRAINING

The week we spent base training was probably one of the best of my life.

I'd watched that first flight on TV in black and white in March 1969. I'd stood wide-mouthed and teary-eyed at Farnborough in 1972 as the prototype was put through her paces in front of the crowd. I'd bunked off school to watch the first commercial flight take off in January 1976. I'd raided the rear galley of fine leftovers when I worked in the Aircraft Library putting all the maps and books on board, and sat absolutely dumb-struck in the pilots' seats in the course of my work. Now I was ready to fly her for the first time. Words can't describe the anticipation, the excitement and the sense of privilege and responsibility.

Concorde G-BOAF, the last built (she first flew on 20 April 1979) and the one destined to feature in the iconic last landing photograph over the Clifton Suspension Bridge on 26 November 2003, was ours for the week.

As well as us six trainees, there was a team of instructors, managers, instructors who were both training and checking out new instructors and engineers to keep the aircraft maintained. The cargo holds were full, not with the usual Louis Vuitton luggage belonging to the rich and famous drinking the finest champagne in the cabin, but with spare tyres and tool kits.

It was a cold and damp day in February 1999. Our destination for our training was Shannon in southern Ireland. Richard went first and we taxied out at Heathrow with the rest of us crammed into the tiny flight deck watching with excitement and awe. We took our seats as Richard taxied into position for take-off. I chose to sit in the rear cabin, knowing that it was an experience I was unlikely to be able to repeat.

Every take-off in Concorde is with full power and reheat, or after-burner, as it's also known, regardless of the weight or weather. Normal procedure with subsonic aircraft is to use what we call derated power. We calculate in advance what the minimum thrust required is and only use that. It varies with the weight of the aircraft, itself a most flexible figure depending on passenger load and the length of the flight. We don't just 'fill it up and go'. We only uplift the fuel we need, plus sensible reserve amounts of course.

That day there weren't 100 passengers on board. There were fewer than twenty of us. There was no significant luggage. No crates of fine champagne nor chilled trolleys of caviar or smoked salmon. The fuel loaded to get to Shannon was just a fraction of the 95 tonnes or so normally uplifted for a transatlantic flight to New York. Concorde was, by comparison, as light as a feather. It was still going to be full power and reheat though, rather than any derated power.

That first take-off experience as a passenger was something else, but still nothing compared to what I was to experience in a few days' time when it was my turn to be at the controls.

Shannon is normally a perfect airfield for base training. It's used regularly by many airlines and not just because the legendary seventeenth-century thatched tavern Durty Nelly's is just ten minutes away, serving fine food and silky smooth Guinness. This was my third visit there for base training. It has a long enough runway, isn't too busy with commercial traffic and the surrounding area isn't too populated. Think aircraft noise issues. It has a fairly good track record for good weather too, being fairly close to the coast, with the warm Gulf Stream coming in from the Atlantic. It could rain though and when it did it lasted for days on end. That's exactly what happened that week in February 1999. Richard managed a couple of circuits but the cloud base was right on the limit so the session was soon aborted. We adjourned to the pub to plan our next move. The forecast wasn't good.

The managers and training captains literally produced a map of Europe and searched for an airport that had the same qualities as Shannon, albeit with better weather. The following morning, with Ron at the controls in the left-hand seat, as the captain under training, we launched and headed south, out over the Atlantic Ocean and down into the Bay of Biscay. As our flight path was over the sea we had no restrictions, so rather unusually Ron's first take-off was quickly followed by a transition through the sound barrier and onwards and upwards to Mach 2 and 60,000ft. For the first time we saw the curvature of the earth and the ink-black sky above us stretching into space and on to infinity. We felt the metal window frames in the flight deck become too hot to touch as the temperature on the nose of the aircraft reached 127°C. It was -60°C outside. All too quickly it was time to decelerate and descend and return to the normal airways populated by subsonic airliners.

Our arrival in Seville was nothing short of spectacular. Concorde had never been there before and thousands of people turned out to welcome us. It was like going back to 1969, with the surrounding roads jammed solid and our every move covered by TV cameras.

Each of us four pilots had to do a minimum of thirteen take-offs and landings, and while this was going on Liam and Mike took turns on the flight engineer's panel with their instructors, Ian Fellows-Freeman and Trevor Norcott, watching over them.

For training flights like these, where all we were doing was take-offs and landings, there were limitations on the fuel we could carry, a maximum figure for take-off and a minimum for landing. This meant that, unlike base training on a conventional aeroplane, where you could bash the circuit for hours on end, we were limited to sessions of about an hour. In between each session there were engineering checks to be completed, paperwork to be done, refuelling and, inevitably, the odd tyre change. We were going to be in sunny Seville for about three days.

My turn eventually came late in the afternoon of Thursday, 18 February 1999. I was to fly Concorde for the very first time. It was to be an experience like no other in aviation. It was to be up there with my first solo at Booker almost twenty years previously. And some. Thousands of pilots had gone solo in the nearly 100 years since the Wright Brothers first flew in *Kitty Hawk* in 1903, but the number who had flown Concorde was still in the low hundreds. This was to be one of the greatest experiences of my life.

I was the team photographer. I've written about my interest in making movies for Dreamflight and how I'd learned to film and edit, so I'd taken a decent SLR camera along with me and my Sony VHS camcorder. Both would be museum pieces now, but I'd managed to film everybody's first take-off and landing. I handed my precious equipment over to Ron as I climbed the steps to enter G-BOAF. She was gleaming in the late afternoon Spanish sunshine, raring to go. The word 'Seville' was in bold letters on the top of the terminal building now in view above the special white high-temperature paint on the fuselage. At the top of the steps I paused and looked left and could see the nose of the aircraft with that trademark long pitot tube pointing directly at the setting sun. It would be a race against time as we couldn't fly the circuits in the dark.

Les Brodie, Flight Training Manager, was already in the captain's seat on the left and he settled me into the co-pilot's seat for the first time. The seat controls for up and down and back and forth were just like the simulator and thankfully everything else looked familiar and fell neatly into place. It wasn't long before we established communication with the support engineers on the headset plugged in by the nose wheel. The passenger door closed with a soft thud and the steps were wheeled away to the edge of the parking area. We were really going. I thought I'd be nervous but, no, there wasn't time for that; a feeling of excitement and disbelief were perhaps rumbling through my stomach slightly. Either that or the paella hadn't been a good idea for lunch.

The engine start routine was soon under way. Most conventional aeroplanes have a thing called an auxiliary power unit (APU) to provide the compressed air and electrical supply needed, but Concorde wasn't fitted with one, to save crucial weight. Giant umbilical cords, or rather two big rubber pipes, linked the underside of the aeroplane to a rather noisy and smelly air start truck that had been towed into position alongside. Talking of noisy and smelly, it wasn't long before the first two Rolls-Royce Olympus engines, the inboards on each side, were winding up to idle power with a crescendo of raw jet noise and a slight vibration through the floor accompanying the power. Mike Hollyer was working the flight engineer's panel just behind me under the watchful eye of Senior Flight Engineer Pete Carrigan. Mike brought the engine-driven generators online and checked their frequencies and outputs before releasing the ground support team with their equipment. Concorde now sat purring away on two engines, sending a whiff of kerosene every now and again through the air-conditioning systems to remind us upstairs that she was very much alive now. Bleeding compressed air from our two running engines and directing it through various engine start valves, Mike was quickly able to get the other two engines, the outboards, turning and burning and then bring their generators online.

With the after start checklist complete, it was time for me to ask Les for 'nose to five' and he reached across and moved the nose/visor control down two slots and I watched in amazement as the glass heat shield first slid down inside the nose and then the long pointy thing itself gradually dipped in salute to the, now even lower, ball of fire slipping slowly towards the horizon.

'Speedbird Concorde Alpha Foxtrot request taxi,' told air traffic control we were ready to go. I reached down and released the parking brake and she started moving straight away, the thrust from those Olympus brutes just on tick over being more than enough to get us rolling towards the runway. I'd been used to taxiing big aeroplanes. The 747, after all, was one of the biggest and you'll remember that was like sitting up on the fourth floor of a block of flats and steering them around by looking out of the letter box. Concorde was unique though. I was sitting 37ft, or over 10m in new money, in front of the nose wheel and 100ft/30m in front of the main undercarriage. I've never driven an articulated lorry, but I'm always amazed at how they get those things round tight corners in small villages without taking the roof off the post office. Well, not too often anyway. This was a similar precision exercise and it really wouldn't have been a good career move if I'd cut the first corner and sunk up to our axles in the grass. Thankfully Les had done this before. Well, now, come to think of it, he hadn't actually. Because Concorde training flights were so rare, Les was actually getting checked out as a base training captain, so this was his first time teaching a novice Concorde pilot how to taxi and then fly the real aeroplane. All five seats on the flight deck were occupied with trainers training trainers to train trainees.

We taxied out for take-off with now just minutes to spare before sunset and close of business for the day. I was the last of the trainees to fly. This was my big moment. If only the world would stop spinning so fast and we could delay the onset of nightfall for just a few more minutes.

Concorde has no flaps like a conventional aeroplane so we didn't have to run those out for take-off, but instead complete numerous other checks and procedures along the way, all ticked off against the now familiar before take-off checklist. We had, of course, rehearsed all this in the simulator back in the training hall at Filton, just down the road from the burnt hotel, but all that now felt a million miles away. This was for real.

'Speedbird Concorde Alpha Foxtrot, you're cleared for take-off,' came through our headsets simultaneously. This was that precise manoeuvre we'd practised over and over again that started with a countdown from three.

The reheats were armed as we turned on to the runway. I was steering with a tiller in my right hand linked electrically and hydraulically to the nose wheel and I rolled out onto the runway centreline. Over 3km of glistening tarmac lay ahead of me with a big orange ball now sitting just above the far end in majestic glory enhancing the silhouette of the city off to the left ahead.

Concorde has a very special wing, full of twists and turns, sloping gently towards the ground with highly swept-back leading edges and a unique delta-wing profile, completely different in shape, form and function from any conventional aeroplane. In any other flying machine, as soon as you start to accelerate down the runway and the air starts flowing over and under the wing, a pressure differential starts to form with lower pressure on the topside, so that the miraculous force of lift starts to take the weight off the wheels and eventually, with the amount of lift increasing in proportion to the aircraft's speed, enough lift is generated to take the craft into the air. The principle's the same whether it be a two-seat Cessna or a 500-tonne A380. Concorde's wing didn't generate any lift at all during the take-off run.

That's why it was always full power with reheat regardless of the aircraft weight. We needed to get to that vital lift-off speed and get the wing working as quickly as possible. The lighter the aeroplane, the faster it went. A Concorde departing for New York from Heathrow with 100 passengers would have had up to 93 tonnes of fuel on board and an all-up weight of about 185 tonnes. And that would shift. We had five of us on board and fuel for two hours of flight. This was going to be quick.

The simulator is great. We'd practised this next bit over and over again, just like astronauts preparing for their first mission. We all knew who was going to say what, who was going to push and pull – that was my job – and who was going to monitor very carefully all the instruments and indicators and initiate emergency stop procedures, an aborted take-off, should things not go to plan.

'Three, two, one, now' … I pushed all four throttles fully forward until they'd go no further.

'Speed building.'

'Power set.'

'Oh fuck.'

The last two were my words, possibly actually said out loud, as I was thrust backwards into my seat.

'100 knots.'

'V1.'

'Rotate.'

The simulator was good. Very good. But it can't prepare you for the noise, the smell of the kerosene through the ducting, the bouncing of the flight deck, the sheer acceleration of this absolutely incredible flying machine. We were airborne in seconds. At the call of 'rotate' I had to gently pull back with the control column in my right hand at 3 degrees a second and raise the nose until I nailed a pitch attitude of 18 degrees. And then we had to level off. At just 2,000ft. Mike chopped the power to a pre-calculated TLA, a throttle lever angle literally marked on the throttle quadrant on the central pedestal. As he did so I pushed. I told you my job was all about pushing and pulling. I progressively but firmly lowered the nose by about half, fine-tuning the attitude as I did so, to achieve level flight. At 2,000ft. No more, no less.

I'd been warned how quickly it all happened and how the training captains had run a book of the greatest altitude reached by a novice Concorde pilot in his attempt to level at 2,000ft. I was told the record was 7,200ft.

The undercarriage had been tucked away just after take-off. Even that was an incredible piece of engineering. Concorde sat very high off the ground. She had to in order to stop the tail hitting the ground on landing when she came in at 11 degrees nose up. The undercarriage legs were longer than half the width of the fuselage, so that when they folded inwards in the normal manner they would have met and become entangled with a nasty metallic grinding noise, not very conducive for streamlined supersonic flight. The clever engineering chaps had solved this problem by making each leg telescopic so that when the landing gear retraction process is commenced, the first event is that hydraulic motors run to retract the legs a few inches inside themselves, before they fold inwards. Look carefully at the wheels when you next visit Concorde in a museum and you'll be able to identify all these moving parts.

With the undercarriage having gone through its complex retraction process, I turned the aircraft right-hand downwind, a turn through 180 degrees putting the sun now directly behind us and the runway from which we had just departed back alongside us again, down on my right-hand side. Thankfully Mike had remembered to cancel the reheats after take-off so I was able to limit the speed to the planned 250 knots. With a touch of tailwind that was pretty close to 300mph, so it wasn't long at all before we were back at the other end of the circuit and ready to turn in for my first landing.

Air traffic control announced that it was now official sunset and we would have to stop. Les was negotiating with them. Something like, 'Oh go on, please, just one more', but they were adamant. This was to be my one and only landing this day. Les came back into training mode just at the right time to give me those few last-minute reminders about how to achieve a good touchdown.

Because Concorde has no flaps or slats, extendable devices on the front and back of conventional wings that increase its size to give more lift, she has to come in at a much greater angle of attack. No steeper, and only 20 to 30 knots faster than a normal airliner, but with the nose pointing 11 degrees up in the air rather than the normal 2 to 3 degrees. We wouldn't have been able to see the runway for landing had some clever chap not come up with this concept of a nose that could be lowered. Hinged just in front of the flight deck and operated hydraulically, with the visor already down, the nose was lowered to the fully down, 12.5-degree position and just out of our line of sight, making judgement against the horizon tricky sometimes. The early test pilots commented on this, so little flip-up bits of metal were installed on the coaming that we could raise to help us reference the horizon and keep the wings level.

Using the red and white precision approach path indicators (PAPIs) guidance lights alongside the touchdown point, I made small corrections to the power with my left hand to adjust the rate of descent very slightly to nail the 3-degree approach path.

Landing a conventional aeroplane is a co-ordinated manoeuvre called a flare. You gently close the throttle and pull back on the stick to raise the nose and reduce the rate of descent, holding it steady until the main wheels behind you gently kiss the concrete. Then you lower the nose and stand on the brake pedals.

Landing Concorde, like most manoeuvres in the aeroplane, is just that little bit more precise. The actions are similar but for a different reason. Just before you touch the ground you chop the power by closing the throttles at 15ft above the ground. Judging this was aided by the flight engineer calling out the heights from a very accurate radio altimeter. As the large delta wing approached the ground it would tend to squeeze the air between it and the runway, which had the effect of trying to tip the nose forward. I'd have to pull progressively back on the control column, not to raise the nose, but to stop it from dropping. In fact, it was vital I didn't raise the nose because I would have hit the back of the aeroplane on the ground. You've probably noticed they actually fitted a small retractable wheel at the back just in case I got this bit wrong.

Once the main wheels were down it was a case of flying that nose wheel down to the ground promptly, applying maximum brake pressure with your feet and pulling full reverse thrust with your left hand. All while trying to finish off the leftover caviar. Only kidding. We didn't have that on the training flights. The brand they served on the New York flights though was something very special, so I'd been told.

The deceleration on Concorde was nearly as exciting as the take-off and I was soon to discover that it was customary to warn the passengers what they could expect to avoid frightening the living daylights out of them.

Well, I'd done it. I'd just flown Concorde for the first time. The landing was fine and we'd do many more tomorrow. We taxied in and shut down. It was just after 6 p.m. I was mentally drained. The whole flight including the taxi in and out had lasted just twenty-four minutes (5.56 p.m. to 6.20 p.m.). The steps came back alongside and I was ready to find a cold beer, but what happened next was totally unexpected.

We had been in Seville for three days now and there was still much media interest, and crowds of onlookers appeared each time the Olympus engines started up in readiness for a few more circuits. Unbeknown to me though, that first circuit I had just flown, as the sun was setting, had been covered live on the 6 p.m. news. I was still in my pilot's seat soaking up what had just happened and talking it through as a debrief with Les, when, out of the blue, a TV crew appeared in the cockpit and interviewed me live on the telly about what it was like to fly Concorde for the first time. I felt like a rabbit caught in the headlights. Still coming down from the elation of what had just happened, I fought to put some eloquence into my description of my first flight, rather than come across as a gibbering idiot. It was a sudden introduction to the spotlight and the high-profile role to which I had just been inducted.

We had all flown now. Even though I had only completed that one circuit, it was a milestone reached. A celebration was called for, so Mike Bannister, the chief pilot, hosted a wonderful dinner in the hotel restaurant. As I considered a glass of fine Rioja, he tipped me the wink that the plan was to 'get me finished first thing in the morning'. So a sober celebration it was then.

After an early night we were back alongside 'Alpha Foxtrot' as the sun came up. It was a chilly start to the day with overnight clear skies, but it was to warm up nicely as the day progressed. By 8 a.m. we were ready to go again. Mike Hollyer was back in the flight engineer's seat under the supervision of the more experienced Dave Hoyle, and training captain Les Brodie was back in command.

We taxied out and flew for just over an hour. We could have got halfway across the Atlantic in that time, but we never went above 2,000ft nor further than 5 miles from Seville Airport. We pounded the circuit. CAA approval had just been granted to drop the minimum number of landings required to qualify to thirteen. You had to be able to fly approaches and decent landings with and without the instrument landing system (ILS), and ultimately with that disabled, as well as the PAPIs. They are a bank of four lights to the side of the runway abeam the touchdown point. They give you an accurate visual indication of a 3-degree glide slope or approach path. The ideal path will be dictated by two red lights and two white lights. Too high and you get three, becoming four white lights, and too low, they all turn red. Red lights are rarely a good thing in aviation. There's an old joke about when they all turn green you are really in trouble. Because you're looking at them through the long grass. That's an old joke though, so I won't tell you that one.

The picture out of the window is so different in Concorde from any conventional aeroplane that it does take some getting used to. After another twelve circuits that morning though, I had produced consistently safe landings with ultimately no electronic nor visual glide slope indications, just 'seat of the pants, mark-one eyeball' judgement.

By 9.30 a.m. on 19 February 1999 I had completed my Concorde training. Or not.

The paperwork was sent off to the CAA. Much money changed hands behind the scenes and I was issued with a type rating certificate to show that I could legally take the controls of a Concorde and fly it competently.

All I had done by now, though, was to learn about all the technical aspects of the aeroplane, complete my simulator training to handle potential abnormal situations and learn, in the real aeroplane, how to do take-offs and landings. Operating the aeroplane on the edge of space at twice the speed of sound with 100 VIP passengers behind you was a whole different world. Route training was next.

ROUTE TRAINING

Concorde had already been in service for twenty-three years. That first flight to Bahrain way back on 21 January 1976, when I was still a schoolboy, had heralded the start of supersonic passenger services. The route eventually extended to Singapore but it was the transatlantic market that was to become the backbone of the Concorde operation. British Airways eventually owned a fleet of seven Concordes and Air France a similar number.

Much has been written elsewhere by esteemed and knowledgeable authors who were there at the time about the design and development of Concorde, about the politics behind the scenes and the other airlines, including Iran Air and Pan Am, who placed orders for Concorde but later withdrew them. I'll not delve too deeply into that arena here.

It's widely known that the Russians built, and put into service, their own version of Concorde, the Tu-144. It was far less sophisticated and design errors at the outset meant it was never going to succeed. The Russians flew their 'Concordski' first and took it supersonic before Concorde, but a tragic crash at the Paris Air Show in 1973, in which their second prototype broke up in flight, meant the project was doomed.

The Americans were keen to develop a supersonic airliner too but wanted to go faster than us and carry more people. Their ambitions were too great at the outset and made the whole project too technically challenging and costly. The Concorde project was, for sure, controversially very expensive, but the Americans spent more than us and never got further than a wooden mock-up. Concorde went on to succeed for twenty-seven years as the world's only supersonic airliner.

There were environmental concerns even in those early days. Concorde was fitted with four Rolls-Royce Olympus pure jet engines. They had been lifted out of the Vulcan delta-wing nuclear bomber and were from a pure military background. They were updated and fitted with a reheat system to provide enormous amounts of thrust. They were very noisy.

Some might say that jealousy was an underlying factor, but, either way, initially the Americans would not permit Concorde to operate into the USA because of environmental concerns, particularly noise. New York's Kennedy International Airport, rather like Heathrow and many others, was surrounded by built-up, noise-sensitive residential areas. They simply didn't want Concorde rattling their windows twice a day.

A few months after the Bahrain inauguration though, permission was granted for Concorde to commence flights to Washington (Dulles) Airport. It was a great success, but anti-Concorde protests were still significant further north at Kennedy.

It's quite normal for major international airports to have noise-monitoring sites set up at various positions around the airport. Some are right at the end of the runway. Others are perhaps in a village several miles away. They aren't secret and the data they collect is readily available to airlines. Each site has a maximum noise level associated with it. They measure the decibels of every aircraft passing overhead and any airline exceeding the limit is automatically fined.

A familiar sight on British roads nowadays are yellow boxes containing radar-based, speed-measuring cameras. They are there to enhance safety, so they aren't hidden. Some enthusiastic drivers, of course, know to speed up in between them without risking being caught and then brake hard back down to the limit approaching the next camera.

A similar tactic was taken to prove that Concorde could operate safely out of Kennedy Airport and comply with all the noise restrictions. Much development work took place in the simulator at Filton and with a real test aircraft in Casablanca to produce a unique noise abatement procedure that could be used in New York. This had all been part of the original development work and the noise data had been presented to the Port of New York authorities. They still wouldn't let Concorde in until a judge ruled in 1977 that the ban on Concorde was illegal and should be lifted immediately. There was an appeal that failed and a trial proving flight was finally set up for 19 October 1977, twenty-one months after Concorde had entered service. It was a great success and commercial services were given the green light and commenced a month later with British Airways from London and Air France from Paris. These flights operated for another twenty-six years until the eventual retirement of Concorde in October 2003.

That noise abatement procedure was crucial to the success of the operation. It was the most precise manoeuvre ever flown by a civilian pilot in a civilian aeroplane. The mastering of it was to form a crucial part of my route training.

As an airline pilot you only trained and qualified to fly one type of aeroplane at a time. They are complex machines after all. With route training the clue is in the title. It's a question of flying a variety of the routes upon which your chosen aircraft operates in a scheduled and commercial role. You'll remember my 747 training with the deer food in Osaka, for example. Travelling the world and having the opportunity to spend time in far-flung places is one of the big attractions of the job. Some colleagues said to me, 'Why do you want to go on Concorde? It only goes to New York. And you only get twenty-four hours there.' It was a fair point, but those of us who applied to join the Concorde fleet weren't doing so for the variety of global destinations. Nor the money, but that's another story.

My route training therefore was to spend the next two months going backwards and forwards to New York. At twice the speed of sound.

On 25 February 1999, just six days after returning from Seville, I was at the controls of Concorde G-BOAB ready to operate my first commercial flight on the morning BA001 to JFK. We had eighty-five passengers on board, so just fifteen empty seats and therefore a profitable operation. Captain Les Brodie was in command again and I was flying under supervision. I'd been to New York before, of course, in the 747, but this was going to be a whole different day out.

Like many fathers that morning, I'd said goodbye to my girls after breakfast and left the house about 7.30 as they were getting their school uniforms ready. I saw other mums and dads walking towards the station with their briefcases on their way to work. It was a Thursday, so they probably only had one more day that week to endure the daily commute in the crowded train into Waterloo. It took me just twenty-five minutes to drive to Heathrow and then a short walk to our operations centre on the northern side of the airport. This was the start of my new job. I was guaranteed a seat by the window in my new office. With the best view on earth. And beyond.

We had learned all the flight planning principles in the classroom sessions but Les took me through them for real in the ops centre. We studied the weather patterns over the Atlantic carefully. I was familiar with these charts from my 747 days. Winds and storms over the Atlantic could have a significant effect on flight times and routings in a conventional aeroplane flying at 39,000ft. They were virtually irrelevant though for Concorde operations as we were going to be cruising half as high again, somewhere between 58,000ft and 60,000ft, and way above all the weather systems. Winds would be light and, cruising at 1,350mph, a wind of 20 knots would have minimal effect on our flight times.

The routings across the Atlantic for subsonic aeroplanes are called North Atlantic tracks and they are revised every day. The prevailing winds are from the west, so heading out to the USA from Europe, the routes are plotted to avoid the headwinds. Most traffic goes westbound during the day and returns overnight. The night tracks are different and designed to offer a ride in the strong tailwinds. This is why it can be an hour quicker coming eastbound across the Atlantic compared to going west.

There were two supersonic tracks across the Atlantic. With the winds having little effect, they were fixed and it's not as if you were going to come across anybody else up there going the other way.

We completed the flight planning involving Flight Engineer Roger Bricknell in the fuel planning decision-making. We ordered 94.6 tonnes for our busy flight to New York. Then it was down the escalator, grab our bags and board the bus to take us out to the aircraft parked on Gate V14 at Terminal 4. From our seats at the pointy end we could see through the visor, currently raised in the sleek, streamlined position, into the Concorde lounge. Our passengers were perhaps enjoying a glass of bubbly or catching up on some last-minute business calls. Anyone flying Concorde for the first time was likely admiring the sleek lines of the thin profile of the aeroplane, looking down on her from in front and slightly above.

With their luggage preloaded in the small hold in the belly or the larger one in the rear, and any coats taken by hand into the small on-board wardrobes, the passengers were invited to board about twenty minutes before departure. So we could get the brakes off and record yet another on-time departure, we would aim to close the front door by 10.25. Just like in Seville, we had to start two engines on the gate, both the inboards, so we could power all the aircraft systems from them before disconnecting from the ground air and electrical supplies.

'Speedbird Concorde One, you are cleared to push,' was the clearance we got from air traffic control before we released the brakes on time at 10.30 and asked the driver of the tug, connected to the nose wheel, to push nearly 185 tonnes of Concorde back into the cul-de-sac. We'd start the other two engines during pushback and, once the tug was clear, lower the visor and the nose to the 5-degree down position, giving us a clear view of the taxiway ahead.

Roger completed his vital checks of all the aircraft systems, with the hydraulics all pressurised correctly, the engine-driven electrical generators all on line satisfactorily, the fuel transfer valves all set to their required positions and the engine oil pressures and temperatures all rising steadily. His flight engineer's panel is vast, such that to reach the extremities he had to slide his seat back and forth and up and down. I could hear all this activity going on behind me as I moved the control column between my knees forwards, backwards, left and right, to check all the flying controls responded as they should. The surfaces themselves were moved by conventional hydraulics, pressurised to 4,000psi, but their actuators, powered flight control units (PFCUs), received electronic signals from all my pushing and pulling, the first 'fly by wire' system in civilian aviation.

Concorde doesn't have conventional flying controls. Any 'normal' aeroplane has a separate tailplane with surfaces, elevators, that move up and down as you push the control column forwards or pull it back. These elevators, in flight with air flowing over them, pitch the aeroplane up or down to bring about a climb or descent. Moving the same control column, or side stick on some aircraft, left and right moves similar surfaces on the main wing, called ailerons, up on one side and down on the other, to cause a roll to the left or the right. Because Concorde only had one large delta wing, with a series of twists and turns built into it, it had these control surfaces combined and named, most appropriately, elevons. Located right at the back of the wing, either side of each pair of engines, they were not visible from the flight deck, so we had indicators on the instrument panel that displayed their movements in response to our inputs. Surface movements were minuscule in flight at high speed but we needed to check that full unrestricted movement was available when stationary.

All systems go. Air traffic clearance received. A nod from Les that we were set to go and I lowered my left hand to the parking brake lever, releasing it and moving it gently forward. Even fully loaded, the idle power alone of those four Rolls-Royce Olympus engines was sufficient to set Concorde in motion as we headed towards the matrix of taxiways that was going to take us from Terminal 4, across Runway 28L, currently being used for landing traffic, and across to the other side of the airport and the start of Runway 28R.

It was similar to Seville as far as handling the aircraft was concerned, but today we had eighty-five passengers behind us. The cabin crew were taking them through the important safety demonstration, before collecting in the crystal champagne glasses that had already served our VIPs with some of the world's finest champagne.

As we taxied out more checks and preparation work took place. The engines guzzled something like 1,400kg of fuel, about 1,750 litres, just to get to the take-off point. Roger, sitting behind me on his highly manoeuvrable and unique seat that would command a fortune nowadays on eBay, was running through all the before take-off checks, including shifting fuel towards the rear of the aeroplane to set up the aircraft centre of gravity so that it sat exactly 54 per cent of the way along the aeroplane, the perfect position for an optimum take-off.

There was a fairly short queue that morning and we had to take our place within it. You could feel the eyes of passengers in other airliners nearby, straining at their windows, watching the timeless lines of Concorde slip alongside them. The pilots too, were in awe, an American voice coming over the radio asking if he might sacrifice his place ahead of us in the queue, so that they could watch us depart. Concorde had been doing this twice a day for twenty-three years, but still the eyes of the world watched with amazement, enthralled by one of man's greatest technical achievements of all time.

'3-2-1, now.'

Once again, the phenomenal acceleration kicked in. The reheats all lit up. Flames were shooting out of the back of the aeroplane. I knew what to expect this time, so there were no expletives. When Les called 'rotate', I eased back on the control column, commanding the elevons to move just enough to change the airflow over the wing and initiate the enormous vortices of lift that were going to suck Concorde into the air. The nose pitched up at 3 degrees a second, a purely visual manoeuvre judged by the rate at which the horizon disappeared down the windscreen. Bringing my eyes in, I refined the target attitude, the angle I needed to achieve for the initial climb out, to 13 degrees, by referring to my attitude indicator, a large ball-shaped instrument with a blue segment above a horizontal line, representing the sky above, and the lower half black. Remember, if you ever saw it the other way up, then we were all in trouble. At the call of '240 knots', I'd raise the nose further so as not to exceed 250 knots, our initial climb-out speed.

'3-2-1, noise,' called Les. Roger was poised with his left hand over the four white piano keys at the back of the throttle quadrant, and his right hand on the four throttles. At the precise, pre-calculated time for the temperature outside and the weight of the aircraft, he killed the reheat and pulled the four big levers back to the pre-determined thrust lever angle (TLA). It was my job now to maintain 250 knots precisely, lowering the nose again to 12 degrees, and fly most accurately during this critical noise abatement procedure. Windsor Castle slipped by on my side about 3,000ft below, which was a clue.

As we passed 6,000ft, Roger gradually increased the power, and the noise, and we would increase our rate of climb proportionally until we were high enough not to be a nuisance to those going about their business on the ground. As we accelerated above 250 knots (280mph), Les leant across to my side and raised first the nose and then the visor using a small lever that was positioned just in front of me on the left-hand side of my panel.

It all went very quiet. Now we were fully streamlined and set up for high-speed flight. This retractable nose and visor, or droop snoot as it was nicknamed, was a vital feature of the aeroplane. Without the nose lowered we wouldn't be able to see the runway for take-off and landing and without it raised we would have no protection from the intense heat we would experience in supersonic flight. It was designed and developed by a long-established British family engineering firm, Marshall of Cambridge. Thankfully, the early test pilots were successful in persuading the designers that their original idea of having a metal heat shield, while ideal for its intended purpose, was far from ideal from a pilot's perspective. Even with all this modern technology and autoland systems, it's still a good idea for pilots to be able to see where they are going.

We levelled off at 28,000ft or Flight Level 280, to be technically correct, and set course for our 'acceleration point' in the Bristol Channel, midway between the north coast of Devon and coast of South Wales. We accelerated to our subsonic limit of Mach 0.95, 95 per cent of the speed of sound, so already significantly faster than the 747 that had taken off before us and was cruising at Mach 0.86.

Behind me the champagne corks popped, the finest Scottish smoked salmon was prepared and the individual pots of the best Russian caviar were being laid out ready to go out into the cabin. Each was presented with a fine mother of pearl spoon, of course.

Just sixteen minutes or so after take-off we were 'ready for the burn', akin to a Space Shuttle going into orbit. We were about to go supersonic.

The regulars behind us knew what to expect in the cabin, but Les demonstrated for me, as it was my first day in this new job, a typical form of words to explain to those experiencing the sound barrier for the first time what they could expect. They would experience two slight nudges in the back as the reheats lit up in pairs, he explained. There was no need to fasten seat belts, nor don helmets and hold on tight. They might notice a ripple or two on the champagne, but all in all, it was about to be a non-event. And that's the whole point. That's what was so incredibly clever about Concorde.

I was using the autopilot by now with the associated controls on the glare shield between us at eye level. As the power increased, with Roger taking care of the engine controls and reheat, I adjusted the pitch of the aeroplane to achieve and maintain maximum indicated airspeed. That was 400 knots below 33,000ft, but as soon as we went through that altitude, I'd chase the speed limit indicator as it moved clockwise around the airspeed indicator towards its ultimate limit of 530 knots. As we gained height the air got thinner and colder. The speed of sound varies with temperature, so effectively came down to meet us.

During the transonic acceleration, the centre of lift, the point about which the total lift acts on the aeroplane, moves rearwards. To counteract this and stop the aircraft pitching nose down, the centre of gravity had to be moved rearwards. Think balancing a pencil on your finger. The flight engineer would do this by transferring fuel from the centre of the aeroplane (remember, we had thirteen fuel tanks – numbered one to eleven), to Tank Eleven, which was located right back in the tail of the aircraft. That fuel was used for ballast effectively during the supersonic part of the flight, and transferred forward again when we decelerated.

Somewhere just above 30,000ft we would punch through the sound barrier. The air molecules ahead of us could no longer hear us coming and jump out of the way. Ever wondered why a pigeon sitting in front of you in the middle of the road always happens to get out of the way just in time? It feels the air parting to let you through. From here on in, we had to force our way through the air, compressing it in front of us with our streamlined profile with the long pitot tube on the front of the nose feeling the associated temperature increase first.

We were really guzzling fuel at this stage of the flight with full power and reheat, over 11 tonnes (12,000 litres) an hour. That's each engine! We couldn't keep this up for long. We didn't need to though. 'The burn' to take us, not into orbit, but well through the sound barrier, only lasted ten to twelve minutes to get us to Mach 1.7. Then we could dispense with the reheat. The fuel flow would halve again and Concorde would do what no other aeroplane, civilian or military, before or since, has been able to do. It would accelerate and climb without reheat (or afterburners) until it reached its maximum speed of Mach 2, twice the speed of sound.

The engine intakes were the secret behind this incredible achievement. And it is appropriate to use the word 'secret'. The designs were very carefully guarded at Filton in the late 1960s and were the subject of various espionage attempts from, shall we just say, 'overseas'?

The Olympus engine was only part of the complete power plant, as the whole unit was known. The reheat and nozzles on the back were fundamental in enhancing the dry thrust from the engine and the intakes at the front made up the third segment to control the air coming in the front.

A series of ramps, or doors, inside the intakes moved down as the aircraft went above Mach 1.3 to slow the air down before it reached the engine. These were controlled by the first digital computers in aviation. They had back-ups, of course, and did switch channels quite regularly, but it was quite reassuring to see the flight engineer was provided with a switch for each one labelled 'open' and 'close'. He would have to put his tea down if he ever had to use those, as it was a most crucial operation.

As speed built up, the intake ramps became more efficient, effectively squeezing and compressing the air going into the engine, akin to a supercharger or turbocharger that we take for granted on modern cars. By the time we got to Mach 1.7 the intakes were providing a boost of about 25 per cent, so we could shut down the reheat. Incredible. We'd only just got colour television, remember, when they designed and built all this. And it was still working fine twenty years after the internet was invented.

By now, we were just forty-five minutes or so into our flight, so nearly a quarter of the way to New York. Our actual flight time today was three hours and eighteen minutes. Behind me the six cabin crew, working in cramped galleys at either end of the aircraft, were preparing to serve the main course. Whether it was a fine piece of beef or a tender lobster, I can't recall, but whatever it was that day, it was certainly the finest.

It was a real skill to serve up to 100 people swiftly and efficiently without giving the slightest hint of rushing. The first course was cleared away around now and I was astonished when a tea tray was brought in by one of the cabin crew and placed on the floor. It had three mugs of strong tea upon it, which was most welcome, but there were three pots of the world's finest caviar to go with it. This was elevenses like I'd never experienced before. I was to go on to learn that it was a bad day at work if there weren't three pots of caviar left over for the flight crew after all the passengers had been invited to partake of this exquisite delicacy. I was intrigued by the way it was presented with the mother of pearl spoon. Everything was done properly, of course. Caviar was an acquired taste. I soon acquired it.

I'd last flown this route in a 747 a few months earlier. It had taken over seven and a half hours and the crew food was more like school dinners and certainly not eaten with a mother of pearl spoon. To be fair though, we were looked after well. The jumbo jet cabin crew would often send any leftovers from first class up the spiral staircase into the 'lion's den'.

As Concorde got lighter, burning fuel at 20 tonnes an hour, we gained altitude. Unlike a conventional airliner, an expression I realise I'm using frequently, we didn't have to cruise at a particular assigned altitude. Travelling westbound, airliners traditionally cruise at even numbers, say 38,000ft, and eastbound, odd numbers, 37,000ft or 39,000ft. This reduced the chances of bumping into somebody coming the other way. At a closing speed of over 1,000mph. Subsonic aircraft of the day couldn't go much higher than these sort of altitudes, but Concorde was certified up to 60,000ft, more than half as high again. There certainly wasn't going to be anybody else up there, apart from perhaps your sister ship going the other way 100 miles to the south, or Air France on their supersonic crossing, but again, well separated laterally. Our cruise procedure therefore was to leave full power set and just drift up and down slightly with temperature changes and the reducing aircraft weight at anywhere between 55,000ft and 60,000ft.

On this, my first supersonic oceanic crossing, I was totally enthralled by the views, which even two years later, when it all ended abruptly, I never took for granted. We were soon cruising at Mach 2, twice the speed of sound – 1,350mph, a mile every two and a half seconds, 23 miles a minute, faster than a rifle bullet, and so on and so forth. Facts that were simply jaw-dropping, and in an aeroplane that first flew when the Beatles were still topping the charts.

We were so high, we were above all the weather. You could look down on the puffy white clouds rushing by below and wonder if they might develop into afternoon thunderstorms. It didn't matter if they did. They certainly wouldn't reach up to us. There was no turbulence. We were above all the jet streams (the strong winds that create all the global weather patterns). You could see the curvature of the earth on the horizon with the sky quickly turning an eerie inky black above us.

We were the highest people on earth. Apart from six. The astronauts on the International Space Station were up there somewhere, 250 miles to be more accurate, circling the globe every ninety minutes at 17,000 miles an hour. They weren't eating caviar from a mother of pearl spoon though, so they were welcome to it.

Being an airline pilot isn't only about physically flying a plane, albeit a big fast one, with your hands. We have automatic pilots that need telling what to do, rather like making inputs to a sophisticated computer. So, it's all about managing an operation, about considering the 'what-ifs?':

'What if an engine fails?'; 'What if a hydraulic pipe splits and we suddenly lose one of the three hydraulic systems?'; 'What if a passenger suddenly becomes ill and an urgent diversion is needed to save his or her life?'. These and umpteen other scenarios, whether supersonic or just crawling along at 500mph, are one of the main responsibilities of an airline pilot – planning for something that might never happen in your entire career, but would be managed safely and efficiently if it did. Les and I spent what little spare time we had discussing all these possibilities and reviewing the facilities at our emergency diversion airfields, whether they were in the Azores, Iceland or Newfoundland.

There were few scenarios that required immediate responses in subsonic aviation but supersonic flight was different. Engine surges or a failure of a ramp in an engine intake, for example, had to be dealt with immediately. There wasn't even time to refer to the appropriately named quick reaction checklist. Items had to be completed initially by memory in such rare emergencies and involved all three crew members working as a team.

The flight engineer would be best placed to manage the situation technically, perhaps transferring to an alternate hydraulic source, or shutting down an engine, while us pilots would fly the plane. At Mach 2 things happened very quickly, an obvious statement I know, but some of the more severe failures needed an immediate deceleration to subsonic flight.

Remember, we had pumped all the spare fuel into the rear tank to keep the centre of gravity aft. If we left it there as we slowed down, the aircraft would eventually tumble out of its flight envelope, which means out of control. And that's what we call 'a bad thing'. Shifting fuel around the aeroplane was a complex and crucial procedure and was the flight engineer's job. If he was too busy dealing with an emergency, that responsibility fell to me. I couldn't possibly reach around and get to all the switches and valves on his panel, but above my head was a big red, guarded, emergency use only, fuel forward transfer switch, which was a potential life saver.

Thankfully, my first supersonic oceanic crossing went without a hitch, as in fact did virtually all of those that followed. We discussed much during the cruise. Even though I was an experienced long-haul pilot, having spent nine years flying 747s, I was very much the new boy.

We had time to enjoy lunch, enjoy the amazing views and entertain our guests. Yes, it was a different world pre-9/11. The flight deck door was always open. Passengers were welcome to pop in and see what was going on, even join us on the spare jump seat for take-off or landing if they were that keen. I guess there was a degree of security in that the flight deck was so cramped that the flight engineer, sitting sideways at his panel, formed a natural barrier between any over-enthusiastic passenger and the physical flight controls right at the front. It would have been a brave passenger who tried to get past some of our engineers. Our visitor might be a regular business traveller, somebody having a trip of a lifetime, or a very well-known film star or musician. I'll tell you a tale or two later.

When I had time to stretch my legs in the cabin, I would perform a clever limbo manoeuvre to get round the back of the flight engineer's seat and saw first-hand the evidence, which I'd read so much about, of how the aeroplane grows by 8 inches in flight. The temperature on the nose reached 127°C and the whole airframe would heat up proportionally. The special aluminium alloy of which she was made was designed to expand with the heat. There is no truth in the myth that you got more legroom as the flight progressed, but the expansion was quite clear within the flight deck. The flight engineer's panel sat flush up against the rear bulkhead on the ground but in supersonic cruise you could get your fist in the gap. Sideways. If you visit Concorde in a museum it's quite likely you'll see a pilot or engineer's uniform hat crushed in there. On the last ever supersonic flight of each aeroplane it became a ritual to put a hat in there, knowing it would be crushed as the airframe cooled again, and it would remain there for eternity. Or until the moths got to it.

Les even had time to tell me a little about the Concorde crew car club. With only twenty or so flight crew on the fleet at any one time, we were a very small family, a group of friends really, and they'd all put in some money and bought a car, which they kept in the car park at Kennedy Airport. I say a 'car' but it was actually one of those big American Jeep-style vehicles, well before we were introduced to SUVs in the UK. You could get six people in and much luggage and ski gear in the boot. Or should I say trunk?

It was quite common for Concorde to leave Heathrow at 10.30 a.m., arrive in New York at 9.30 a.m. and for the crew to be on their way to the ski slopes in New England an hour later.

All too soon, our supersonic cruise was coming to an end. It was time to prepare for 're-entry', or at least deceleration and descent back into the world of subsonic aviation. It was another critical and precise manoeuvre, with each of the three flight crew playing their vital role. I was about to partake for the first time.

Approaching our predetermined deceleration point, taking into account our final achieved altitude, the wind and air temperature, Roger commenced the countdown (in miles) and then gradually reduced the power while I held the aircraft level. If we had just closed the throttles, as you would on a subsonic aircraft, it would have been like flying into a brick wall and we would have been joined in the flight deck by all our passengers and their empty bone china dinner plates.

We started a very gentle descent as the speed drifted back slowly towards Mach 1. The drag (air resistance) increases significantly in this transonic region and then, with no fuss, just an oscillation on the vertical speed indicator as the shock wave moved forward again, we were subsonic. Throughout this manoeuvre Roger had been pumping the fuel, which had been stored in Tank 11 in the tail, forward again. It had been back there in supersonic cruise to keep the centre of gravity aft, remember? That needed to come forward again by the time we were subsonic and then we could use the fuel for the purpose for which it was designed, rather than supersonic ballast.

We slotted back into the world of regular airliners making their way into JFK. Air traffic control vectored us round for an ILS approach onto Runway 04R at Kennedy, which, thankfully, was one of the less complex arrivals and ideal for my first visit. I'd soon go on to get exposure to the famous curved 'Canarsie approach' to 13L.

Just three hours and eighteen minutes after leaving the ground at Heathrow, I managed to replicate my landing that I'd been practising in Seville a week ago. The touchdown was perfect and I knew that Les was monitoring my every move, the ultimate responsibility resting with him of course.

We had pushed back from the gate in London at 10.30 a.m. We shut down on the gate at the British Airways terminal in New York at 2.14 p.m. in London. That was 9.14 a.m. local time. We had delivered our eighty-five passengers safely to the Big Apple over an hour before they had left London. Concorde once again had proved herself as a time machine of the finest order.

We had burnt 78.7 tonnes of the 94.6 tonnes of fuel that we had started with. That's 98,375 litres or 21,640 of our British gallons. We'd travelled 3,000 nautical miles, which is 3,450 of our British miles. Seeing as I've got a calculator to hand, let's take this all the way. Yes it was a gas-guzzling

0.16mpg overall. To carry that number of people, though, you would have needed twenty-five cars. If you took the fuel used for take-off and going through the sound barrier out of the equation, and just considered the fuel burn cruising at Mach 2, with a wink of your eye, you could prove that Concorde was more economical than a Ford Escort. Environmentally friendly? Convinced? No, I didn't think so.

We took the crew bus into Manhattan. That took just over forty-five minutes. It was a 15-mile journey. In that time we had covered over 1,000 miles just a short while ago.

Unlike all my subsonic flights to New York, it was 11 a.m. instead of mid-evening. We had no jet lag, no dehydration, no fatigue. We were ready to start the day. That's exactly what Concorde was all about. In years gone by there even used to be a helicopter service from JFK to downtown Manhattan for Concorde passengers, making 10 a.m. business meetings feasible. I really felt we had done something special that day, that morning, even though Concorde had been doing it twice a day for twenty-three years.

Our hotel was in the heart of the action, on East 55th Street, so I was quickly changed and off out to explore. In fact, it's recently been renamed The Concorde, a tribute to the fact it was the home to all the supersonic crew for many years. A relatively small, family run hotel, a home from home, we were on first-name terms with all the staff there. Abdul, the bell captain, always had a cheery smile and I was back there not long ago for the first time in years and was greeted with a friendly 'Hello John!'

I was soon introduced to the normal Concorde crew routine. After a day out shopping or sightseeing, it was to meet at Hurley's, a typical New York diner, for an early dinner and a couple of beers. Back to the hotel for a full eight-hour sleep, a luxury for a long-haul pilot, and then up bright and early to take the BA002 back to Heathrow.

The day of 25 February 1999 had been a good day, my first supersonic transatlantic flight. My private pilot licence had been issued on 25 July. My commercial pilot licence had been issued on 25 March. This was the ultimate job in aviation. I was very fortunate and could see myself flying Concorde for the rest of my career. I was 41 years old, so only had fourteen years until compulsory retirement, as it stood at the time.

I was wrong. The 25th was to feature again in just seventeen months' time for all the wrong reasons.

THE MOST SPECTACULAR TAKE-OFF KNOWN TO MAN

The return flight the next morning introduced me to my third aircraft of the Concorde fleet, G-BOAG, and the most spectacular take-off known to man in a civilian airliner, the noise abatement departure from Runway 31L, which we had rehearsed many times in the flight simulator.

Subsonic airliners take off with reduced power and climb straight ahead until at least 500ft before making any turns. Concorde didn't. It was full power with reheat, as always, and then as soon as the wheels were off the ground, I heard Les say, 'Positive climb. Turn.' That was my instruction to start a gentle turn to the left, rolling on 25 degrees of bank and simultaneously pitching up to arrest the acceleration and nail a climb speed of 250 knots. It was a precise and critical three-dimensional manoeuvre. Too slow or too much bank and the drag would increase exponentially and you'd quickly be into a dangerous predicament.

The initial flight path took you out over Jamaica Bay, avoiding all the noise-sensitive residential areas. We'd achieve about 2,000ft by the time we reached the exclusive Belle Harbor and Rockaway Park area on the peninsula that formed the southern edge of the bay. Another noise-sensitive area with a yellow box on a pole, or the aviation equivalent thereof.

'3-2-1, noise,' heralded the next phase of this unique procedure. Roger cancelled the reheats and throttled back the engines while I reduced the bank angle and lowered the nose to ensure I could maintain 250 knots with just a fraction of the power I'd had a second ago. The beautiful beaches of the Atlantic coast passed serenely beneath us, deserted at 9 a.m. on this cold February morning. Once out over the Atlantic, with noise no longer a concern, Roger eased the throttles forward again and we climbed and accelerated without further restriction. The burn through Mach 1 followed a few minutes later and, encouraged by Les to 'get the feel of her', I hand flew Concorde for the first time, through the sound barrier and all the way to Mach 2.

We touched down at Heathrow just three hours and nineteen minutes later (exactly the same flight time as outbound) and I was home in time for tea. A fine day in the office.

My route training continued back and forth to New York for another two months. On all these flights we carried another first officer, a safety pilot, until I had gained enough experience to be able to manage the operation safely, should anything untoward happen to the training captain.

All went well. No technical issues to speak of. No two flights were exactly the same, of course, and I flew with different training captains and flight engineers on each trip. As time went on I got to know everyone on the fleet quite quickly as there were so few of us. Faces in the cabin started to become more familiar too, with many of the cabin crew flying Concorde regularly as part of their work pattern on a short-haul rota.

'Rocket Man' was one of my favourite Elton John songs and Lynne and I had been to Wembley Stadium with 100,000 others the previous summer to see 'the boy from Pinner' perform. It was fantastic. Scheduled as a double act with Billy Joel from New York, Elton held the crowd in the palm of his hand for three hours alone as Billy had been taken ill. I'd always enjoyed live music and this was one of the best.

It was a surreal moment when I went out into the cabin, cruising at Mach 2 in 'the Rocket', as Concorde was often called, and bumped straight into Sir Elton in the front row. I didn't know he was on the flight until then. We had a short chat but I was too star struck to remember what either of us had said, but I came away thinking what a lovely gentleman he was. I learned to consult the passenger list in advance from now on so I didn't get caught out should I bump into any of my other heroes. That was indeed to happen in the not-too-distant future.

After another seven supersonic return trips to New York I was ready for my final check flight, my rubber stamp to certify the end of my training. This was nothing different from the previous trips, just with another training captain taking an independent view of my operation, to check that I was safe enough to be released from the training environment.

As in many professions, you never stop learning. You never know everything there is to know. No two flights are the same. I remember way back when I was flying the B727 with Dan-Air, saying to a grey-haired, somewhat distinguished captain, who I was flying with for a day, how much I loved this job, how there was always something to learn. I'll never forget his reply. 'When you've been flying as long as I have young man, you pretty much know all there is to know.' I was astonished. Thankfully, it's an attitude I've never encountered again in the last thirty-five years and now I have been flying even longer than he had at the time, I know it's not true. I'm still learning. That's what makes flying so safe.

On 16 April 1999, off I went to JFK and back again with training captain Roger Mills and flight engineer Jes Wood. It was a routine trip with no issues but significant only in that I passed my line check. After six months my Concorde training was complete.

Roger had been a Concorde captain for many years and was fascinating company. I learned he flew all sorts of historic aeroplanes in his spare time at air shows and displays all around the world. He even kept his own Harvard, a 1940s American training aircraft, at a small airfield not far from New York. It was only a month later that I found myself in the passenger seat of this wonderful historic flying machine with Roger at the controls, enthralled by the power and the noise from the enormous 60-year-old radial engine pounding away in front of us. Just a few hours ago we'd been at 60,000ft together, at twice the speed of sound.

The career of an airline pilot can normally progress two different ways: short haul or long haul. There are pros and cons of each. Flying around Europe, with whichever airline you have joined, you have to accept you will often start work early in the morning. Very early sometimes. You'll fly back and forth to major European cities, or exotic Mediterranean holiday islands, but probably not stop over there. You'll work long days and end up back where you started from. There is no jet lag though, nor nights out of bed, and there is much routine in your life. You'll get the occasional day off in Budapest or Paris, but it's in the employer's interest to keep such slips to a minimum.

In long haul you'll see the world. Literally. There's normally a civilised start time in the UK but, more often than not, a long night flight home again. You'll experience dehydration (so soon learn to drink much water). You'll be constantly jet-lagged, your body never really in one time zone long enough to settle. The flights can seem to go on forever, crossing not just countries but continents, and you find yourself completing a day's work nearly halfway round the world in a completely different climate and culture. Then you'll stay there, though often just for forty-eight hours, sometimes less; but occasionally, where the flights only operate once or twice a week, it can be a mini-holiday.

Concorde had the best bits of both. No early starts, no nights out of bed and certainly no overnight flights. We'd fly in the dark, of course. In fact, in the spring and autumn a most astonishing experience soon became normal. Now, we all know that the sun rises in the east, don't we? Every day, the evening Concorde flight, the BA003, left Heathrow in the dark at 7 p.m. Once established in the cruise at Mach 2 you're travelling at 1,350mph. You are flying faster than the earth is rotating. You actually catch up with the sun that you had seen set over the reservoir to the west of Heathrow before you left. You see the sunrise again, but this time in the west. You touch down in New York, an hour before you've left, in broad daylight and, as you drive into the city, you enjoy your second sunset of the day as it slips behind the Manhattan skyline.

Only on Concorde.

ALL IN A DAY'S WORK – GLITZ AND GLAMOUR

Going to work was fun. It was normal to do about five transatlantic trips a month, either 'the early' or 'the late'. The BA001 left LHR at 10.30 a.m. each day but you'd be in downtown Manhattan by 11 a.m., so had all day in the Big Apple. If you lived a little further from Heathrow you might prefer 'the late'. The BA003 left at 7 p.m. and had you into New York in time for a quick beer and a good night's sleep before a late-morning return the next day. I liked to do a mixture.

I came down for breakfast one morning and the girls were getting ready for school as usual. It was St Patrick's Day, 1999. Natalie asked me what time my flight left that day. I was operating the BA001, so '10.30 as usual darling' was my reply. 'Why?'

'Well, don't go without Chris Tarrant will you?' she said.

Tarrant was then a DJ at Capital Radio and had been covering the weekday breakfast slot since 1987, so for all of Natalie's life and more. Like many homes in the south-east of England, the radio alarm burst into life at 7 a.m. with Tarrant's bright and bubbly voice. He'd been going for an hour already by then and didn't sign off until 10 a.m.

Driving to work, I tuned in and learned that Chris was really looking forward to flying Concorde to New York so he could do a second morning show live from Manhattan on their equivalent of Capital. That show started at 10 a.m. in New York, 3 p.m. back in the UK.

I was still trying to work out the logistics of all this when I pulled into the staff car park next to our operations centre at Heathrow. All became clear though when I reached the crew report centre, where we were thoroughly briefed.

Chris Tarrant was indeed travelling with us. He was leaving his studio in London early, on the back of a motorcycle, continuing to host his show live as he travelled to Heathrow and would sign off as normal from the Concorde lounge at 10 a.m., half an hour before departure. I was told the original plan was for the host of the show after Tarrant's to speak with him live from the flight deck of Concorde soon after 11 a.m., but that plan had been scrapped because of the technical challenges and it would be too much of a distraction for the three flight deck crew.

We had four of us on the flight that day for some reason, perhaps a training flight, but I was the extra one, the safety pilot. Once we were safely established in supersonic flight, I went back to see Chris and explained that, in fact, we could have a go at the live link if he was still interested, because I could help set it up via our spare radio from the observer's jump seat.

With thanks for the kind offer, he took a sip of his champagne and explained, 'It's all done John. We recorded it in the studio yesterday.' Indeed, back at home, Lynne had recorded it all on, wait for it, a cassette tape. You couldn't tell it wasn't live. The DJ hosting the mid-morning show announced, 'And now we are going live to the flight deck of Concorde. How's it going Chris?' With appropriate and most realistic background noise, Tarrant went on to explain, with his usual great gusto, how the reheats had kicked in and given him two nudges in the back and we were now through the sound barrier and on our way to Mach 2. The tricks of radio.

We got Chris to New York on time and he was whisked away to the studio in Manhattan. St Patrick's Day in New York is a big event and the parade was nothing short of spectacular. The Guinness in Hurley's was 'on special' that day and in plentiful supply. I tuned in to Chris's broadcast in New York, which was being transmitted simultaneously on Capital in the mid-afternoon slot back in the UK. Natalie and Jenny were delighted when, as prearranged with Chris, he gave them a lovely mention to coincide with the short car journey home from school just after 3 p.m. He even explained how their dad had taken good care of him on Concorde earlier that day. All in a day's work.

As well as being a great business tool, Concorde was vital in getting film stars to and from their engagements.

Rogue Trader was released in the UK on 25 June 1999 but had been premiered in London's West End four days earlier. It starred Ewan McGregor as Nick Leeson, the banker who had brought down Barings Bank four years earlier. Anna Friel starred alongside McGregor and by the time the movie was released she had made her Broadway debut at the Music Box Theatre starring in *Closer*. The play was critically acclaimed and was playing to a packed house six nights a week. Not Mondays.

During our pre-flight checks at Heathrow on 22 June 1999, a Tuesday, the cabin service director popped into the flight deck and asked if we would mind if Anna joined us for take-off. Dick Maher, the flight engineer, fixed her up with a spare headset so she could follow every move. She loved it and once we were settled into supersonic cruise, explained that she had dashed over from New York, on her only day off, to get to the premiere of *Rogue Trader*, but would be back on stage on Broadway that night.

Taking Concorde in both directions was the only way she could virtually be in two places at once. She'd left New York on Monday morning, been to the film premiere (and doubtless the after-show party) and was back in New York mid-morning Tuesday. After a spot of lunch back in the cabin, Anna joined us up front again for the landing into JFK. It was a sporty, curved 'Canarsie approach', another precise manoeuvre with me at the controls, straightening Concorde up and levelling the wings, just seconds before touching down on Runway 13L.

By way of a thank you for her VIP Concorde experience, Anna invited the three of us to her show that evening, a welcome change from the usual dinner at Hurley's. Sadly, we had to decline the champagne she had laid on in her dressing room afterwards, sticking to the cranberry juice instead, as we were taking 'the early' back the next day. All in a day's work.

Occasionally it becomes necessary to travel as a passenger as part of one's work. First class, of course.

On the day in question, 5 July 1999, I had to travel to JFK on a Boeing 747 to pick up Concorde, G-BOAF. It was part of a charter operation for Bath Travel based in Bournemouth.

The next day, we brought eighty-three passengers from New York to Stansted Airport, just to the north-east of London, in three hours and twenty-six minutes, most of it at twice the speed of sound. We stayed overnight in a hotel near Stansted and then flew 'AF' to Boscombe Down in Hampshire to collect another seventy-one passengers and whisk them westbound at Mach 2 to New York. We did a lot of work with Bath Travel in and out of Bournemouth and Boscombe Down, often tied in with cruise passengers. Funnily enough, the short hop from Stansted to Boscombe Down was sold out. We had 100 passengers who had paid £299 to experience a short ride on Concorde, albeit not at Mach 2. That would have taken some explaining.

The runway at Bournemouth was long enough to land Concorde, but too short for take-off on a transatlantic operation with 92 tonnes of fuel on board, so we would launch from Boscombe Down instead.

Anyway, there I was sitting in 4K. That's at the back on the right for anyone who's not familiar with the first-class cabin on a 747. I was settling into my seat and had already been presented with my first glass of champagne. I'd had my jacket taken by the stewardess and hung in the wardrobe at the front of the cabin and was looking through the *High Life* in-flight magazine to see what movies I might be able to enjoy during the long Atlantic crossing. This flight was going to take about seven and a half hours, more than twice as long as I was now used to.

Entrapment was a film that had just been released and I was hoping it might be in the schedule for the day. Starring Sean Connery as an art thief and Catherine Zeta-Jones as an investigator out to catch him, it was going to be perfect entertainment after lunch. I was disappointed though to see it wasn't listed. It was too new, I guess.

As I was leaning forward to put the magazine back in the rack, I sensed a presence behind me. It was a strange feeling. Maybe my subconscious had picked up a voice or something, but I sat back and looked up and there was Sean Connery standing right there. He sat down next to me across the aisle. I must admit, I was all of a quiver. Whatever a quiver is.

Off we went. Drinks and a fine lunch were served and after lunch Mr Connery leant across and struck up conversation with me. We spoke about flying and the pros and cons of crossing the Atlantic in a 747 versus Concorde and got along rather well.

It was Natalie's birthday coming up in three weeks' time. She was going to be 9 and both her and Jenny loved watching James Bond films on a Sunday afternoon. I came home with a rather special birthday card that read 'Happy Birthday Natalie. Best wishes, Sean Connery.' She thought that was rather cool.

Although I couldn't have predicted it at the time, a couple of years later I was a captain on an Airbus flying short-haul routes. I always sat sideways in my seat during boarding, so I could see out of my peripheral vision what was going on in the cabin. During boarding one morning, a passenger stuck his head in the door to say 'good morning', as was quite common. I looked up and there was Pierce Brosnan. It was Jenny's birthday in a couple of weeks and, you guessed it, I came home with a card 'Happy Birthday Jenny. Best Wishes, Pierce Brosnan.' So both my girls had a birthday card from a James Bond.

Now my grandson, Harvey, is getting into the more modern Bond films and only recently I met Rami Malek when I was captain on his flight to New York on the B777. He had just been in London for the premiere of *No Time to Die* with Daniel Craig. So Harvey's got a personal card now, from a Bond villain. All in a day's work.

It was always a special pleasure to fly with a colleague who I had been on the training course with. We had spent six intense weeks in the classroom together and were then split into two separate crews for the nineteen simulator sessions. I was paired up with Captain Ron Weidner and Flight Engineer Mike Hollyer. We had formed a special bond during those months training together, a very special time for all of us.

Ron tells a good story. It soon became the talk of the fleet.

Ron plays guitar and had a few fine examples in his collection at home. On a flight from New York to London in the spring of 2000, one of the cabin crew came into the flight deck bearing tea for all and explained that one of her passengers had a few guitars, including a new one he had just bought in New York, and he wondered if he might visit the flight deck to show Ron. The autopilot was engaged, the flight progressing smoothly at Mach 2 and lunch had been cleared away so it was a perfect time for visits to the flight deck.

Paul McCartney came bounding in with a guitar under his arm. Presenting Ron with said instrument, he asked him to show how he could play. Ron explained that he knew McCartney was left handed and being of the opposite dexterity himself, wouldn't be able to play a note. Paul went on to describe how he had just bought the guitar in New York for his only son, James, who was, in fact, right handed.

Ron took the guitar and started strumming 'Yesterday'. Very well, by all accounts, and so much so that Paul started to sing along. It was, I understand, quite special.

A couple of weeks later, I was paired up with Ron and Liam, also from my training course. We were on board preparing for the evening BA004 flight from New York and Ron was reviewing the list of passengers who were due to join us shortly. 'My friend Paul McCartney is with us again tonight,' he exclaimed.

I went back to the cabin mid-flight and found McCartney chatting and joking with the cabin crew in the front galley. He was everybody's favourite passenger, always full of fun and very down to earth. He drew cartoons and signed my girls' autograph books. I explained how we had all heard about his last flight with Ron and his supersonic duet and were 'dining out' on the story. 'I am as well, John,' he said. 'I'm telling all my mates too, because when I was a kid growing up in Liverpool I never dreamt I'd be singing at twice the speed of sound.' All in a day's work.

Talking of famous musicians, I thought I really ought to see what I was missing out on in New York. My frequent visits there often just led us to a local bar for a couple of beers and a burger.

I was at home one day when I had this urge to research what was coming up in the next few months. I was excited when I found that Eric Clapton and Friends were appearing for one night only at Madison Square Garden (MSG) in a few months' time. It was a special benefit concert to raise money for Eric's drug rehabilitation clinic that he, as a former addict, had conceived and opened in Antigua the year before, in 1998. And the tickets went on sale tomorrow.

I was taking the early morning Concorde to JFK 'tomorrow', so I decided immediately that I'd go straight to MSG to buy as many tickets as I could. I didn't even know if I was going to be able to get there on that 'one night only', let alone find others to join me, but I'd worry about that later.

We left on time at 10.30 a.m. and arrived in JFK on time at 9.25 a.m. That still seems impossible but it's true. By 11 a.m. I was in the queue at the MSG box office. I knew it was my time to be served when the nice lady boomed 'next!' from behind the glass partition. I explained that I wanted the maximum four tickets for the Eric Clapton concert on

30 June, 'Please'. That last bit threw her. It's not a word that's used much in New York.

'When do they go on sale?' she asked me, which I thought, was a bit strange. 'Today,' I offered with a quizzical edge to my voice. 'Well we won't have them until tomorrow then. You'll need a Ticketmaster outlet.' That stopped me in my tracks somewhat. I was leaving early the next morning, so coming back to MSG tomorrow wasn't an option.

I managed to ascertain that there was indeed a 'Ticketmaster outlet' not too far away in a local record shop. Who remembers those, I wonder? Great places to browse for an hour or two. I was soon back on my BA bike and accomplished my mission successfully. All I needed now was to ensure I was in New York on that 'one night only' and hope I had three others on the crew who fancied joining me.

As always, there were two Concorde flights to JFK that Wednesday. The BA001 would leave LHR at 10.30 a.m. and arrive at 9.25 a.m. The evening BA003 would leave LHR at 7 p.m. and arrive at 5.55 p.m. The show started at 8 p.m., so the evening flight might be a bit tight given the long drive into the city. I bid for both though and was assigned the evening trip.

Jenny was due to start at her new school, Sir William Perkins's in Chertsey, the following September, and that afternoon, Wednesday, 30 June 1999, was the induction/welcome afternoon to which we were all invited. That started at 1.45 p.m., and Eric Clapton was on stage at 8 p.m. In New York.

I left the school at 4.20 p.m. and drove straight to Heathrow to go to work. Max Robinson, one of my favourites, was the captain on G-BOAA that night and he offered me the opportunity to fly the outbound sector. He'd bring the flight back the next day. We left a minute early with seventy-seven passengers, not a bad load for the evening flight, which was often a bit quieter than the morning one. The flight time was slightly longer than average at three hours and twenty-four minutes, but we were still on the gate in JFK seven minutes early at 5.48 p.m.

As we took our seats in MSG that night, Eric Clapton came out on stage. Perfect timing. I'd left Jenny's school at 4.20 p.m. in Surrey and I was in Madison Square Garden in downtown Manhattan for 8 p.m. Only on Concorde. It was a fantastic show. I know it was because I've just watched it again on YouTube, twenty-three years later while writing this chapter. And I had no problem finding three new friends to join me, by the way. All in a day's work.

It was a routine flight out to JFK on the BA001 on 16 February 2000. The return the next day was far from routine, unique in fact.

We had a phone call at the crew hotel in downtown Manhattan delaying us by an hour. Concorde G-BOAG had a problem with the captain's seat. A spare part was required and it was arriving on the early morning Concorde service from London, which was due in just after we were scheduled to depart. It wouldn't take long to fit, so the one-hour planned delay seemed reasonable. The passengers would be contacted personally and appraised of the situation. All good so far?

There are two ways to move the pilots' seats back and forth: electrically and manually. The captain who had brought 'AG' in from London the night before on the evening BA003 service had passed on verbally that the fore and aft movement of his seat was 'a bit notchy' when moved manually, but was fine electrically.

By the time we got to the aeroplane a bit of a saga was developing. Overnight the engineers in New York had found the cause was a broken nipple on the end of the cable that was attached to the manual operating handle. They had carried out a temporary repair quite satisfactorily and updated the engineering head office in London appropriately. That's when the problem started.

The bods in London didn't approve of this temporary repair, so dispatched a replacement cable on the BA001 from Heathrow. We were all set to go, passengers and baggage loaded, aircraft refuelled and most of the paperwork completed. The BA001 parked up alongside us and a couple of minutes after she'd shut down, somebody rushed into our flight deck clutching a cable. 'Five to ten minutes,' he said, the back of the seat already having been removed and the whole procedure wasn't any more involved than changing a brake cable on a kid's bike. That is, assuming you've been to the bike shop and bought the correct cable.

You're probably one step ahead of me here. It was the wrong cable. It didn't fit. We were back to square one and now had a potential PR nightmare on our hands, having kept our passengers updated throughout, including the bit about 'five to ten minutes to fit, then we'll be on our way'.

Now, aeroplane maintenance, whether it be Concorde or a small Piper, is strictly controlled. No bodge jobs are allowed and everything has to be recorded and accounted for. So to be fair, the temporary repair was somewhat debatable, as it wasn't a procedure authorised by the aircraft manufacturer. Any faults, no matter how minor, are written up by the flight crew in the aircraft maintenance log (AML) and they must either be fixed before the next flight or delayed until a later date.

Some faults, of course, must be fixed before the next flight, a hydraulic leak or an engine problem for example. But with other more minor defects we would consult the allowable deferred defects manual and the engineers would sign it off as an ADD, to be repaired at a later date, but within the time limit prescribed in the manual.

Under the paragraph about the captain's seat it just stipulated that it must be moveable fore and aft manually and electrically. We figured we were able to do that. The electric system was fine. Even if we didn't have the temporary repair to the cable, we could still move the seat manually now the back cover had been removed. The flight engineer had easy access to the lever in the back of the seat to which the end of the cable would normally be fitted. If needed, he could lift that lever and the seat would move manually. We were complying with the requirements. 'Let's go.'

Sometimes a degree of pragmatism and common sense is required. But as well as that, we also needed a signature in a book. The defect had been written up in the AML and had to be signed off.

We were in one of those rolling delay situations. 'Just another ten minutes,' we kept telling the passengers, each time with a decreasing degree of conviction. Incredibly, nobody was prepared to sign the aircraft off as serviceable. The flight was cancelled.

The passengers, by now quite understandably somewhat miffed, returned to the lounge. They were rebooked on the later BA004 service. The next day, we were tasked with flying an empty Concorde back to Heathrow. Because our flight had been cancelled there was now a spare aeroplane that needed repositioning back to base. I dread to think how much all this had cost.

We had an extra night in New York. I went shopping. Not to Macy's, Bloomingdale's or any of the fancy stores on 5th Avenue. I went for a wander round Oddjobs. A flight engineer friend of mine had told me about this place. 'Great for DIY bits and pieces and all those odd little things you never knew you needed,' he'd told me. It really was full of all sorts of strange things. I'm not much of a DIYer, so I didn't need any screwdrivers or wrenches, but I did come out with a couple of rabbits.

I'd always enjoyed picking up gifts or clothes for my girls from far-flung places around the globe and when I saw these two, I didn't hesitate for a moment. Perhaps I should have done, because then I might have considered how daft I was going to look in my BA Concorde pilot's uniform, walking through a crowded terminal at JFK with two enormous cuddly rabbits, one bright pink, the other bright blue. And where was I going to put them when we got on board? There certainly wasn't room in the flight deck.

Luckily we had no passengers. They were the size of a small adult, so had a seat each in the front row, 1C and 1D on the right-hand side. We had a cabin crew with us, with nothing to do of course, so they had to find some way to amuse themselves. Each time I went back in the cabin for a stretch these two rabbits were in an even more compromising position. Thankfully, they didn't breed. They're 22 years old now and they haven't grown either.

All in a day's work.

THREE BREAKFASTS IN A DAY

Soon it was time to venture further afield.

Over the twenty-two years that Concorde had been operating prior to me joining the team, she had been to numerous destinations around the globe. The scheduled routes had included Bahrain, Singapore, Miami, Washington, New York, of course, and the jewel of the Caribbean, Barbados.

With some of the world's most prestigious hotels located along the west coast of the island, Barbados had long been a popular destination for the rich and famous. Just 21 miles long and 14 miles across along the south coast, and only eight and a half hours from London, it was a popular destination for winter sun seekers. The temperature never drops below 25°C and even in the heat of the summer rarely exceeds 31°C. The trade winds bring a cooling breeze from the east, and with no mountainous terrain like some of the other islands, it is less prone to the afternoon thunderstorms that are typical of the region. Grantley Adams International Airport, on the south coast, is well equipped with a long runway, a good instrument landing system and a large open-air terminal that could process 2 million passengers a year. Barbados was a most successful Concorde destination.

Every Saturday morning, half an hour before Concorde left for New York, the roar of four Rolls-Royce Olympus engines would fill the sky as BA273 set off for the Caribbean. I'd flown the route many times in a 747, of course. It was straightforward. Head to Land's End and turn left a bit. You'd sometimes glimpse the Azores mid-Atlantic but otherwise you'd see no land for the next eight hours. Having left Gatwick soon after 10 a.m., it would be mid-afternoon in the Caribbean when you landed, and having queued at immigration with nearly 400 other passengers, holidaymakers would typically arrive hot and tired at their chosen hotel, just in time for a cocktail to go with the sunset. Scrambled egg was more in order with Concorde.

With a four-hour time change in winter and five in the summer, we could leave Heathrow at 9.30 a.m. after breakfast, serve another breakfast or lunch en route and land in Barbados at 8.30 a.m. In time for breakfast, if you were so inclined to partake of three in a day.

My first exposure to this critical operation was on 7 August 1999. It was deemed to be a critical operation because, at 4,250 miles, it was right at the limit of the aircraft's range. Indeed, occasionally refuel stops were required in Lisbon or the Azores. There were limited airfields en route in case of emergency and, unlike Heathrow and New York, Barbados only had the one runway, so if somebody in front of you had a 'whoopsie' on the runway you were a bit stuck. If you know what a whoopsie is? An inter-island prop aircraft could burst a tyre on landing, for example, and if Concorde was next to land then a diversion to St Lucia would have to be initiated without any delay.

There was a special classroom training session required to cover the intricacies of the Barbados operation. I was introduced to high-level increment (HLI) fuel. This was an approved procedure where, even when the fuel tanks were supposedly full, you could override the shut-off valves and squeeze in another 1,200kg (1,500 litres) or so. It's like filling your car up before a long journey and, rather than accepting that first click when the pump shuts off, you pull the nozzle out a little, squeeze the trigger gently and get a few more litres into the tank and the pipe leading to it. It was about then that I would normally manage to shoot it all over my shoes. Refuelling a car, that is, not Concorde.

This HLI fuel procedure was approved by the aircraft manufacturers and the airworthiness authorities and introduced in the mid-1990s. It was common procedure on the longest flights – to Barbados, for example.

Using HLI fuel, we loaded 96.8 tonnes of the stuff for my first supersonic trip to the Caribbean. And none of it went on my shoes.

I was in good hands. The flight engineer on this trip was Ian Kirby. His nickname was Brains. He knew more about the aeroplane than I ever would, so if we had any technical issues along the way, if he couldn't fix them, nobody could. Ian had started his career as an engineering apprentice at BAC Weybridge, where much of the design, development and construction work of Concorde had taken place. Ian told me how, as a teenage apprentice, Barnes Wallis, of Bouncing Bomb fame, used to sit on the top of the stairs outside his office and motivate the youngsters at the beginning of each week. Ian's life has gone full circle. After an exciting career, peaking at flying with me to Barbados, he went back to Brooklands, now a museum, to work as a volunteer guide on Concorde, the VC10 and other exhibits.

I was also reintroduced to 54 per cent C of G take-offs, instead of the 53.5 per cent used at lighter take-off weights. Again on flights where we needed to squeeze every last little bit out of the aeroplane, there was a procedure whereby we would move a little bit more fuel rearwards into Tank 11 in the tail and move the centre of gravity (C of G) slightly further aft than normal. Remembering that Concorde didn't have any flaps like a conventional aeroplane, this rearward C of G procedure meant that the elevons would be drooped slightly to counterbalance its effect and act, just a little bit, like flaps. That would give us a bit more lift, increase our take-off performance and meant we could carry more fuel or passengers, as appropriate. The teams on the ground had to be very careful boarding the aeroplane though, because if all the fuel went in the back first, followed by the passengers in the rear cabin and their luggage, the aeroplane would have tipped on its tail and that wouldn't be good.

Just three hours and forty-six minutes after lift-off at Heathrow, we touched down in Barbados. That was less than half the time the 747 had taken. Much less. It wasn't even 10 a.m. and we were on our way to the hotel in no time. We'd used 86 tonnes of fuel and landed with over an hour's worth left after all.

We stayed for just twenty-four hours on this occasion, so having left home on Saturday morning, I was back home in time for dinner on Sunday and had enjoyed twenty-four hours in Barbados. That was the magic that was Concorde.

The normal Concorde schedule in the winter season was just one flight a week on a Saturday. Had the aeroplane been turned around and come straight back we could have legally flown there and back in a day, just like a short-haul trip to Tenerife and back, but because the schedules dictated the aeroplane sat on the ground for four hours we had to wait to take the next flight back. A week later.

These trips were popular, of course, so we shared them out fairly among us over the season. It wasn't everybody's cup of tea though, so it wasn't unusual to get three weeks in Barbados each winter. We had an arrangement whereby, if there was a spare seat, we could take somebody with us, so Lynne had her introduction to supersonic flight in November 1999. The captain had his wife with him and the flight engineer took his daughter. We all had a wonderful week away before the short hop back again the following weekend.

We were coming to the end of the twentieth century, the end of the millennium, a once in a lifetime experience. Literally. Parties and celebrations were being planned all around the world but I volunteered to work. Concorde was to be part of the London celebrations. Instead of the usual fireworks at midnight, a spectacular display was planned around the Millennium Wheel, later to be renamed the London Eye. Planned with military precision, we were tasked with swooping over the wheel at the exact moment the 8 p.m. firework display concluded. We were part of the grand finale.

We take satnav for granted in cars nowadays but back at the end of the last millennium they were very rare. My car, a Vauxhall Omega, was a top-of-the-range variant and as well as heated seats and powered steering, it had an early GPS satnav system. As part of the planning for this special mission, I drove with Jenny up to London, parked briefly right close to the Wheel so I could note precisely the latitude and longitude and feed it into Concorde's navigation system in the evening.

We left Heathrow at 7.30 p.m. and circled over a radio beacon to the north-east of London. I was with Mike Bannister, the Concorde chief pilot, and Keith Brotherhood, who incredibly I'd been in the Scouts with thirty years previously. We had measured the distance from the radio beacon to the Wheel precisely, taken the wind into account and used a suitable airspeed – just 250mph, so very slow for Concorde – to calculate to the second the moment we had to leave the Lambourne beacon and track inbound to the city. We got it spot on but the cloud base was right on minimums and we couldn't come any lower safely, so the effect was somewhat muted. It was, nevertheless, a privilege to be involved in such a historic event. I was back home by just after 9 p.m., where our house party was just getting going.

Concorde was conceived in the 1950s, first flew in the 1960s and went on to fly over 2 million people through the '70s, '80s and '90s, and here we were entering the twenty-first century. The operation was still successful, popular and profitable and showed no sign of coming to an end. The aeroplanes, even though they were over 20 years old, were in as good a shape as a 3-year-old subsonic aeroplane. They flew far fewer hours for a start, and every time they went supersonic, they got hot enough to get rid of any corrosion-causing moisture that might have found its way into the airframe. Some of the electrical components would play up every now and again, but were generally easily replaced. The plan was to continue the operation for at least another ten years. Sadly it wasn't to be. An eventful year lay ahead.

THE CHARTER FLIGHTS WERE FUN

Flying as a passenger on Concorde was expensive. Very. Senior business executives, film stars, lottery winners and pop icons were the only ones who could afford it. The extensive charter programme brought Concorde to 'normal people'. There were short subsonic flights to Bournemouth or Birmingham, usually to get the aircraft in place for a transatlantic charter flight. The most popular trips were the ninety-minute 'Round the Bay' trips that we did with Goodwood Travel or Bath Travel and other small tour companies. The passengers would meet up in a hotel by Heathrow for a welcome reception and be taken by bus straight to the aeroplane, often parked in a remote spot at the airport to give premium photo opportunities.

With only half the fuel needed to get to New York, the take-off was sporty. We would take the standard route down to the Bristol Channel, light the burners and take 100 Concorde enthusiasts through the sound barrier and on up to Mach 2 and the edge of space. The route would take a long, lazy, left-hand climbing turn out over the Atlantic and the Bay of Biscay before deceleration and a return to Heathrow over the south coast. There was a light lunch with unlimited champagne and each passenger was presented with a certificate signed by the captain.

We would carry an extra pilot or flight engineer on these trips. It was a busy operation and part of the fun, and the challenge, was for all 100 guests to visit the flight deck during the short trip. Smartphones and selfies hadn't even been thought of, but things called 'cameras' were in abundance.

I enjoyed being the extra pilot, 'the PR' as we were known. As well as hosting all the visits to the flight deck, I'd give a running commentary throughout the trip. I'd describe the take-off, the two kicks in the back as the reheat kicked in to shoot us through the sound barrier, and everything in between. Armed with a list of people who were along celebrating something special, and there were normally quite a few, I'd give them all a mention by name along with their seat number.

Much champagne was drunk on these flights, not by the crew I hasten to add, and it was a pleasure and a privilege to be able to share my enthusiasm with 100 like-minded 'normal people'.

It wasn't uncommon to do several Round the Bay trips in one weekend. Sometimes 'the Bay' was the North Sea if we were flying from Leeds, Birmingham or Manchester, but the principle was the same.

Dad had never flown, apart from one very short hop to Jersey way back in the early 1950s, well before I was born. He was quiet, introverted, didn't like crowds of people around, was particular about what he ate and what the temperature was like in the room. An aircraft cabin certainly wasn't an attractive environment for him.

He had always been fascinated with my work, though – always keen to hear how my latest trip to some far-flung part of the globe had gone. Now I was on the Concorde fleet his thirst for knowledge of all the technical aspects of supersonic flight was vast. Dad was soon going to be 80 years old and I hadn't given up on getting him to come on one of my flights. I'd dropped hints and asked him outright many times over the years, but to be fair, spending eight or more hours on a 747 just to be in the same aluminium tube as me wasn't that appealing. I understood. Now Concorde was a different matter. A short flight perhaps?

He eventually agreed.

On Sunday, 12 March 2000, just three months before his 80th birthday, Dad took Mum's arm as they walked into the Renaissance Hotel at Heathrow to check in for the Goodwood Travel supersonic charter flight that was to take them to 11 miles above the surface of the earth at twice the speed of sound.

There had been many questions driven by the apprehension that was linked to such a significant trip, mainly centred around the catering arrangements. It wasn't unusual for Dad to take his own food with him on days out, whether it was to the theatre to see a Christmas pantomime or a family trip to a London museum. Concorde was no different. I assured him it would be OK to take his special sandwiches made with his special bread.

After I'd dropped them at the hotel, trying to keep a low profile as I was in my pilot's uniform and knew I'd be meeting everyone in the check-in queue a little later, I made my way to our operations centre to meet the rest of the crew.

I was 'the PR' pilot on this flight. The captain was my good friend from my training course, Ron Weidner. Ron was always most eloquent on the public address system and gave all the passengers a lovely warm welcome and introduced all the crew. He explained how it was a very special flight for me as my mum and dad were on board before handing the microphone over to me for my commentary.

Indeed it was a very special day. I was so proud of Dad and when I popped back into the cabin to see them both, I was delighted to see the Sainsbury's bag with his picnic was still under the seat in front of him and he was getting stuck into the smoked salmon. He and Mum had a wonderful day. It did occur to me though, as I posed for a photograph with them in the cabin, how different life would have been had they not taken me in for a few weeks back in early 1958.

I'd rigged up a small cassette tape recorder with its microphone taped to the earpiece of a spare headset on the flight deck, so I could record my commentary and the special mention I was going to give Mum and Dad. It worked a treat and sat around in my study for many years after. Twenty years, in fact, until Jenny retrieved it and created a wonderful birthday present for me by getting it digitised and on to a USB memory stick, which was beautifully presented in an engraved wooden case.

We didn't know it, that lovely Sunday in March 2000, but Concorde was shortly to have her life curtailed, as was Dad.

Situated 31 miles north of the Arctic Circle, Kangerlussuaq is Greenland's major air transport hub. It lies at the eastern end of one of the largest fjords, some 190km long with its estuary on the west coast. The airfield itself is only 160ft above sea level but is surrounded by snow-covered mountains on all sides. The view from the flight deck of Concorde, as we approached from the west right along the middle of the fjord on 28 May 2000, was nothing short of spectacular.

Kangerlussuaq (I'm just showing off that I can spell it now) was formerly known as Sondrestrom and the major airport there, with a whopping 2,800 × 60m runway, was originally an American air base set up in the Second World War. During the 1990s it became a popular destination for Concorde charter flights organised by our friends at Goodwood Travel. Only in the summer though.

I'd been to Anchorage ten years previously in the B747 and found it never got dark in the middle of summer, but here the sun actually remained firmly above the horizon on the Summer Solstice. Bloody cold and dark in winter though, I should imagine.

The Concorde passengers were in for something very special. Not only had they experienced flight at the edge of space and at twice the speed of sound, but when we landed in Greenland (not going to push my luck with the spelling again) they were whisked away on a small turboprop aircraft to go even further north. They would sail around glaciers and have fine food and wine in the midnight sun while we Concorde crew had to amuse ourselves in the airport hotel within sight of the wonderful aeroplane that had carried us there. She looked absolutely beautiful, like a resting swan, sitting out there with the sun reflecting off the snow-capped mountains all around her.

We were good at amusing ourselves in far-flung places around the world and we set out on our day off in a couple of Mitsubishi Shoguns with some local guides to explore the nearby glacier. They cooked some strange things on a barbecue on the ice. We didn't ask, but all very tasty though.

Prior to that we'd noticed three flying boats arrive at the airport. It was, after all, a major staging post for any flying machine with a limited range crossing the North Atlantic. This was a sight to behold, so along with one of the other Concorde pilots and our flight engineer, I wandered out to see if we could have a chat with the crew.

They enthralled us with their adventurous tales and we soon learned they were on their way from Canada via Greenland, Iceland and Scotland to a flying boat reunion in Southampton. They invited us on board the Catalina and showed us around, but all too soon it was time for them to get under way to keep to their tight schedule.

We positioned ourselves on the tarmac at a safe distance and watched in awe as these 60-year-old amphibians fired up their engines. A spectacular sight and sound indeed. They started taxiing out in line astern towards the eastern end of the airfield ready to take off in a westerly direction and climb slowly along the length of the fjord before turning east over the mountains.

It was about that time that Derek, our flight engineer, started leaping up and down in a rather peculiar manner and shouting all sorts of strange things. He'd just realised he had left his backpack in the cabin of the aircraft we'd visited. It contained his passport, licence and wallet apart from anything else. All vital documents, as without them being in one's possession one could not operate as aircrew. Our friends at Goodwood Travel would be friends no more when they learned we were to be marooned in Greenland for the foreseeable future. Well, at least until the Catalina had reached Iceland and arrangements made for said backpack to be returned somehow.

Derek could run. Run like I've never seen a flight engineer run. Unless the only bar in town was about to close of course. He shot up the steps of the control tower, several at a time, and disaster was averted when the air traffic controller was able to stop the aircraft before they applied take-off power; the relief was audible when the captain's window slid back and Derek's bag dropped, in a most unceremonious manner, onto the tarmac below. A narrow escape indeed and our return supersonic flight back to Heathrow left punctually the following morning.

In all my years of travelling the world and by now 42 years old, I'd never been to Paris, so when an opportunity cropped up to be one of the pilots on a Concorde charter to the French capital, I jumped at the chance. This would be a wonderful opportunity to find my way around the city so that I could plan a future weekend there with Lynne.

When I checked in at our ops centre I was the only one who was disappointed to be told that we weren't going to be accommodated in a city centre, four-star hotel as would be the norm. It was Gay Pride weekend and all the hotels in Paris were fully booked, so we were to be put up in a wonderful historic château way out of town. That scuppered my plans somewhat but, hey ho, it was going to be a fun weekend regardless.

We flew 100 passengers supersonic out over the now familiar Bay of Biscay and into Charles de Gaulle before adjourning to our château. Very impressive it was too, but the crew took pity upon me and, as it was a lovely afternoon, offered to take me into the city and show me around. The concierge kindly drove us a few miles to the nearest train station and off we went. I saw, for the first time, the Eiffel Tower, Notre-Dame, the Arc de Triomphe and all the other wonderful landmarks.

We had a fine dinner on the Champs-Élysées, accompanied by some fine wine, naturally, but all too soon it was time to start the long and complex train ride back to the countryside. We were all getting a bit sleepy on the way back but made sure we didn't miss our stop. The plan was to alight at the local station, from what was probably the last train arriving there that night, and then just grab a taxi from the queue in the rank outside the station.

It was all going very well until we found there wasn't even a taxi rank let alone a taxi to put in it. There was no answer when we called the château, so no concierge to come and collect us. It was too far to walk and we were exhausted.

The thought of a Concorde crew sleeping on the benches in the station was not the sort of glamour to which we were accustomed. It looked as if that was going to be the only option, though, until a kind local resident took pity upon us and drove us back to our majestic accommodation complete with ancient four-poster beds. He has probably been telling the same tale about the Concorde pilots he found settling down for the night on the platform for years since.

The next day we had a leisurely, sumptuous breakfast with fine French croissants and coffee, then explored the wonderful grounds and the château itself before heading back to Concorde late afternoon for the next charter flight, again via the Bay of Biscay at Mach 2, to Heathrow.

It was 25 June 2000. A month from that day, supersonic flight was to change forever.

We had an arrangement whereby, as long as we weren't landing overseas, we could take a friend or family member along for the ride on the spare flight deck jump seat. My girls were 10 and 13 and an ideal opportunity presented itself on a weekend in early July 2000.

Lynne had been to Barbados on Concorde. Mum and Dad had enjoyed their supersonic experience. Now it was time to get Jenny and Natalie up there too. My sister, Lucille, was living in France, so it wasn't going to be easy to get her on a Concorde trip, but it was something we could think about one day in the future. There was no hurry after all.

I'd volunteered to be the PR pilot again on a series of five flights over the weekend of 8–9 July. One of the other pilots was keen to get his children along too, so we came up with a cunning plan.

Natalie joined me on the flight deck from Heathrow to Birmingham, a short subsonic flight with 100 passengers. Lynne shot up the M40 in the car with Jenny and we swapped the girls over there. Jenny came on the second flight, Birmingham back into Birmingham but via a supersonic tour of the North Sea.

Jen was 13 and was by now developing a healthy interest in aviation. She was in the Air Cadets and had spent much time on the 747 flight deck with me growing up. She was grinning from ear to ear when she took her place alongside me on the spare jump seat on the Concorde flight deck as the four Rolls-Royce Olympus engines came alive again for the second time that day.

The take-off from Birmingham was another spectacular event, with crowds of people lining the perimeter fence and cameras clicking away furiously as we roared over their heads with full power and reheat. We cut back to the reduced-noise setting quite quickly, with me commentating over the PA system explaining every change in noise and configuration, including the raising of the drooped nose as we accelerated through 280mph. I'd spent time before take-off explaining to Jen what all the main switches and levers did and she seemed to take it all on board.

In no time at all we had covered the 100 miles or so to the east coast and set off up the North Sea. Clear of land, we were now approved for supersonic flight. I explained to our guests, as normal, what they would experience as we went through the sound barrier. The main feature was, you'll recall, two nudges in the back as the reheats were switched on in pairs, the inboards first, followed a few seconds later by the outboard engines. These were operated by four white switches towards the rear of the central console. Jen was given the opportunity to take part in this operation. It was quite simple really, but I'd obviously not made the bit about 'two at a time' clear enough. Instead of two separate nudges in their backs, that day our guests got one big kick.

We landed back into Birmingham late afternoon and adjourned to our overnight accommodation. The city centre hotel wasn't quite as exotic as our French castle of a couple of weeks previously, but it was comfortable. Instead of dinner on the Champs-Élysées we went to Pizza Express in Birmingham. If only the other diners knew that the large party on the table in the middle of the restaurant was a complete Concorde crew and a few 'hangers on'.

The captain was Stewart Bates and it was always good to fly with Stewart. He'd got in touch with me a couple of months previously as I was part of the crew operating a charter flight to Tenerife. Stewart's son, Tim, was a doctor on board a cruise ship that was going to be berthed in Tenerife while we were there. He wondered if we might be able to show him and his team of nurses around Concorde during our time on the ground. It was a pleasure to do so, of course.

Many years later, I had cause to contact my local GP to seek advice on some minor ailment or other. A call-back was arranged and the doctor came on the line. 'I met a Concorde pilot once called John Tye …' he said. Tim Bates, with no connection to our locality, was now my GP. It's a small world.

We did three charter flights the next day, via Manchester and the North Sea again, before returning to Heathrow. We carried 500 'normal people' that weekend, plus a few family members on the jump seat. By 'normal people', of course, I mean *not* the rich and famous who would think nothing of spending £7,000 for their supersonic flight across the Atlantic. These charter flights sold for something like £299 for a subsonic hop to £699 for the full supersonic experience. We could have filled them day in, day out all year long, but British Airways had to find the right balance. They weren't that profitable compared to the scheduled flights and we didn't want to wear the aircraft out prematurely. After all, she was going to be in service for many years to come.

In just over two weeks from now that plan was to change dramatically.

A DISASTROUS DAY – 25 JULY 2000

I'd flown the BA002 supersonic Concorde service from New York the night before and got home about 7.30 in the evening as usual. I had two days off before my next trip – the morning BA001 from Heathrow on 27 July.

It was the middle of summer. The children had finished school and, like any father, I was treasuring my time away from the office having fun with the kids.

I had one thing I needed to deal with on my days off. The family TV, an old Ferguson, had been playing up for ages. It was a 26in screen in a large wooden cabinet, fashionable for the time, when flat screens twice the size were still a long way off. The picture was intermittent and the colour way off the spectrum, occasionally improved by a firm thump with a flat palm on top of the cabinet. In those days, you didn't just throw them away when TVs developed a fault and replace them with another flat screen purchased through the internet. You took them to the local TV repair shop.

That's where I was on the afternoon of Tuesday, 25 July 2000. Jenny had come with me and she was waiting in the car outside the small family run business in Ashford, Middlesex, just a short distance from Heathrow, while I dropped the faulty Ferguson off for repair.

I wasn't in the shop for long and when I returned to the car, Jen was sitting quietly and the radio was turned off. I'd left her listening to music. She broke the news to me that Concorde had crashed. There had just been a newsflash with the briefest of details and she had thought to cushion me from the shock and break it to me gently. She didn't know at that moment if it was a British Airways or Air France aeroplane. We soon discovered the dreadful truth and by the time we got home, just before 4 p.m., all the TV channels were bringing us the latest updates, including that sickening video clip, shot from the cab of a passing truck, of an Air France Concorde struggling into the air with a massive fire coming from its underside, soon to be followed, after it passed out of sight behind a street sign, by a fireball and plume of black smoke that signalled the end of that short flight.

The world was in shock. British Airways cancelled their evening BA003 Concorde service, but resumed services the following day. I flew the BA001 to JFK as planned on the 27th but it was a most sombre trip.

Our family was in shock. Our neighbours were in shock. The world was in shock.

Dad was particularly shaken by the accident that afternoon and I went over to see him at the family home in Sunbury the next morning. It was only six weeks since he had taken his first proper flight, that supersonic trip around the Bay of Biscay with his own sandwiches.

He had had his 80th birthday and was getting quite frail. He'd had a few funny turns over the last few weeks too. The circulation in his legs was very bad but he could still walk up and down the garden OK and to church every Sunday.

I remember walking up and down the garden with him that morning trying to ease his worries about me flying Concorde. I was scheduled to fly back to New York the following day, 27 July. He wasn't happy about me going. I explained how, while at this stage we didn't know what had caused the accident, it was surely a freak event that couldn't possibly happen again. The aircraft had been in service quite happily, after all, for twenty-four years. He eventually relaxed somewhat but the shock and the worry hadn't done him any good.

I flew that service to New York the next day.

Lynne met me at the airport when we got back to Heathrow on 28 July and broke the news that Dad was very unwell in hospital. After I'd left him on the Wednesday he'd had a massive stroke. Mum took the decision not to tell me, knowing how important it was that I flew Concorde. He was in a coma and was unlikely to recover. Lynne took me straight to the hospital. I spent time with Dad talking to him, trying to make him smile, telling him I loved him and thanking him for everything he had done for me over the last forty-two years. There was no physical response but I think I saw an eyelid flutter slightly before he slipped quietly and peacefully away. He'd hung on to life until he knew I was safely back from New York. It was five days after the Concorde crash.

An investigation into the tragic accident got under way immediately. A total of 113 people died that afternoon: 100 passengers, six cabin crew, three flight deck crew and four on the ground when the aircraft crashed into a hotel in the village of Gonesse, just two minutes after take-off.

Despite the total destruction of the aircraft, the team of investigators gathered sufficient evidence, including eyewitness reports and video footage, to quickly determine the approximate chain of events that had brought the aircraft down.

Aircraft accidents are normally brought about by a chain of events rather than a single incident. Some of those events might be a mechanical failure. Some might be what we call human factors, like workload management or poor communications among the crew. The analogy of a Swiss cheese with all the holes lined up on the fateful day is often used.

By 15 August, just over three weeks after the accident, the preliminary findings had been released and the UK CAA reviewed them and made a decision to ground the entire fleet of Concordes, pending modification.

A titanium metal strip some 43cm long had fallen from the engine of a DC-10 aircraft that had taken off five minutes before Concorde. The Air France Concorde was at, in fact, (illegally) 800kg over, its maximum structural take-off weight. As I have already mentioned, unlike a conventional aeroplane, where the wings start to generate lift and take the weight off the wheels soon after it starts rolling down the runway, Concorde's wings do nothing until the nose is raised. All the weight of Concorde, some 185 tonnes, was on the wheels when it struck the metal strip at nearly 210mph.

The right front tyre on the left-hand side exploded and broke into large pieces, which were flung in every direction. One piece, later calculated to weigh 4.5kg, hit the underside of the wing with tremendous force at over 300mph. Like all aeroplanes, the fuel tanks are mostly located within the wings, and one was completely full. Tank No. 5 took the impact. It didn't puncture directly, but the impact set up a shock-wave within the tank such that it ruptured slightly further forward. A massive fuel leak developed.

The tyre explosion also damaged the undercarriage and its associated electrical cables and hydraulic pipes. The hydraulic failure meant the undercarriage couldn't be raised as normal, so they were stuck with much extra drag (air resistance), which impeded significantly their ability to accelerate. The electric cables that were cut flailed about in the airflow sparking, which was the ignition source for what quickly became a massive fire.

While the flight crew, two pilots and a flight engineer, couldn't see what was going on underneath the aeroplane, they had fire warnings and indications in the flight deck, which led them to shut down one of the engines immediately and another started to surge (misfire in automotive terms) as it ingested the disturbed fiery airflow.

There were other significant factors though, including serious errors made by the flight crew and the maintenance engineers, and much has been written elsewhere in more detail about the accident.* All these years later, it's widely considered that there might have been a different outcome if these human errors had not been made. The official line though was that a single piece of metal on a runway had brought down the world's only supersonic airliner after twenty-four years of safe operation.

The chain of events had to be broken so that could never happen again.

The CAA telephoned British Airways on the morning of 15 August to give them twenty-four hours' notice that the Concorde fleet would be formally, temporarily, grounded the following morning. An urgent board meeting was convened at BA headquarters.

As that call came through, I was on board Concorde G-BOAC BA001, preparing for our 10.30 a.m. departure to New York. The passengers were boarding, the fuel was loaded, the champagne was being chilled and the pre-flight checks were going well.

There were four of us on the flight deck, as it was a training flight. I was the extra safety pilot with the responsibility of overseeing the whole operation to make sure nothing was missed.

As normal we started the first two engines on the gate at 10.28. We disconnected from the ground support services and at 10.30 precisely were cleared by air traffic control to push back from the designated Concorde gate right in front of the VIP lounge at Heathrow's Terminal 4. We were in the middle of the cul-de-sac parallel to the terminal building, just about to ask the tug driver beneath us to disconnect his tow bar and clear the area, when air traffic control called us again. They wouldn't normally disturb us at this critical stage unless it was essential.

'Speedbird Concorde 001, Ground.'

'Go ahead,' we replied.

'Speedbird Concorde 001, message from the company [British Airways]. Return to the gate.'

We knew there was nothing wrong with the aeroplane so we enquired as to why. Knowing the radio frequencies are monitored by external agencies and aircraft spotters, no further information was forthcoming. We asked the

---

*   Concorde *by Mike Bannister and* The Concorde Story *by Christopher Orlebar.*

tug driver to tow us back on, instructed the cabin crew to put the doors to manual and, thinking it was perhaps a bomb threat, shut the engines down.

The jetty was quickly positioned alongside the aeroplane, and being at the back of the flight deck I was the closest to it and met the aircraft dispatcher as she arrived at the opening door.

'What are you guys doing back?' she asked me.

'I kind of hoped you'd be able to tell us that,' I replied, and then the penny dropped.

Realisation dawned upon us simultaneously that Concorde had been grounded following the accident. We later learned that the BA board meeting had quickly decided, 'If we know that Concorde is going to be officially grounded in twenty-four hours, how can we possibly let the BA001 depart this morning? Call it back.'

We had a Concorde aircraft in New York being prepared to operate the reciprocal flight from JFK to LHR. That was immediately cancelled, but before the passengers had arrived at the airport, and the aircraft was flown back empty. All seven of the fleet were therefore at Heathrow ready to be mothballed and modified.

We had some sixty passengers to whom we needed to explain the situation. Looking after our customers is a big part of the job and I found myself taking care of Queen Noor of Jordan and her party and a lovely elderly French lady, who I remember fondly.

This lady was travelling with a tour group to New York from her home in the south of France. The rest of her party were flying subsonic from Nice, via Paris to New York, but this lady, well into her 80s, had always dreamed of flying Concorde, so made her own way to Heathrow to fly supersonic that day. She was so understanding, but it made me sad to think that she might never get her Concorde flight.

It didn't occur to me at that stage that I might not get another either.

Once we had done all we could for the passengers and entrusted them to our wonderful colleagues in our ground-based customer services team, we were taken by bus back to the Compass Centre, our operational headquarters. We were given a thorough briefing and as I drove slowly and sadly back around the airport perimeter road on my way back home, the news broke on the car radio that Concorde had been grounded.

We had no idea at this stage how long we would be on the ground for. My six-monthly simulator check was scheduled for six days' time, on 21 August. I drove to Filton on the Sunday night as normal and met up with my captain, Paul Mallinson, and flight engineer, Alan Walker, early the next morning ready for the first of two four-hour sessions in 'the box' being checked by training captain Stewart Bates. You remember, the one whose son is my GP? It went well. Very well, in fact, and I treasured the glowing handwritten report that Stewart presented me with, not knowing if it would be my last.

Much work went on in the months that followed.

The cabin crew flew not just on Concorde but on the subsonic European routes as well, so life for them went on pretty much as normal. The captains, senior first officers and flight engineers were told to stay at home on gardening leave.

The Concorde fleet and engineering management team got together with the air accident investigators, the CAA, Airbus and their counterparts in Air France to plan a return to service programme. If any one of the events in that chain could be neutralised so that it could never happen again, that was all that was required. Each event was assessed individually and it was decided that all of them should be addressed:

1. Metal piece on the runway – policy introduced that the runway be swept before every Concorde departure.
2. Tyre exploded into large, destructive pieces – tyre redesigned to break into small, harmless fragments.
3. Fuel tank ruptured, causing massive fuel leak – Kevlar bulletproof linings installed in critical tanks close to the undercarriage.
4. Damaged wiring sparked and ignited the fuel – wiring armour-plated in steel sheaths and electrics isolated from the area before take-off.

The project was extremely successful, with the British and French teams to be commended for their effective teamwork and dedication.

British Airways was keen for Concorde services to New York to resume and continue well into the twenty-first century. The aeroplanes had plenty of life left in them as they only flew a fraction of the hours logged by subsonic aircraft. They took the opportunity to modify the cabin, designing and installing new seats and toilets and other passenger-service items. They kept in touch with key corporate customers during the programme, even hosting them in the hangars at Heathrow, where they could witness, first hand, the modifications taking place.

The return to service programme was going to take the best part of a year. Concorde flight crew would have immaculate gardens if they were allowed to remain on gardening leave all that time.

We were approached after a few weeks and asked to consider which aircraft types we would like to transfer on to temporarily. When Concorde returned to service we could all return to our supersonic lifestyles.

Most of the Concorde captains had less than five years to go until their compulsory retirement age of 55 and had flown the mighty B747 before they came to Concorde, so it was fairly straightforward for them to return to the jumbo.

I was 42 and a Concorde senior first officer, so had the opportunity to take promotion and become a captain on the short-haul Airbus fleet. Normally, a first officer will have months to prepare for his command course, the ultimate pinnacle of your career, by studying all things non-technical and attending residential management-training courses. Whether you are a first officer or a captain, your flying skills need to be to the same high standard and you're tested regularly in this arena, but as a captain you have to be able to manage a team of up to twenty-four people for ten days, on and off the aeroplane, all around the world. People you've never actually met before. You have the ultimate responsibility for hundreds of lives a day in the most hostile environment: an aluminium tube 8 miles above the surface of the earth. You don't want to think about it too much really.

I had the option of taking this career step with no preparation, or taking the easier route and remain as a senior first officer, but transfer to the 747 that I'd flown before.

I like a challenge. When I enquired about the Airbus command course and when it might start, the answer was along the lines of 'next Wednesday'. It was certainly going to be a challenge. It's quite common for pilots to undergo training to become a captain. That's called a command course. It's also quite common to undergo a conversion course. That's training to fly a different type of aircraft without changing rank, but a command/conversion is the two combined: learning a new aircraft and how to be a captain at the same time.

Apart from the charter work in Dan-Air, I'd never flown scheduled short haul. I'd never flown a modern 'glass cockpit' aeroplane. I'd never flown an airliner without a flight engineer to look after me. And find the cheapest breakfast in town. How was I going to manage?

Opposite page, from top left: Concorde nose in Seville; me on the flight deck at Seville; taxiing out for my first take-off; Seville, February 1999.

Clockwise from top left: Seville, February 1999; Jenny and Natalie on Concorde, 8 July 2000; with Mum and Dad, 12 March 2000; Concorde ground school at Filton. That's me, far left, pointing enthusiastically; Flopsy and Topsy, or whatever their names were, our only passengers from JFK on 18 February 2000.

6

Back to Subsonic Flying (2000 to 2022)

A Funny Graunching Noise

Manage I did though. I started my training to become an Airbus captain on 14 November 2000. There was a residential Essentials for Command course first, learning management skills and all about the legal responsibilities, enough to frighten anybody off if you thought about it too much. Then it was into the classroom to learn the technical side of the aeroplane. Unlike the 'chalk and talk' style of the Concorde ground school, with long, leisurely lunches and the excitement of hotel fires, this was self-taught, computer-based training. All very boring really, but you had to pay attention or you wouldn't pass the exams at the end of it.

The simulator training followed, about ten sessions in all, the first couple settling in flying this new hi-tech, glass-cockpit aeroplane from the left-hand seat, before moving on to managing complex, unusual situations with make-believe passengers and cabin crew. Then it was time to go flying. In a real aeroplane, into unknown territory – Europe.

The small bedroom at home was a makeshift study with a steam-driven computer and printer that doubled as a photocopier. 'What are you doing, Daddy?' asked Jenny as she came in on her way to the bathroom to brush her teeth before going to school. She had caught me, red-handed, photocopying pages out of her school atlas. 'I'm going to Oslo tomorrow darling and I don't know where it is,' I explained, slightly embarrassed.

Finding my way around Europe at 500mph was all part of the training, and learning how to manage snow in Sweden (I did find out that Oslo was actually in Norway though) in the morning and busy Italian air traffic control in Rome in the afternoon brought much variety to the new job. Like my Concorde training and 747 before that, I'd fly the routes with experienced training captains until I was ready for my final command check.

That's a most bizarre experience. It's one of the most significant events in the career of an airline pilot. I'd been a first officer, a co-pilot, became a senior one after four years' probation, for thirteen years, the second in command. Now I was to undergo a test: a check flight on a regular service to see if I had developed all the attributes to be let loose as a British Airways captain.

It was 25 January 2001. Yes, there's the 25th featuring once again. There were more stripes in the flight deck that day than you'd find in a tiger reserve. There was a training captain in the right-hand seat with four stripes on each shoulder and the same on the sleeves of his jacket. I only wore my standard three each side until I'd earned the right to another. Behind us sat an even more senior training captain with another sixteen stripes spread symmetrically about his uniform. He was the examiner and was to take no part in the operation. It was a requirement that he hadn't been involved significantly in my training so that he could take an independent view of me, observing not just my flying skills but more importantly my management, leadership, communication and decision-making skills. We call them non-technical skills.

The captain in the right-hand seat, my co-pilot, was to have no training input whatsoever, unless safety was going to be jeopardised, of course. He was to play the role of a competent co-pilot, but lacking in initiative. He wouldn't come out with any helpful hints or tips. Put simply, he would do what I asked of him to the best of his ability, not making any deliberate errors, but wouldn't be proactive or helpful. I'd been warned that it was a very lonely experience with little or no social interaction.

So Roger (the examiner), Dave (training captain but pretend competent co-pilot) and I set off to catch the crew bus out to the aeroplane on its parking gate at Heathrow's Terminal 1. The cabin crew were already on the bus, having met and completed their own briefing separately; my first role as leader, as captain, was to give them an update on the flight time, weather conditions and any other relevant operational details, including why there were so many stripes on the bus today.

Roger had included in his briefing to me that nobody would pull any stunts, make any deliberate mistakes, nor do anything to trip me up during the day. That was comforting, but then he added, 'We don't need to. Something always crops up.'

The bus pulled up alongside our shiny new Airbus A319, G-EUPT. She looked wonderful. Not in a way that Concorde looked wonderful when you pulled up alongside but she almost seemed to have a smiling face. Was she welcoming me or did I see a little wink from the corner flight deck window? Was she planning something to catch me out on my big day?

It's normal to see much activity round an aircraft an hour or so before departure. Engineers are checking and topping up the oil in the engines. Cleaners are cleaning, caterers are catering, refuellers are refuelling and baggage loaders are, well, you can figure that one out I'm sure.

Today was different though. There were two vans parked right at the front of the aircraft and there was a huddle of people around the nose wheel. That wasn't good. Something was amiss. I couldn't believe it. I hadn't even got off the crew bus and there was Roger's 'something always crops up'.

I popped on my hat. It didn't have any gold (or platinum in BA) braid on it yet. That hopefully would be added in a few hours' time, but to all intents and purposes, I was the captain. I walked, albeit with my slight limp, in an authoritative but friendly manner, over to the group of engineers huddled around the nose wheel. There's actually a pair of them (the nose wheels) but we use the singular term. There was some head scratching going on but not a spanner nor hammer in sight.

The aeroplane had recently arrived from another European flight and the inbound pilots had reported a slight 'graunching noise' taxiing in to the parking spot after landing. They were investigating and undertook to keep me posted. There was no point me standing around overseeing their investigations, so I returned to Roger and Dave, updated them and led the crew on board to commence our pre-flight procedures. I think I might have seen a slight smile appear at the corner of Roger's mouth. He was there, after all, to assess my ability to manage situations, both normal and abnormal. It was starting to look like he might have some material to work with.

About fifteen minutes before departure three of the engineers appeared on the flight deck. The number of engineers present is usually in proportion to the severity of the problem they are faced with. Other factors might include overtime rates and the proximity to the end of the shift, of course.

The boarding of the passengers was almost complete. The cabin crew were smiling, taking coats from the businessmen and women and hanging them in the Club wardrobes. The well-known boarding music, an adaption of 'The Flower Duet', was creating an ambience of calm and tranquillity in the cabin. We could have done with some of that where I was sitting, feeling somewhat lonely.

Their verdict was, 'We can't find anything wrong. We'd like you to take it and report further.' Great!

Any faults, minor or major, with an aeroplane are recorded, written up by the pilots in the aircraft maintenance log (AML) and each one must be addressed before the next flight. Minor issues can, of course, be deferred until a later date; for example, 'bulb in front toilet failed' and, in the engineer's 'action taken' column alongside, 'bulb to be replaced within ten days' would be quite normal.

Alongside the previous pilots' report of the 'graunching noise' from the nose wheel, the engineers wrote: 'Ground checked. No fault found. Please report further.'

Pilots like black and white. Clear-cut decisions are easy to deal with. We work from checklists. We have strict procedures. The challenging part of being a captain is what we call 'managing the grey'.

We closed up on time and called air traffic control for permission to start engines and push back from the gate. We were advised of a forty-five-minute ATC slot delay. It was busy on the route, so there was a queue. Parking gates were, as usual, at a premium, so we were offered what is called a remote hold. I'd never had one of these before. They were rare in long-haul operations and certainly something we couldn't entertain on Concorde. Commonplace in Europe during winter, though.

There were procedures to follow. We had a checklist. It was black and white, so I'm sure I could handle this, even if my co-pilot wasn't being that proactive with the support from the right-hand seat.

I shared with Dave that my plan was to taxi out to the remote hold, a preassigned parking spot away from the terminal, where we could shut the engines down and await our turn for take-off, and assess any 'graunching' along the way. Roger made some more discreet notes.

Thankfully, as we set off up the taxiway it was smooth and silent. I made a turn to the left at the end, gently on the tiller knowing the cabin crew had started the safety demonstration and were standing in the middle of the cabin demonstrating how to fasten and unfasten seat belts. A sudden input from me would scatter them into passengers' laps in a rather ungainly manner and that wouldn't be a good look.

No graunching. Good, it was going well. We'd wait out our forty-five minutes and then be on our way to Oslo with no further hiccups. I might even go out and talk to some of the passengers once we had shut the engines down at the remote hold and use some of those PR skills I'd brought with me from my supersonic days.

The final turn into the holding area was to the right. There it was, a distinct 'graunching'. It was a very good description. Metal on metal. It was faint, not dramatic and probably not even noticeable in the cabin. But it was there. I'd only been flying the Airbus for three weeks. Dave and Roger had twenty-odd years' experience between them. I tapped into that experience with questions like, 'Have you ever heard that before?' and, 'Do you have any thoughts?' Dave offered up a 'no' and a shrug of the shoulders, and Roger even less. He was, after all, there to assess my decision-making processes, my 'management of the grey'.

I elected not to shut the engines down at the remote hold, as would be normal, until we had decided what to do. It was a question of considering the commercial implications of a further delay, but second only to safety of course. I sat quietly for a few moments gathering my thoughts. The other two sat just as quietly, probably having already gathered theirs.

I considered the facts. This aeroplane was just a few weeks old, fresh out of the Airbus factory in Toulouse. We were at our home base where engineering facilities were plentiful. We were going to Oslo, where they weren't. The weather at Oslo was awful. It was snowy, icy, cloudy, windy and anything else you could think of with a 'y' on the end. The main thing was the runway could be slippery, with a potential crosswind fore-cast. There was something not quite right with the nose wheel, the one that did the steering. I'd finished considering all the facts. I presented them to the others and got some more shoulder shrugging and 'whatever you think John'-type support from Dave. Roger carried on making notes.

I must stress at this stage that this was all 'role playing' from them to see if I could make the grade as a captain and not be afraid to make tough decisions. If this scenario had only held itself back until after my check ride, I would have had all the support in the world. Flight crew are pro-fessional at working as a team, contributing ideas and suggestions with minimal 'authority gradient', and communication is always open and effective. Today though, I was effectively alone. They would only come out of role if I was about to drop a rather large proverbial 'clanger'.

'Dave, please tell ATC we need to return to the gate. I'm not taking this aircraft.'

There. I'd called it. An aircraft change on my final command check. Gulp.

The logistics of that called upon all my management skills. I had to break the news to the crew and then the passengers. Operations had to source another aircraft. Did we have enough crew hours to complete the mission or did they need to call out a standby crew? Roger searched for a new pen. His notebook was nearly full and we hadn't even left Heathrow.

Well, we managed the aircraft change. We left for Oslo an hour and a half later on a new machine. The flight went well. We were later than planned, of course, so the weather had deteriorated even further. The cloud base was 'on the deck'. The wind was blowing across the com-pacted snow on the runway, so an automatic landing was appropriate.

There's actually quite a lot involved in that, not like in the movies. We touched down smoothly. Thankfully, the steering from the nose wheel was perfect.

It wasn't until we got back to Heathrow at 9 p.m. that I had any idea how this was going. Was I to go home as the newest captain in British Airways or had I made a dreadful commercial decision, caused many missed connections and cost the airline thousands of pounds? That thought had been nagging at the back of my mind all the way back down the North Sea.

We shut the engines down on the gate back at Heathrow. I bade a final farewell to the passengers, who were gathering their belongings ready to disembark over three hours behind schedule. We'd been held up further in Oslo by the bad weather. It had been a long day. I was exhausted.

Roger leant forward and spoke. Just about the first words he'd said since we'd left the operations centre some eight hours ago. I've forgotten everything he said after 'congratulations'.

Goodness me. What a day! Role playing now over, Dave and Roger reverted to their normal friendly selves. I'm sure if we'd been overseas we would have adjourned to a local hostelry and shared a few beers. I asked each of them what they would have done. Would they have taken the original aeroplane? One said 'yes'. The other said 'no'.

Roger was most complimentary in his thorough debrief and written report that followed. I'd put safety first, used all my resources, such as they were, to make a judgement call. I'd 'managed the grey' most effectively. His report read:

> John has completed his Command Check to a very high standard. The check was complicated by technical problems requiring a return to stand and aircraft change. AWOPS conditions at OSL required auto land. All of this provided a very heavy workload. John was very positive and assured in his command in circumstances that he had not previously experienced. One or two elements of knowledge that could have been improved but these were also dealt with in a sound and appropriate manner. John will make an excellent addition to the Airbus fleet. Promote to captain. Well done. RS.

AWOPS, by the way, is 'all weather operations' or, more simply, it was foggy and you couldn't see a blooming thing.

I followed up the issue with the graunching nose wheel with the engineering department. They had stripped the assembly down in the hangar and discussed the matter with Airbus. It was established that a faulty batch of nose wheels had come out of the factory with no lubricant in the bearing assembly. A fleet check was called to identify others before they even started graunching. Rectification took place. I had made the correct decision that day and possibly averted a more significant incident.

TO STAY OR NOT TO STAY

I had my interview for my next new job less than a month later on 21 February 2001.

I hadn't even flown the Airbus for the first time when I'd been stopped in the corridor by the flight training manager on the Airbus fleet. I was still in the simulator phase of my training. 'I understand you used to be a training co-pilot on the 747 John. Make sure you apply for the vacancies I'm putting out tomorrow.'

The interview went well, as did the other aspects of selection that followed, and I was appointed as a training captain on 6 April 2001.

I'd already benefited from a significant pay rise for the promotion to captain and now I was to be paid an extra £11,000 a year for this next step up the career ladder. I'd only put my hand up to fly the Airbus for a short period while Concorde was grounded rather than stretch out the gardening leave.

The Concorde return to service programme was well under way. The modifications to the tyres, fuel tanks and wiring were all progressing as planned. She could be back in the air and soaring to the edge of space again within a year of the grounding. All was going to plan. Once all the modifications had been completed and approved by the authorities on at least one airframe, test flying could begin. The target was to achieve that early this summer. They'd need their pilots back soon.

I spent the spring and early summer of 2001 enjoying life as a British Airways captain flying around Europe. As the weather improved and even the northern parts of the Continent started to become warm enough to enjoy, I found I was enjoying the new role enormously. More than I thought I would, in fact. I liked the challenges of the busy environment. I was discovering places I never knew anything about. I might be walking in a park in Latvia one afternoon or enjoying a free day in Budapest the next. The flights were normally only a couple of hours long and we would do anything between one and four in a day. The Airbus was a delight to fly with its light fly-by-wire joystick falling neatly to hand. Instead of the monster of a control column rising from the floor in front of you between your knees, as I'd become used to on all my previous airliners, we had a fold-out table, so lunch in flight was a much more civilised affair. My dry-cleaning bill for uniform trousers halved as well because I didn't spill my dinner all over them.

I enjoyed the interaction with the passengers too. There were plenty of opportunities to greet them when boarding or to stand in the doorway as they left us. I learned to put some variety and a touch of humour into my public-address announcements. Those PR flights in Concorde commentating had taught me much. It was most satisfying to see my customers disembark happy and having enjoyed their time with British Airways.

The happiest group I had were on a sixty-minute flight to Glasgow back in early February. We arrived three hours late after snow and ice had caused chaos at Heathrow. I'd ventured into the Shuttle lounge during the delay, despite being told, 'You'll get lynched up there, they're really pissed off', by one of the ground staff. It was quite daunting at first. I felt as if I was walking into the lion's den for a moment, but with my jacket and hat, now adorned with much platinum braid, I soon had 150 people in the palm of my hand. They appreciated I couldn't solve the problem, but had taken the time to come and explain what was going on and I soon built up quite a rapport with them, which continued until we arrived in Scotland to a rapturous round of applause. There wasn't much left in the on-board bars by then though, so I think that had helped.

Life was good that summer. I was working harder than I ever had as a pilot. The days were long. The early starts were a bit of a struggle, but at least it was light when the alarm went off at 4 a.m. The variety was wonderful. No two days were the same. I was getting the hang of this. The work was satisfying and fun. I'd better make the most of it though because I'd soon be returning to Concorde and my supersonic lifestyle. Or would I?

The letter came on 12 June 2001:

I am writing to tell you that the Concorde pilot retraining programme
is anticipated to begin from 1st August 2001. In line with these expectations, we now need to know who wishes to return to the fleet ...

'Gulp!' Another decision needed making.

We moved into our new house on 1 July 2001. Concorde took to the
air again on 17 July.

We had lived very happily in our third house in the small village of
Upper Halliford, part of Shepperton, for eight years. It was a mile or so
from the girls' school in the centre of town and it had quite a rural feel to
it with the garden centre close by and within earshot of the church bells of
Lower Sunbury, where Dad had tinkered with the sound system all those
years ago. We had lovely neighbours and the children could play happily
and safely in the quiet street. Both the girls learned to ride their bikes
there and we have many happy memories, whether it was playing in the
snow or splashing in the paddling pool in the small back garden.

The promotion to captain and then rapidly to training captain brought
about a significant pay rise, so it triggered thoughts about making one
final house move.

We'd already seen that during the 1980s and '90s property prices had
risen significantly and bricks and mortar were clearly a good investment. When you're talking in terms of significant percentage increases,
surely the more you've got invested the bigger the potential gains were.
We decided to stretch ourselves one more time, take on the largest mortgage we could and make that final significant house move.

We found a lovely five-bedroom detached house in Shepperton that
backed on to a tributary of the Thames. It faced south and even had a weep-
ing willow tree at the end of the garden on the river bank. We could have a
small boat on the mooring too. It was idyllic and tucked away in the quiet
historic part of Old Shepperton. The bus stop was right outside and that was
where the girls could jump aboard and ride to their new senior school in
Chertsey. Jenny was already there and Natalie was due to start in September.
We made plans, got the mortgage approved and put our house on the market.

We were really upset when we were beaten to it. This would have been
our home forever but a property developer had seen the potential to make
some improvements and a quick profit to boot.

Friends of ours were always keeping an eye on property that was
coming on the market locally and gave us the details of a house in

Walton-on-Thames. This was in the days before you sent links to websites via emails and the typical A4 summary from the estate agents didn't really impress us. I remember thanking them, but saying, 'I don't like the look of that and there's no way we can afford it.'

A few days later we took a sneaky drive by regardless. We've been here ever since.

In the process though, we had rather burnt our bridges financially as far as returning to Concorde was concerned. I would have had to forego the two significant pay rises and peel all that platinum off my jacket and hat and return to senior first officer salary and status to get back to my former supersonic lifestyle.

I replied to that letter of 12 June with a heavy heart, but a well thought through response, declining the offer to return to Concorde. That simulator check I had passed with flying colours back on 21 August the previous year was indeed my last one. In fact, the next time I was to fly that simulator it would be as a museum exhibit at Brooklands Museum in Surrey.

I'd flown 149 sectors in Concorde as operating pilot, logged 535 hours and twenty-five minutes and carried 8,920 passengers, some subsonic, but most at twice the speed of sound. On top of that, I'd been the PR, the commentator, on many, many charter flights and helped put a big smile on hundreds of other 'real people's' faces. It had been a tremendous privilege and it was a job like no other, that I would have done happily forever. And without being paid, but don't tell the boss that.

Sadly, I would never see the sun rise in the west again.

The plan was to return Concorde to service gradually with just one flight a day to New York and then build up the network slowly, with a question mark still hanging over the Barbados route and the charter operations. They only needed a handful of pilots to get the operation started and there had been a core group who had kept current in the simulator at Filton as part of the return to service programme.

17 July 2001. '3-2-1, now.'

It was sports day at St Nicholas School in Shepperton and Natalie, in her last few days there, shot off the starting blocks in the egg and spoon race. Proud parents cheered the children on. The noise was extreme and only just drowned out by the sound of four Rolls-Royce Olympus engines passing overhead.

It was eleven months since her last flight and the chief pilot, Captain Mike Bannister, and CAA test pilot Jock Reid took Concorde G-BOAF (the very machine I flew in Seville) on her first test flight with all the post-accident modifications incorporated. The world's press were covering the take-off at Heathrow, just 4 miles to the north of Natalie's school field, and the long noise abatement gentle right turn from Runway 09R brought Concorde just to the south of Shepperton.

It was a route I'd flown many times and once Jenny had started secondary school, 3 miles to the west in Chertsey, I could get both their schools perfectly during morning break. We were a few minutes late one day and Jen's geography teacher had to pause mid-sentence and looked skywards in a rather unimpressed manner as she waited for the noise to fade before continuing, muttering something about Concorde. Jen felt herself blushing slightly, knowing that it was her dad.

The test flight went very well. Late in the afternoon the aircraft landed as planned, not back at Heathrow, but at RAF Brize Norton, where it would undergo further testing. The evening news covered the flight in detail with footage of Concorde taking off from Heathrow in glorious sunshine but landing three and a half hours later in torrential rain at Brize. Mike came down the aircraft steps protected by his impressive Concorde-branded umbrella and announced the success of the test flight to the waiting media throng. By the time the excitement had died down, one of them had pinched his umbrella.

However, less than two months later disaster would strike again and the world would change forever.

11 SEPTEMBER 2001

9/11 was one of the world's worst terrorist attacks. Four airliners were hijacked in flight in the USA and deliberately flown into the Twin Towers of the World Trade Center in New York and the Pentagon in Washington. Three thousand people died and the tragedy kicked off a global recession. Air travel in particular was badly hit. I flew an Airbus to Stockholm and back that afternoon, leaving Heathrow shortly after watching the collapse of the Twin Towers.

Concorde was on her way to New York. The plan was always to fly halfway there and come back again. This was a proving flight rather than a test flight, the final phase of the return to service programme. The aeroplane had performed perfectly throughout the testing regime and on 11 September there were 100 passengers on board for the first time. Airline employees chosen from the enormous dedicated team of engineers and ground staff who had worked long hours tirelessly on the programme were being used to check out all the support systems before going live again. The check-in procedures, baggage loading, catering, toilets, immigration procedures, etc. all had to work seamlessly before we could start welcoming back our supersonic VIP passengers.

When Concorde returned that day from her supersonic proving flight halfway across the Atlantic and back, the atmosphere was initially one of joy, excitement and celebration. By the time the aircraft door had been opened and the dreadful news relayed to those on board, that changed to just the opposite. Apart from the shock of the event itself, it didn't take long to realise that Concorde's future success, with New York as the only viable destination initially, was suddenly in serious doubt.

Concorde did return to New York two months later. It was the lift the city needed. Supersonic services recommenced on 7 November 2001. British Airways and Air France took an aeroplane each, full of VIPs, dignitaries and members of the press. They parked nose to nose, just like they had done twenty-five years previously. They were met by Mayor Rudy Giuliani, who welcomed them with open arms and said, 'Do me a favour. Spend a lot of money.'

The return to service programme had been a tremendous success. British Airways had modified five of their seven aeroplanes in the knowledge that they could do the other two should demand ever recover sufficiently. It had been a monumental task with hundreds of people involved. British Airways, Air France, Michelin, the British and French authorities and others had all pulled together, just like they had done fifty years earlier, to get Concorde flying. All we needed now was bums on seats.

Initially bookings were promising. The novelty factor kicked in, but they soon tailed off again. Businesses around the world were struggling as the recession got deeper and deeper. Remember, 80 per cent of Concorde passengers were senior executives and bankers. Quite a few regular Concorde passengers had actually perished in the World Trade Center.

'We cannot foresee the day when we can be seen to be including Concorde in our corporate travel plans,' said one executive, over lunch at

BA's headquarters. That sentiment was echoed far and wide. The writing was on the wall.

Despite the best efforts of the marketing department, demand for supersonic transatlantic air travel never recovered to anywhere near viable levels. Maintenance costs were spiralling and eventually, on 10 April 2003, British Airways and Air France made simultaneous announcements that Concorde would be permanently retired later that year.

You couldn't get a seat for love nor money after that. People from all over the world begged, borrowed or perhaps even stole the money to buy a seat on Concorde. It really was the last opportunity of a lifetime.

If I had a pound for every person I've met since who said, 'I wish I'd ….' You can guess what followed and I would have been very wealthy.

The iconic grand finale, when three Concordes landed back at Heathrow simultaneously – well, as close as you can get to simultaneously with three aeroplanes and two runways – is a vision many will remember forever. That was 24 October 2003. We were on holiday in Barbados and I watched the event being broadcast live globally, in a beach bar, with a rum and coke in my hand. And a tear in my eye.

The aircraft were loaned to museums at significant locations around the world, including New York and Barbados. The last ever flight of a Concorde was good old 'Alpha Foxtrot', my favourite, to her final resting place, back where it all began in Filton, Bristol, on 26 November 2003. The last ever. Ever. She will never, ever fly again. I was there as a guest with my family to witness that sad but historic event.

THE BEGINNING OF THE END

I returned to Filton in January 2018 with two other Concorde pilots, John Eames and Christopher Orlebar, author of the acclaimed *The Concorde Story*, to entertain 500 guests who had paid £99 each to have a fine dinner under the wings of 'Alpha Foxtrot' and hear our funny stories. The love and enthusiasm for Concorde will never fade.

Thousands of people were involved in Concorde over the fifty years of her design, development, operation and eventual retirement. The designers, the draftsmen and women, the engineers, the ladies who stitched the seat covers together in the 1970s, the pilots, cabin crew, the politicians

… the list goes on. Most people know somebody who was involved in Concorde one way or another. Today, it's the volunteers in museums in Europe and the United States who keep the dream alive for future generations to marvel at the past. To be able to look back at when 'ordinary people' could fly to the edge of space, cross the ocean at twice the speed of sound, faster than a rifle bullet, see the curvature of the earth and the sun rise in the west.

I visit Brooklands Museum in Surrey regularly and delight in seeing the expression on the faces of young children as they look up at the curvature of the wing and the pointed nose with its telltale scorch marks, and their parents try to explain that, despite looking so futuristic, Concorde is actually a thing of the past.

In an era where space travel is almost taken for granted, I am honoured and most privileged to have been one of only 134 pilots who flew Concorde for British Airways. It was a dream come true. There were more US astronauts who flew in space during that period.

The Concorde family has many generations and, like any family, reunions are wonderful events. There's sometimes a grumpy uncle in the corner or Grandad might have a drop too much sherry but there's much merriment and reminiscing.

One such event is a most prestigious dinner for Concorde flight crew, so pilots and flight engineers, and their distinguished guests. Held at the RAF Club in Piccadilly on the first Friday of March, the closest to the anniversary of the first flight on 2 March 1969, it's a wonderful opportunity to catch up with friends and colleagues. We all have a very special bond. Whether you were there right at the beginning in 1976 or involved in the grand finale twenty-seven years later, we are all part of one, not very big, family.

It's a family, a club, that's only getting smaller as the years roll by and eventually, just like Second World War veterans, there will be nobody left who was actually there, flying Concorde to the edge of space.

At the 2017 dinner we were summoned in a most ceremonious fashion (lots of hollering) from the downstairs bar and herded upstairs to the grand banqueting room. Disaster was narrowly averted. I was engaged in entertaining conversation with two 'legends' of the Concorde fleet, Christopher Orlebar and Peter Horton, both now sadly departed. Now I don't walk too well, as you know, and I'm rather vulnerable on a staircase, but Peter and Chris were just above me and walking with the aid of sticks.

The walking sticks became entangled and it was just a question of how many veterans would be taken out in the massive tumble down the marble staircase that, for a moment, seemed inevitable. Is there a technical term for an avalanche of Concorde pilots?

THE BRACKLEY MEMORIAL TROPHY

Exactly sixteen years after that spectacular day when three Concordes landed back at Heathrow in that iconic grand finale on 24 October 2003, a significant event took place in the City of London. A celebration and the ultimate recognition of the part Concorde had played in aviation history took place at the Guild Hall.

On 24 October, the Brackley Memorial Trophy 2019 was awarded to the British Airways Concorde fleet by the Honourable Company of Air Pilots. The terms of reference for this award are that it is 'awarded to an individual, a complete aircraft crew, or an organisation, for an act or acts of outstanding flying skill, which have contributed to the operational development of air transport or transport aircraft'.

Lynne and I were privileged to attend the Annual Trophies and Awards Banquet at the Guild Hall that night. This was one of those 'oh wow' moments, to use the polite expression, when we first took sight of this magnificent building across the square and then entered through the enormous double wooden doors. It's been used as a town hall for several hundred years, but it's not just any old town hall. They started building it in 1411 and it took them twenty-nine years to finish it, longer than Concorde was in commercial service. The Grand Hall where the banquet was being hosted was, quite simply, amazing.

It was an honour to be invited to the banquet but the honour didn't end there. I was only invited to go up and receive the award on behalf of all the 134 pilots and fifty-seven flight engineers who had flown Concorde for British Airways. Goodness me! Why?

I'd assumed it would have been received by one of the well-known pilots. One of the former chief pilots or somebody who had contributed much to the success of the operation during the formative years, but no, they asked me. I'd only been a first officer on Concorde, albeit a senior one, for three years towards the end of the era, but Captains John

Hutchinson and Mike Bannister, former chief Concorde pilot, put my name forward as somebody who was there at the end and who was still flying for British Airways. There's only so many times you can use the word 'honour' but I'll slip it in again there. It served to remind me that, regardless of how long you flew Concorde for, or the seat you occupied, we all shared that same special privilege of having been a Concorde pilot.

Concorde wouldn't have been such a success story without the thousands of other people involved in the air and on the ground. John Dunlevy joined me on the stage to represent the dedication and skill of all the engineering team, and Suzanne Gordon-Wilson on behalf of all the cabin crew.

What an evening that was.

Brackley Memorial Trophy with John Dunlevy and Suzanne Gordon-Wilson.

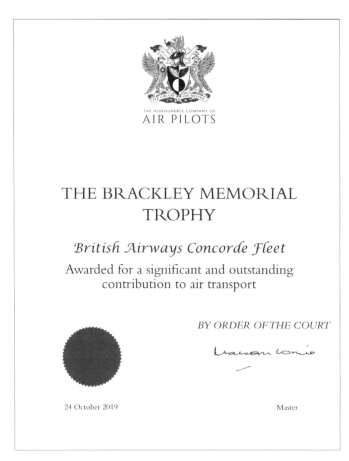

The Brackley notation certificate. (Courtesy of Mike Bannister)

ONE NEW MESSAGE

I continued flying the Airbus A319/320/321 around Europe until August 2007. I really enjoyed the role of training captain alongside that. It was what I call 'real training'. Brand-new cadets fresh out of flying college would have their first posting on to the Airbus fleet and it was uplifting to see their enthusiasm and pride to be wearing their sparkling new British Airways uniform with two platinum stripes on each arm.

It was commonplace for senior first officers to gain their promotion to captains on the Airbus fleet, either by changing seat, a 'right to left', as we call it, or by transferring from another aircraft type, just as I had done. With my own command training fresh in my mind, it was most rewarding to help others develop into this management role.

I spent time in the simulator on the instructor's panel conducting training and checking, and took new pilots, either captains or co-pilots, on their line training trips around the European network.

The route structure was vast and there was much variety on a daily basis. When I had flown around Europe in my Dan-Air days, it was mainly on charter routes, typically the Greek Islands or the Balearics, for example. The BA Airbus routes were mainly to European cities and not many overlapped with the former Dan-Air routes.

Berlin was one notable exception and it was great to be able to revisit some of my old haunts. Nobody went anywhere nowadays without a mobile telephone. I hardly used mine and in those days they weren't smart enough to do anything with, apart from make calls and send texts. Nevertheless, I took it out with me knowing that Lynne was at home with the children and I wouldn't be home for a few days.

Friday night in the Irish bar in Berlin was still the place to be. The live band were great, covering all the hits from the 1960s and '70s, and the place was rocking. I couldn't possibly be expected to hear my phone ringing in my jacket pocket, especially as said jacket was folded up neatly on my bar stool. Anyway, who was going to call me at 11 p.m. on a Friday night? Lynne was.

Something made me check my phone as I went to the toilet. Perhaps it was the novelty of having such a modern device, or perhaps there was that nagging 'just in case' feeling that somebody had called. A little light was flashing, which was drawing my attention to a new symbol on the screen that I wasn't familiar with. It looked like a cassette tape and eventually I realised through the haze that I had a voice message. I retreated to the tranquillity of the shopping mall in which the bar was located and keyed in the relevant code to retrieve my 'one new message'.

I could barely hear Lynne's voice, it being virtually drowned out by the sound of gushing water. She sounded quite distressed and I was astute enough to realise that this was … a bad thing. I considered the cost of an international phone call from this mobile device might equal my bar bill for the evening but decided I'd better ring home. Quite understandably,

Lynne wasn't impressed with my diction nor pronunciation. I'd either suffered a stroke or had consumed my fair quota of Kilkenny – a fine, smooth Irish ale, by the way.

There wasn't much support I could offer from afar, a common frustration for an international airline pilot, and by the time I had called back, she had handled the emergency well, a common skill for the wife of an international airline pilot.

Lynne had taken a shower before bed. In the process, the whole mixer control had come off the wall and water had come gushing out of the new hole. With no apparent way of shutting the water off, she was at least thankful that it was being contained within the shower cubicle.

The description of this lovely house in Walton-on-Thames when we bought it included the statement that the loft was 'partly boarded'. This fact was, however, lost on our next-door neighbour. Tony was 70, if not a day, and didn't mind in the slightest being called out late at night to help a damsel in distress. That's just what good neighbours are for after all. He knew for sure that there would be a way of shutting the water off in the loft and was up the ladder in no time. He soon came upon that part of the loft that wasn't boarded and his left leg appeared shortly thereafter in the guest bedroom. Luckily no guests were in attendance.

The insurance company were puzzled at first as to how the hole in the ceiling had been caused by the shower coming off the wall in the adjacent bedroom. The loss adjuster, when he visited though, could see we were honest folk, and thankfully Tony's injuries were minor, so they were happy to cover all the damage.

DON'T MENTION THE WAR

During my time flying the Airbus around Europe I met some wonderful people. The pace of work was often frantic, arriving in a European airport perhaps a few minutes late and managing just a quick chat with the engineers or the handling staff you remembered from last week, as it was all hands to the pumps to get the return flight away on schedule.

One hot summer's day, I was conducting my walk-round in a well-known German airport that had been heavily bombed by the British in the Second World War. I was checking the aircraft externally for any damage when I spotted an issue. It was normal during particularly hot or cold weather to connect external air supplies to the underside of the aircraft to pump in conditioned air, either hot or cold as required. The flexible pipes needed to do this are about a metre in diameter and can often be seen snaking their way across the tarmac from the supply unit to the socket underneath the aeroplane.

On this particular day, the ground team had obviously connected it in a hurry and I spotted the pipe was bent at quite an angle, restricting the airflow significantly. Using my somewhat wobbly feet, I started to kick it about in an attempt to rearrange it on the floor and enhance the flow of air to the aircraft.

The ground engineer was well known to us all, a wonderful character with a most colourful vocabulary and a wonderful sense of humour. Now, it's well known that Germans aren't famous for their sense of humour, but this chap had plenty of it.

He saw my dilemma and efforts to straighten the air pipe out and came running across to help me. 'It's no vonder vee lost zee war [and he had me doubled up at that stage] if vee sink vee can get zee air through zee pipe with a kink in it.' He helped me get it straight and walked off chuckling and shrugging his shoulders.

A RETURN TO GA

'GA' is short for general aviation, a term commonly used to refer to flying small aeroplanes for fun. Most airline pilots have some degree of GA in their background. After all, they had to fly small aeroplanes before they were allowed to fly big ones.

For some, that might have consisted of doing just the minimum necessary under the supervision of an approved flying training organisation. For people like me, who gained their commercial pilot licence through the hours-building route, it had been a joy to take family and friends on trips to the Isle of Wight, Le Touquet or the Channel Islands. All that flying back in the 1980s had taken me slowly towards my target of that much-needed 700 hours. It was, and still is, perfectly legal to share the cost of such flights as long as it's just with family and friends and there is no hint of any commercial operation or financial gain for the pilot.

I'd stopped it though once I started flying professionally. I was now getting paid to be up in the sky after all, so why on earth would I want to go spending money on my days off to go flying?

That all changed when we took a family day out to Aero Expo in the early summer of 2006. It's a bit like the Motor Show or the Boat Show but for small aeroplanes, GA. There were the latest flying machines from Cessna and Piper as well as home-built planes, gliders and helicopters. There were trade stands from the companies who sold headsets, maps, special pilot pens and sunglasses. You could even buy those chunky flying jackets that the Second World War Spitfire pilots wore. It was everything linked to general aviation.

Unlike Natalie, my youngest, Jenny, had always had a passion for aviation and she was 18 now. She had been in the Air Cadets, been on gliding courses and gone solo in a glider at 16. She had even spent a couple of weeks doing work experience with the ground crew at Booker, refuelling and handling the aircraft.

This year Aero Expo was at Wycombe Air Park, Booker, right back where it had all started from for me, so it was quite nostalgic wandering around and catching up with old friends and staff from the British Airways Flying Club. Jenny did the same. The ground crew were delighted to see her back there.

There was a long wait for lunch. We'd managed to bag a table outside on the grass so we could watch the planes and ordered sandwiches and cold drinks all round. We'd been warned though that there would be a wait of an hour or so because they were so busy. Jen and I took the opportunity to go for another wander and came back with her booked up to have a trial flying lesson at 3 p.m.

I sat in the back as she took the controls of the Piper Warrior and we took in the delights of Buckinghamshire once again. It had been the best part of ten years since I'd been in a small plane and to see my daughter flying it was something quite special. A thought bubble appeared. And that's often the start of something with me.

I made a few enquiries. 'Training as required, followed by a flight test', was the answer I was given when I asked what was involved in getting my pilot's licence revalidated so I could fly small aeroplanes again. GA was beckoning. I was, after all, a training captain now and earning pretty good money, so wouldn't it be nice to be able to take the family places again with Jen as my co-pilot.

I thought it would take hours of expensive training to get me back up to speed. In the event, it was only forty minutes. It was like riding a bike. You never forget how to do it. About thirty-eight minutes of that was sorting out the landings. A Piper Warrior landing at 70mph is a bit different from a 150-seat, twin-jet Airbus touching down at twice that speed.

The flight test went well on 29 June 2006 and after some admin and a big cheque had been sent to the Civil Aviation Authority, I was once again the proud owner of a private pilot rating or SPA (Single Pilot Aeroplane) rating, as it's now known, for I still enjoy such pleasure flying even now.

Jen went on to get her own pilot's licence after gaining two different flying scholarships and I was the proudest father in the sky when she took me in a small Cessna from Blackbushe to White Waltham and back. I was just a passenger.

I enjoyed taking friends up again, just locally or perhaps to the Isle of Wight for lunch, but was keen to go further afield.

Jen finished university in the middle of March 2008. She had worked hard studying aerospace engineering, a subject I couldn't even spell, let alone understand, so I took her away for a well-earned break in the sunshine.

We took a 747 to Miami, rented a convertible Mustang and drove south down to the Florida Keys. Then we came north again and blasted across the Everglades with her at the wheel. We spent some time on the Gulf Coast near St Petersburg. Where we hired a plane. As you do!

I took a check ride, as the Americans call it, in a Cessna 172, a four-seat, single-engine, high-wing light aircraft, with a cruising speed of 100mph or so. Then we were let loose for the day. I was the captain and Jen was the co-pilot but apart from the take-offs and landings she did all the flying. She took me right across Florida, over the top of, with permission of course, Orlando International Airport. We looked down at the BA 747 parked on Gate 80, right where I'd parked it many times before. We were just 1,000ft above the ground and continued our journey out to Titusville, also known as Space Coast Regional because it was the airfield for the Kennedy Space Center, which was just across the causeway.

Nowadays, we weren't allowed any further east than that. Without getting shot down, that is, but in days gone by, pre 9/11, you could. Way back in 1996 I'd been in Orlando for a couple of days on a layover, again as the Americans call it, and I'd had a check ride at Orlando Executive Airport in a Piper Warrior and took three of my cabin crew out flying for the day. We went east and got permission to circle the Kennedy Space Center at 500ft with close-up views of the gigantic Vehicle Assembly Building (VAB) and even do a fly-past of the runway that the Space Shuttle used to land on. That was something very special and never to be repeated.

Jen and I studied all the space memorabilia in Titusville and took a loan car out to the Space Center itself to marvel at all the history of space exploration and get a close-up view of the launch pads. Then she flew me all the way back across Florida again for tea back in Tampa.

Back in the UK, I was keen to keep my GA flying going but there's only so many times you can take friends up within an hour or so of High Wycombe in a 20-year-old Warrior. I'd been an avid reader of *Pilot* magazine since I'd started back in the 1970s and kept up to date with all the latest developments in the GA world even though I'd moved on from there. In 1998 I read about a new manufacturer on the scene, Cirrus. They'd actually been around for over ten years but were now hitting the big time with the launch of their new Cirrus SR20. This was going to take on the likes of Cessna and Piper and bring GA into the modern world.

The SR20 leapt out at me from the pages of the magazine. It looked gorgeous and could fly four people comfortably at 180mph or more over great distances. It even had a parachute. Not for the occupants, but for the plane itself. In the event of an engine failure, or other serious malfunction, rather than performing a forced landing, as they were called, whereby you would keep the aircraft flying by gliding in a controlled manner, choosing a suitable field close by and touching down gently (oh yeah), you'd just pull the big red handle in the roof. A rocket would fire from just behind the rear seats and within seconds the aeroplane would be dangling on the end of a line from an enormous 'chute. And it would really touch down gently and you'd more than likely walk away. This was a most comforting safety enhancement, particularly for cross-Channel flights, where performing a glide approach and landing at 70mph into a choppy sea, before clambering into a life raft, was surely not going to end well.

Oh well. Dream on. These aeroplanes were clearly very expensive and doubtless no flying clubs in the UK were likely to buy a fleet of them to replace their ageing and slightly smelly Warriors. Cirrus was clearly aiming its marketing at the wealthy private owner and that certainly wasn't me.

Never say never. I got checked out in the Cirrus SR20 on 20 April 2009.

G-OSPY was owned by a small company that had a few advanced light aircraft that experienced pilots could rent. You paid a monthly fee to be part of this non-equity group. I can't remember how much it was, but probably quite a lot. This was, after all, a very expensive and sophisticated aeroplane. You'd then pay an hourly rate recorded by a meter tucked away in the leather central armrest. This was taking GA to an altogether new level. It had that 'new car feel' to it, black leather seats and a glass cockpit, whereby all the flight instruments were incorporated into a couple of large screens in front of the pilot, instead of cogs and vacuum pumps whirring around behind the panel. And it had a big red handle in the roof for emergency use only.

G-OSPY was based at Blackbushe Airfield, near Camberley, so just over half an hour from home and much closer than Booker, so that became my new base for my GA flying.

I was keen to try and tempt Natalie into aviation once again after her childhood remark, 'Aeroplanes smell and I don't like the food'. She was my first passenger on a flight away from Blackbushe in June 2009. I took her to the Isle of Wight for lunch. As you do. She took the controls as we shot across Hampshire and the Solent at 160mph and flew it very nicely. She's been with me several times since and enjoys a nice day out, but never got the flying bug.

The Cirrus is quite a sophisticated aeroplane for an inexperienced pilot with a fresh PPL. It's a big step up from the Cessna or Piper aircraft typically used for training. The older, more basic trainers cruise at about 110 knots, so just under 130mph, which is fast enough for most novice pilots. A Cirrus, though, can travel at nearly half that again, closer to 180mph at altitude. As well as the extra speed, it is more like a Boeing 777 than a Piper Tomahawk. It has the latest navigation equipment with double GPS receivers, a sophisticated autopilot capable of flying RNAV approaches (pilots will understand what they are but basically they are a type of navigation) and big glass cockpit screens with an overwhelming amount of information. It has four sumptuous leather seats and is really, something quite special.

The G-OSPY group had about ten members. We didn't really know one another, unlike a normal flying club, and one would just book the plane online and complete the relevant paperwork before and after each flight.

I was, by far, the most experienced pilot in the group, by now a training captain on the Boeing 777 with over 11,000 flying hours logged. I had let my instructor's rating lapse though, so wasn't qualified to do any formal teaching or check rides.

One of the group members got in touch one day and asked if I wouldn't mind flying with him just as a safety pilot. He hadn't flown for a while and quite wisely thought it would be a good idea to have somebody more experienced and current alongside him for his first flight back. I readily agreed and a date was set. I was flying the evening BA service to Abuja, Nigeria, but didn't have to be at Heathrow until 7 p.m. that fine Saturday, 20 June. So we'd have plenty of time. Or so I thought.

We rendezvoused at Blackbushe, where the aircraft was based, as planned, at 9.30 a.m. Then the first curve ball came my way. He turned up with two of his mates. He hadn't told me anything about that when we'd spoken the night before, so that was a bit rude. More importantly, with four people on board, one has to be careful to check the weight and balance limitations. Most light aeroplanes fitted with four seats can't actually carry four people with full fuel tanks. Luckily, we were within limits, so the mission was still on.

Remembering I was there as a passenger really, not an instructor, I didn't intend to interfere unless something serious or potentially painful was about to occur. It was all about getting this chap's confidence restored really.

We'd decided upon a quick hop to the Isle of Wight for a coffee and back again, only about twenty minutes each way, so I'd be home in time for lunch and then pack for my short overnight stay in Abuja. Maybe even an hour in bed before heading for Heathrow. It didn't quite work out like that.

He'd told me right at the outset that he didn't really know how to use all the complex navigation equipment. He said he 'just wanted to fly it like a Warrior'. That didn't really matter. It was a lovely day, so no real reason not to just navigate by looking out of the window and flying by hand and the seat of the pants, whatever that really means.

He settled down quite quickly and seemed to be keeping up with the aeroplane OK. We were travelling south at about 170mph and it wasn't long before we could see the south coast and the island beyond on the other side of the Solent, separating it from the mainland. There are two airfields on the island and we were heading for Bembridge on the north-east corner. We were cruising along at 3,000ft. Very fast. He hadn't said much for a while, so out of curiosity more than anything I asked how he planned to position himself for landing on Runway 30. We were heading south-south-west and the landing runway was at 90 degrees to our flight path. He told me he planned to join on right base. That means descending and slowing down and simply making one 90 degree turn to line up with the runway, pointing towards the north-west.

A couple of minutes later, I could see that this clearly wasn't going to work. We were too high and too fast, so I politely asked him what Plan B was? I went on to suggest what we call an overhead join. He gracefully accepted my suggestion, flew overhead the runway at 1,000ft in the landing direction, reduced speed to a more manageable 100mph or so and made a series of right turns to fly a standard circuit. 'That's more like it,' I thought, and relaxed again. Perhaps a bit too much though.

I assumed he could land the aeroplane safely. I had no reason to think otherwise. It had just been the higher speeds that had caught him out a bit due to his lack of experience. Now the landing manoeuvre in any aeroplane is called a flare. It's a case of flying the aeroplane down at the prescribed final approach speed (about 85mph in the Cirrus), then closing the throttle and gently raising the nose slightly so you land on the two main wheels first before lowering the single wheel at the front just behind the propeller. He forgot the bit about raising the nose for some reason and as I grabbed the side stick to avert what was, at best, going to be a firm landing, I realised I was too late. The nose wheel hit the ground very hard.

We vacated the runway in silence. He was clearly embarrassed and his mates, who until now had been chattering away in the back and enjoying the views, were somewhat stunned. I felt it was safe to proceed to the parking area though, but out of the corner of my eye spotted the fire truck on the move. It followed us in and pulled up behind us on the grass parking area, waiting for us to shut down and disembark.

'Good afternoon Sir. Would you like the rest of your aeroplane back?' asked the fireman, as he presented us with a few large pieces of fibreglass. Oh dear. This wasn't good. My immediate thought was the fact I was potentially marooned on an island in the English Channel six hours before I was due to be at Heathrow to fly a B777 across Africa. Why hadn't we gone to Goodwood or Shoreham on the south coast? I could have just jumped on a train home.

I suggested to our captain that he might want to dispatch his pals to the cafe to get the coffees ordered, to save him any more humiliation, apart from anything else, while we discussed our predicament.

Upon further inspection and after a couple of phone calls, I established that the aeroplane was safe to fly. The smashed fibreglass that the nice fireman had retrieved from the runway was the shattered nose wheel fairing, an aerodynamic moulding that encased the top two-thirds of each wheel to minimise drag and help achieve the high cruise speeds. The landing had been so heavy the thing had hit the ground and been smashed to smithereens. The solid metal strut that fixed the wheel to the aeroplane, however, was undamaged.

I did feel for this poor chap. He felt awful and after a 'little chat' about the best way forward, he suggested that he had perhaps had enough for one day (and caused enough damage, I thought) and would I mind flying back? 'That's a good idea,' thought I, and luckily, the flight to Abuja departed on time later that day.

We'd been to Le Mans by car a couple of times to see the historic twenty-four-hour car race, a must do for anybody with the slightest interest in motoring. The journey there and back was half the fun, with classic and exotic cars filling the roads from the Channel ports to the iconic race track.

In June 2009 we went in the Cirrus. Just under two hours each way and the runway is right next to the race track. We parked up next to all the millionaires' executive jets and picked up our rental car to pop off to our rather nice hotel to freshen up, before returning to the circuit for the start of the race.

We did this again for the 2015 race, taking our good friends, Arthur and Shirley, from Northern Ireland, who were car nuts and had introduced us to Le Mans in the first place.

I'd found another Cirrus group by then, flying an even bigger SR22 with a turbocharger out of Fairoaks, which was even closer to home.

We somehow found ourselves in the pits at the end of the race. Not quite sure how that happened as we didn't have any of those VIP tags around our necks, but there we were after the team from Porsche had claimed victory and the drivers were arriving back in the garage. One of the three drivers was Australian F1 driver Mark Webber and we were hoping to catch a glimpse of him, but it wasn't to be. We waited around but he was clearly such a big name, he was off doing press interviews somewhere else.

When Le Mans finishes after twenty-four hours at 3 p.m. on mid-summer's day in June, thousands of cars head back out on to the roads, most of them with British number plates heading back for the Channel ports. The millionaires' executive jets line up on the taxiway to whisk them home to the south of France or Italy. We went back to our fine hotel for a lovely post-race dinner with Arthur and Shirley and other regulars whom we'd got to know over the years.

The next day, after all the fuss had died down, we went back to the circuit and the temporary executive jet terminal to file our flight plan for our two-hour flight back to the UK. The place was deserted and they had already started packing everything away until next year but there was one other passenger waiting for his pilot to pick him up and take him to Switzerland. Mark Webber. So Lynne made up for her disappointment of the previous day and we had a lovely chat with Mark about racing cars and flying planes.

'JOHN, WHAT ON EARTH ARE YOU DOING?'

Every commercial pilot has to undergo a flight check every six months. In airline world it's two days spent in a full-motion flight simulator, in uniform to enhance realism, paired up with another pilot and presented with a sequence of abnormal events to manage. There might be hydraulic failures, engine fires and difficult passengers kicking off down the back. There's refresher training too and while it's hard work, it's often fun as well and keeps your skills finely tuned.

In the GA world there are various minimum flying requirements each year to keep your licence valid but you must have a flight test with an examiner every two years. Airline pilots were exempt from this GA test if they were being checked in their day job regularly, but for a period, after a change in European rules, this exemption was withdrawn.

I had to find an examiner to carry out a flight test on me to keep my private pilot licence valid. It was recommended I get in touch with Professor Mike Bagshaw at Blackbushe. Now Professor Mike was the same person I'd been to see when he was the chief doctor at the BA medical centre back in the 1990s. As I explained earlier, he was a senior aero medical examiner for the CAA. I'd been given my diagnosis of spinal muscular atrophy and been fitted with my first leg splint. I made an appointment to see Mike and expected to lose my job that day. This was a serious medical condition after all and surely he would withdraw my Class 1 medical certificate? The

CAA had a most pragmatic attitude towards my predicament. Any further muscle wastage would be slow and, as long as I could still push the pedals OK, that was fine. Nothing was going to change suddenly and cause a pilot incapacitation at the controls.

Here I was in 2017 making another appointment to see Mike, but this time in his role as a senior flight examiner. On initial contact, he didn't remember me. I wouldn't have expected him to. He had played a significant part in my career, not the other way around.

We compared diaries and tried to set up a day where Mike was available to fly alongside me in the Cirrus to which I had access. However, our diaries didn't tie up but it was important we did this test before my rating actually expired.

'Why don't you come down to Blackbushe, old chap, and fly my Bulldog?' suggested Mike, and a date was set.

As I was driving my old Jaguar down the M3 on the agreed date, 25 (there's that date again) August 2017, I thought, 'John, what on earth are you doing? You're presenting yourself for a flight test in an aeroplane you've never even seen, let alone flown, with a bloke who doesn't remember you from Adam. This could all go horribly wrong.' I carried on regardless but somewhat apprehensive.

Mike did remember me when I arrived in the cafe at Blackbushe. It was lovely to see him and he hadn't changed a bit in the twenty-five years or so since our last meeting, although I suspect his characteristic bow tie wasn't the original.

We walked out together to the aeroplane and Mike was pleased to hear my legs were still working well enough to be able to 'commit aviation', another of his favourite expressions.

I sought a briefing on the intricacies of this wonderful aeroplane before we started up, but all I got was, 'It's just like any aeroplane old chap. You pull back and the houses get smaller. Push forward and they get bigger again.' I guess that's all you need to know really.

The Bulldog was a wonderful two-seat military trainer where, unlike many military aircraft, you sat alongside your instructor, or examiner in my case today. Mike's machine was in tip top condition, despite being some 40 years old, and had recently been repainted in its original RAF livery.

It really was a wonderful little aeroplane with excellent all-round visibility and good handling characteristics. I declined Mike's invitation to have its aerobatic skills demonstrated but stuck to the standard flight test syllabus. We did steep turns and stalls, then practice forced landings into a field somewhere in Berkshire. I took us down to just 500ft and lined up with a well-chosen field ready for a gentle touchdown should it have been a genuine engine failure. As the sheep started to look up a bit quizzical, Mike instructed me to put the power back on and climb away.

We then returned to Blackbushe to have my landings assessed. In an aeroplane I'd never flown before, remember, and I'd only had about forty minutes or so by now to acquaint myself with the glide characteristics of this British-built craft. As we came over the top of the airfield Mike had one more surprise up his sleeve. He closed the throttle and kept his hand firmly on it, denying me any access to engine power, and instructed me to 'land off that, old chap.' I did. Perfectly, and allowed myself a sneaky smile. Mike said, 'Very good. Ever thought of becoming a Concorde pilot?'

We wrapped up the aeroplane and then did the paperwork over a sandwich and a cup of tea and headed out to the car park together. I didn't know until then that Mike was also a Jaguar car fan and my gleaming XK convertible was parked behind his, even more gleaming XJ. We had the inevitable chat about cars before leaving to go our separate ways. Except I didn't.

I'd had a wonderful morning. I was on a real high. The last time I'd seen him was when I expected my flying career to be snatched from me and here we were flying together at long last. My flight in his Bulldog had been a real privilege.

I fired up my Jaguar and engaged drive but then turned it off again. I was sitting outside the headquarters of Aerobility. A wonderful charity based at Blackbushe, they have a small fleet of aircraft adapted for disabled pilots, including pilots with no legs. They have a hoist to help people out of their wheelchairs and into the pilot's seat. This is a fantastic organisation.

I wanted to give something back. I'd had a fantastic career and felt most privileged to have been given so many opportunities despite my leg issues. There was a big poster outside the Aerobility office advertising raffle tickets they were selling for their grand draw to be held in a few months' time. I went in and the receptionist told me more about the wonderful work that they do. The raffle tickets were £10 each and I bought quite a few. I just wanted to do something to help disabled people have the opportunity to enjoy the magic of flight.

I fired up the Jag for a second time and set off home.

Wind the clock forward about six months. I was sitting in the late after-noon sunshine in Antigua after flying the Boeing 777 (I'd transferred to this by now) there, pleased to feel the warmth on my body after leaving Gatwick a few hours ago on a bitter, grey November Saturday. It was Saturday night back home, and I didn't know it but the Aerobility Charity Ball was in full swing at a hotel near Heathrow. The leader of the Red Arrows had been called on to the stage to draw the winning raffle ticket for the grand draw. I suspect you're one step ahead of me by now. A friend of mine was in attendance and my phone pinged as a text message arrived at the speed of light across the Atlantic. 'John. I think you've just won a Breitling.' Indeed, mine was the winning ticket and I'd won a £5,000 Breitling B1 pilot's watch. I felt guilty rather than elated at first but when I went to Blackbushe to meet the Aerobility CEO, Mike Miller-Smith, and be presented with this precision timepiece, I learned that Breitling were a most generous sponsor of Aerobility and donated a top of the range watch annually to be auctioned. All the proceeds of the raffle had gone directly to the charity.

Talking of Aerobility, I've another quick tale to tell.

During the Covid lockdown of 2020 a fundraising virtual air show and auction was put together with all the great and good from the aviation world contributing to a live YouTube broadcast. It was great viewing and that's just what we did as a family that Saturday. There were live updates on the progress of the auction throughout the evening and the event was hailed as a great success as it came to a close at 10 p.m.

Jen said goodnight and went up to bed but came right back down again with her phone in her hand. She gave me a quizzical look and said, 'Daddy, I've just had a text from the leader of the Red Arrows [a friend of hers]. Is that right you've won the wing-walk experience?' Oops! Yes, I'd slipped in a winning bid in the closing seconds and was to be strapped to the top of a Boeing Stearman biplane for a 100mph ride through the skies of Gloucestershire. Jen had done just that a couple of years previously as part of another Aerobility fundraiser, and anything she can do … etc. She went on to raise even more sponsorship to do it again, but that awful long Covid knocked her sideways for over two years, so she had to postpone. We're going to fly together and have it booked for summer 2023. I'll let you know how we get on.

I'm now on my fourth Cirrus, still based at Fairoaks, and we've had some wonderful trips away with family and friends. We've been to Cannes in the south of France, four hours each way, but it's mainly Le Touquet or the Channel Islands again.

In February 2022 our grandson, Harvey, aged 7, had a rugby tournament on the Isle of Wight. His mum, Jenny, was still suffering from long Covid and lacked energy and stamina. The five-hour journey by car and ferry was going to be a real drain on her and with their campsite right at the end of the runway at Bembridge, it seemed the obvious solution. Out of 280 attendees, Harvey was the only one to fly in. And out again on the Sunday afternoon. It took twenty-one minutes from Fairoaks. He took it all in his stride, thankfully; but one day, when he's older, he'll realise that was something quite special.

While there's an age limit of 65 to fly commercially, there is no such restriction on GA, so as long as my health, ability and bank balance permits, I hope to keep my GA flying going. It's fun after all.

The Tye family, October 2008.

Natalie and Jenny,
October 2008.

BACK TO THE LONG-HAUL ROUTES TO FINISH ...

I did my last flight on the Airbus on 27 August 2007, an uneventful short hop back from Paris in just under an hour. The next time I'd be airborne it would be in an aeroplane three times the size and capable of, literally, flying the world.

Back into the classroom again to learn all the technicalities of the Boeing 777, which was now the backbone of the long-haul operation as it was at least 23 per cent more efficient than the four-engine Boeing 747. Then followed the simulator training, just ten sessions, all four hours long, to learn how to fly the aeroplane and handle abnormal situations.

I did my last simulator session on 2 October 2007. We didn't have to go base training, circuits and bumps in a real aeroplane, because the simulator was so good it was categorised as what they call 'zero flight time'. My first flight would be a few days later to Beijing and back. Or not.

I'd had some problems with my tummy during the ground training. The rumblings after lunch had become quite a talking point in the quiet classroom and I was getting pain occasionally, not to mention other rather unpleasant symptoms. Like a typical bloke, I tried to ignore it, but presented with a twelve-hour flight to China in a few days' time, I had an attack of wisdom and went to get it looked at.

A well-placed prod from Philip Bearn, consultant general and colorectal surgeon, had me pinned to the ceiling with pain and within hours I was under general anaesthetic having been diagnosed with appendicitis.

When I woke up, though, Phil said, 'The good news is there was nothing wrong with your appendix, but I took it out anyway. The bad news is that you have Crohn's disease and I've had to remove about 18in of your bowel.' I've lived with it ever since, controlled by medication.

Needless to say, I missed my first flight to Beijing and managed to avoid it, in fact, for the rest of my career.

When changing fleet in an airline you retain your status, so I was transferring across as a captain and hopefully I'd be able to upgrade again soon to become a training captain. Right now there were no training captain vacancies, so it gave me an opportunity to build my experience flying on the numerous routes that made up the 777 network.

It wasn't until four years later, in 2011, that vacancies arose, so I had to go through the whole training captain selection procedure again, for the third time in my career. Luckily, I managed to fool them once again and was appointed training captain B777, a position I held for the rest of my career.

The trips were variable. The shortest was Tel Aviv, just over four hours, and the longest, Singapore or Buenos Aires, some fourteen hours or so. We'd carry an extra pilot on anything over about eight and a half hours and the extremely long flights required two extras. There were strict procedures about rest and bunk beds were fitted on most aircraft to facilitate this, a secret compartment above the front passenger cabin. After all, some of these working days were seventeen hours or so long, taking into account all the pre-flight procedures.

It was good to revisit some of my favourite haunts from the 747 days but also to expand my global experience further. It was quite something when I landed in Sydney for the first time in October 2008; every long-haul pilot should do this at least once. You can't get much further from home. Despite a forty-eight-hour layover each way in Singapore, I still found it very tiring. All the way to the other side of the world and back again in just over a week was a bit too much for me. A trip for the young-sters, I thought, although I did it twice more after that.

The Maldives appeared on the route structure for the winter schedule in October 2009. Wow. I'd seen the pictures in all the travel programmes and Sunday supplements. Beautiful turquoise sea, hundreds of tiny idyllic islands surrounded by coral reefs teaming with tropical fish, large, small and very colourful. I just had to go.

I'd learned over the years to grab opportunities when they came along. You never know when they're going to disappear again. I put in a bid to go to the Maldives the next month. It was going to be a popular request but I was fairly senior and was delighted when my roster was published and there it was. A night flight down across Europe, the Mediterranean, Egypt, Saudi Arabia and then hundreds of miles across nothing but ocean … to paradise. I suggested to Lynne that she might like to come along. After all, this might be our only opportunity.

We made arrangements to get the cats looked after and the bins put out on the Sunday night. I bought Lynne a staff standby ticket but I could see she had a good chance of spending the night in a business-class seat.

I hadn't flown this route before so there was much preparation required. We had home access to all the operations manuals, my own set filling a shelf in the study, and I even had my own atlas now. I didn't need to borrow the girls'. There were special procedures for flying in African air-space and there was only one runway in the Maldives large enough for a Boeing 777. It was located on a small island next to the capital island, Malé, with the nearest alternative runway in Colombo, Sri Lanka, about an hour and a half to the east. It wasn't quite like Gatwick and Heathrow, just ten minutes apart by air.

The weather forecast was reasonable so we didn't take any extra fuel, just enough to divert to Colombo and have a reserve of thirty minutes. flying time plus 5 per cent contingency to cover any eventualities along the way. Fairly standard figures.

We broke out of the bottom of the thunderstorm at about 500ft above the sea with the windscreen wipers going full pelt. That wasn't expected. It wasn't a problem because there was an instrument landing system installed at Malé that we could use down to 200ft, landing to the north on Runway 36. The sea wasn't the stunning turquoise I was expecting, but it would surely brighten up though.

Flight crew have to clear customs and immigration just like anybody else and in Malé we have to have our luggage X-rayed. My preparation for the trip had centred mainly on operational matters and I'd failed to pick up that, while alcohol is served freely on the outlying resort islands, it isn't permitted to be brought into Malé. The bottle of our favourite champagne, that I'd thought might get our romantic weekend in the Maldives off to a good start, was confiscated from me at this point in the proceedings.

It's normal for the crew to board their own bus when they exit the arrivals hall at any airport and be whisked away to their crew hotel, but in the Maldives crew transport takes on a different form. Everyone is handed a life jacket and invited to board a crew boat to whisk them off to another island. I'd pushed the boat out though – did you see what I did there? – and booked a private thatched villa on the idyllic island of Bandos, about twenty minutes by speedboat from the airport. The rain was torrential but eased off by the time we arrived at our resort.

Thankfully, it didn't rain the next day, our only full day off, but it remained cloudy and windy all day. The sea looked like the English Channel. On a bad day. There was nothing turquoise in sight.

Oh well. You've got to take the rough with the smooth.

From the Slum to the Palace

Once of the most thought-provoking places I visited was the Dharavi slum in Mumbai, the largest in India, with a million people living in a square mile in one of the world's most populated cities. *Slumdog Millionaire* had been filmed there and a TV documentary in the UK had followed presenter Kevin McCloud spending a week living there.

I'd spent much time in the slums in Delhi in my 747 days with Manoj and Raju, the child movie star, so I knew what to expect. I went to Dharavi a couple of times and each was a most wonderful experience. Yes, it was filthy and the poverty was shocking but once you could see beyond that it was inspirational.

These people had nothing. Nothing material, that is, which most of us take for granted. They weren't saving for a new Porsche or the latest designer handbag. They had happiness and a wonderful community spirit though. There were umpteen different religions all living in close proximity. Happily. I met a Sikh gentleman who was crafting a most detailed model of a temple out of wood as a gift for his Hindu friend living close by. I played cricket with the children, who used a broken piece of fence panel as a bat. I was shown some of the cottage industries where women and, yes, children, pick plastics out of piles of waste and process it for recycling. That was quite shocking but not once did I hear anybody complaining. They were some of the happiest people I've ever met, the adorable, wide-eyed children with brilliant white teeth especially.

I'm not totally naive and I'm sure that along with what I witnessed, there was doubtless sadness, bitterness, poor health, crime and other awful goings-on, but my colleague summed it up oh so well after a stunning day in Dharavi: 'These people have got more in life than I'll ever have.'

'Wow, that was a weird day,' said Natalie, as we drove out of the gates of Buckingham Palace.

Jenny had been very involved in a wonderful aviation charity, the Air League, and had been particularly active in creating opportunities for young people to seek out a career in aviation. For her dedication she was to be awarded the Marshall of Cambridge Medal, sponsored by the long-established family aviation maintenance company of the same name. Jen was to be presented with this most prestigious award at the Air League Annual Reception. Normally held at St James's Palace, it was this year shifted down the road to Buckingham Palace, to be hosted by the patron of the charity, Prince Philip.

A programme of events was sent out in advance and a dozen or so award recipients were to be presented to the Duke of Edinburgh himself. I asked Jen if she knew who that chap above her on the list was. The name Sully Sullenberger didn't immediately ring any bells with her, but once I explained how he was the pilot who landed the Airbus in the river in New York, she knew exactly who I was talking about. We spent the evening in Buckingham Palace with Sully and his lovely family.

We drove up in our Volkswagen Golf, pulled up outside the gates, where tourists were gazing into the car trying to work out who we might be, before the police did a security check and called for the gates to be opened so we could drive right on in. I was glad I'd cleaned the car.

As very proud parents, we watched Jen going up to meet Prince Philip from very close by. He was wonderful and had a joke and a firm handshake for every recipient that evening. Natalie had been very quiet and enthralled by the whole sequence of events. She spoke those immortal words as we left to go back home to the real world.

Until two years prior to this wonderful evening in Buckingham Palace, I had been a training captain on the Airbus with British Airways, the same aircraft that Sully had been flying the day he hit the flock of geese on departure from La Guardia. A surreal moment that evening was when I found myself in conversation with two other Airbus pilots, Sully and Yves Rossy. Rossy was a Swiss adventurer in his spare time and had just made history by crossing the English Channel, looking like a cross between Superman and Buzz Lightyear, with a wing and a jet pack on his back. My time flying the A320 had been all rather normal compared to their adventures.

Just a few weeks later, on 24 June 2009, the telephone rang. I was on standby so it wasn't a great surprise. The arrangement was that, following a call from our operations department, I had to be able to present myself, all 'booted and spurred', ready to fly anywhere in the world within two hours. Fortunately, I lived fairly close to Heathrow, but it wasn't unknown for pilots who lived further afield, perhaps in Scotland or North Wales, to sit out the periods of standby duty in a camper van in a motorway service station, just so they could be within two hours.

I sat up straight when I realised it wasn't the guy from operations but our chief pilot in person. Was I at all interested in a trip with him and one other to Seattle tomorrow to pick up a brand new Boeing 777 from the factory? Was I? You bet.

We travelled out as passengers on the scheduled service. Before that, though, we'd partaken of the wonderful refreshments in the first-class lounge at Heathrow. After all, we were travelling first class. Well, two of us were anyway. It became apparent, shortly before boarding, that there were only two first class-seats left and one in club (business) class. One would clearly go to the boss, but who should have the other one? I was wrong. Dave, the chief pilot, took three scraps of paper, wrote our three names on and screwed them up in tight balls before putting them in the proverbial hat. Very fair, I thought, and totally unexpected. Somewhat embarrassingly, he lost as well and took his seat in the still very comfy business class.

After a night in a hotel near the airport in Seattle, we made our way to the Boeing factory. We were treated like VIPs. There was much hand shaking and a private guided tour of the Boeing factory was laid on, before a sumptuous three-course lunch was served in the management dining room. No wine of course. We were shortly to become the proud owners of a brand spanking new multimillion dollar aeroplane and fly it back home to the UK.

After lunch there was even more hand shaking and handover ceremonies. There was a red carpet to traverse and a ribbon of a similar colour to cut before we could go on board. It had that 'new car smell' to it once we were inside. Not the normal, somewhat unpleasant 'eau-de-Boeing', as we call it. Remember Natalie's wise observation about 'aeroplanes stink?' This one didn't.

The first thing I noticed, being the observant type, was that there were no seats or bulkheads fitted. You had an uninterrupted view from the front, all the way to the back. That felt weird. Dave had done these delivery flights before and told us of a wonderful in-flight game that had been invented and caused much amusement. It required two players. Each would put one end of a toilet roll in the rear toilet on their side of the aeroplane, one on the left and one on the right. They would then carefully unroll the toilet paper, laying it out along the entire length of the aeroplane. The game commenced once each player had returned to the rear of the aeroplane and on the count of three would hit the flush button on their respective loo. The winner was the owner of the first toilet roll to be completely consumed by the respective toilet. All very immature of course, but then this was a delivery/test flight and it was important to check out all the aircraft systems.

Now, it was quite unusual for three pilots to be left with an empty aeroplane without a cabin crew to look after them. After all, we'd become accustomed over the years to leftovers from first class or, in my case, pots of caviar served with a mother of pearl spoon. Tonight we had to fend for ourselves.

There were limited cooking and tea-making facilities installed. Probably just as well really. We would have got in one hell of a mess. The nice people at the Boeing catering department had supplied us well though. We weren't going to go hungry. There was one oven fitted, so we were given a selection of hot meals in foil trays. All we needed to do was figure out how to work the oven. There were bags of crisps, or 'chips', as the Americans call them, sandwiches, cheese and biscuits and all sorts of things. No caviar though, nor mother of pearl spoons. There were no 'bev-makers', units to make tea and coffee, so that was provided in a couple of enormous, and I mean enormous as only the Americans can do, flasks. We were all set for the night ahead.

Now, there were three pilots and this brand new aeroplane was going to do one take-off and one landing on its first flight with British Airways. There were three of us, of course, as it was a long night flight and we legally needed to be able to take in-flight rest. We had no bunks fitted yet though, so had to improvise with sleeping bags on the floor.

I had no ego nor burning need to do either of these 'firsts', so I offered to be the third pilot, P3, and to take care of all the catering and stewarding duties. Once we were ready to go, for example, I put the doors to automatic, which meant that if we needed to get out in a hurry, the escape slide would inflate and, after removing any high heels of course, we'd be able to exit the aeroplane, just like in the pictures on the safety card.

I took my role seriously and, while the other chaps were doing their pre-flight checks, served them with tea and sandwiches and attended to their every need. I'd seen how easy this cabin crew work was after all. As we taxied towards the runway I started to clear everything away, just like I'd seen the cabin crew do umpteen times. After a quick look round to make sure I hadn't missed anything, I took my place in the P3 seat, in the middle of the flight deck behind the other two, where I had a bird's-eye view of everything. It's where the flight engineer used to position himself for take-off on Concorde and the old 747 Classic. There's a rather rude joke that goes something like this. 'What's the similarity between a flight engineer and a stage coach driver?'

'I don't know. What is the difference ...'

Answer: 'They both sit behind a pair of ar★★holes.'

It was a flight engineer who told me that of course.

Anyway, here I was assuming the position of a stagecoach driver. My role, in all seriousness, was to monitor carefully the actions of both pilots and make sure nothing was missed.

Dave did the take-off. She had been test flown, of course, by the Boeing test pilots, but this was the first flight of G-YMMT in British Airways ownership. Funnily enough, we weren't going to Heathrow, but to our big engineering base in Cardiff, Wales, where the seats were going to be fitted and other BA-specific items before she could go into commercial service.

She left the ground with much enthusiasm. She wanted to fly, that was for sure, and being empty, of course, there was nothing holding her back. As we left the ground, though, there was a tremendous bang. Much crashing and banging from behind us brought about worried looks from the chaps up front. 'Don't worry,' I said, 'I'll go and investigate.'

Now my only responsibility in life had been to make sure all the galley equipment was secure for take-off. Do you remember those enormous flasks I told you about? The big shiny ones that were full of tea and coffee. Well, once I left the flight deck it became immediately clear that I hadn't quite fulfilled my duties. Not quite. One of these was in a very sorry state, having fallen off the galley worktop as the aircraft lifted off, and deposited its contents, about three American gallons of black coffee, all over the galley floor.

I stuck my head back in the flight deck and announced 'coffee's off. chaps', which didn't go down too well with a ten-hour night flight ahead of us, before beating a hasty retreat. Remember that bit about 'the new car smell?' It wasn't there any longer.

Thankfully, when we got to Cardiff, the engineers said, 'Don't worry about that. The first thing we're going to do is to rip out all these carpets and put our nice BA ones in. Phew!

I carried on working in the flight simulators and flying the global routes, cutting down to a 72 per cent part-time contract in 2015.

This was known, rather appropriately, as the wind-down scheme. It was aimed at pilots over a certain age (55) to give them the opportunity to prepare slowly for retirement. It was basically two full-time months, followed by a month off duty, but in that month off, you had to do one short trip to keep you current.

It was well known in our profession that a sudden step into retirement wasn't necessarily a good thing. It wasn't just a job you were walking away from, but rather a significant lifestyle change. Preparation was required. For many couples, it was the fact the pilot was away for much of the time that kept the relationship back home alive. A month virtually off in every three gave you that time to feel what it was like to be at home all the time. It was rather nice actually and gave the body a chance to get back into a routine, so surely a health benefit.

Most of our passengers in the Concorde years were business travellers but on the B777 the profile varied enormously depending on the route. The Caribbean, naturally, was mainly leisure traffic, whereas New York, Shanghai, Chicago and many other city destinations were popular with businessmen and women.

I met a few celebrities and well-known people, but nowhere near as many as on Concorde. I carried members of the royal family and their entourage, too.

The morning after the closing ceremony of the 2012 Paralympics in London I flew a B777 to Antigua and Prince Harry joined us in business class. He kept a very low profile and I don't think any of the other passengers even spotted him. During disembarkation in Antigua, he skilfully kept his head slightly bowed with a plain baseball cap hiding the bulk of his face. I was in the doorway as usual bidding farewell to all our customers and he just took his place in the line. Neither the person in front, nor immediately behind him, had a clue.

Prince William and his team were shattered after their gruelling tour of China when they took over the first-class cabin for the thirteen-hour flight back from Hong Kong in March 2015. They slept virtually all the way home.

It's normal for the cabin crew to subtly prevent passengers from other cabins from disembarking until all the first-class guests have left and today was no exception. Except that Prince William had popped to the toilet, so we couldn't really hold the other 250 people up indefinitely. Disembarkation was scheduled as normal, via Door 2 Left. That means the passengers in First walk towards the back of the aeroplane to reach it while everyone else comes forwards. There's a well-known expression about knowing you've made it in life when you get on board a BA jet and turn left instead of right.

Passengers therefore arrive from three directions (through the galley as well as front and back) and converge on this single door. We made the exit available to the remaining passengers but after a couple of minutes

I saw Prince William emerge and start making his way towards the exit with his head slightly bowed and his baseball cap lowered. I stepped in front of a lady who was walking at quite a pace and was somewhat miffed that I'd halted her progress suddenly. As she started to protest, muttering something about a connecting flight, I said politely, 'I won't keep you a moment madam.' That's about as long as it took for Prince William to duck out of the door miming a silent 'thank you' to me, accompanied by that wonderful smile that reminded me instantly of the night I went go-karting with his mother. I needed to detain my lady in a hurry no longer and she scurried off completely oblivious to the fact she was following the future King of England up the jetty.

And Then Covid Struck

It was the last week of February 2020. I was enjoying the sunshine in Cancun, Mexico, during a forty-eight-hour layover there. Like everyone else, I'd been following developments on the news and it was starting to get a bit scary, to say the least. We'd had regular updates from our managers in British Airways but it bothered me that it had been rather quiet the last few days.

I met up with the rest of my crew for happy hour in the beach bar at 5 p.m. as planned and the conversation initially centred on this strange virus that was sweeping its way around the globe. I remember saying something about how I thought our industry was about to be hit by something more catastrophic than ever before. I'd been around a long time by now. I'd seen at first hand the effects of the Gulf War, SARS and 9/11. Aviation is a fragile business. It's one of the first industries to be hit by a major global event. This was coming at us like an express train. It was going to hit us hard. And fast. The youngsters looked at me as if I was a silly old fool and suggested I ordered another tequila before the bell rang.

I didn't fly again for almost six months. And that was a cargo flight to Mumbai. I suspect most of those youngsters on my crew that day were made redundant.

Within no time at all we all found ourselves self-isolating and social distancing. Lockdown came along and it became illegal to even leave your home apart from to obtain essentials from the local shop. There was panic buying of toilet rolls and flour, of all things.

The air around Heathrow was silent. The blue skies above were completely clear and not being criss-crossed by the usual white contrails of intercontinental passenger jets, their pilots, like me, sitting at home twiddling their thumbs and worrying about their futures.

Me, I started writing a book.

The toll on society was enormous, not just the rising death toll, but the dreadful effect it had on people's mental health. Single parents confined to small flats with young children and elderly relatives locked away in care homes, with no contact with their families. It was dreadful.

The hospitality sector was closed. Travel and tourism died. The government stepped in with welcome financial support, while the staff in the NHS worked flat out to save lives.

British Airways was reported to be losing £20 million a day, with their fleet grounded but staff costs still a burden. Redundancies were inevitable and thousands were laid off. Those who remained took significant pay cuts.

Some of the B777s had their seats removed and were reconfigured into cargo aircraft. Special procedures were developed for these operations and the authorities granted dispensations for pilots to operate, in double-sized teams, to Hong Kong and straight back, a duty day of some twenty-seven hours, to collect tonnes of vital personal protection equipment (PPE).

Over the months that followed more cargo flights were introduced, with the airlines desperate to source any income they could find. Instead of my normal jaunts to the beaches of the Caribbean, I found myself taking 50 tonnes of rubber to Halifax, Nova Scotia.

Pilots have to be kept current. Captains must complete a landing every thirty-five days. A take-off too, but for each landing there's normally one of those thrown in as well. All pilots are subject to a 'three in ninety' limitation as well but with the flying programme slashed to well under 10 per cent of the normal operation, it was going to be impossible to keep everyone current. Initially, it was thought we'd be back to normal within a few months, but that soon became an optimistic dream.

Pilots were eventually furloughed and redundancies were announced, the first ever for pilots in BA's 100-year history. Training captains like myself worked in the simulators keeping as many pilots as possible current by carrying out recency training sessions.

The sound of the two Harley-Davidson motorcycles pulling up behind the crew bus was deafening. It was early April 2021 and restrictions were easing in the USA. I had a box I wanted to tick, so I'd booked a Harley for a day. There's a scheme in the USA whereby you can rent motorcycles from private owners and the kind lady who owned this brand new Softail had offered to deliver it to the hotel as I arrived. Her wife followed on an even bigger machine to run her back home again after formalities were complete. The faces of my crew were a picture. 'Yep. That's mine for the day,' I explained.

Next morning I set off early. This thing made a hell of a racket as I cruised through the streets of Long Beach soon after 7 a.m., having been awake for hours with an eight-hour time change. I headed for Malibu, up to the north. I had visions of cruising along a long, smooth tarmac road with my shades on and the sun glistening on the Pacific Ocean alongside me, like something out of a cult 1970s movie. The reality was much different.

The traffic was horrendous. There were traffic lights every half a mile and they were always red. The fumes from all the trucks were suffocating and, having taken all my heavy protective clothing from home, it was sweltering every time I stopped. I must admit the cold beer I swallowed when I got back to the air-conditioned hotel at the end of the day was like no other. I'd ticked a box though and it was fun. I think.

It was virtually two years before restrictions were lifted across the globe, slowly at first and sometimes they were suddenly reintroduced when a new variant of the virus popped up in South Africa, for example. It was late 2021 and early 2022 before people started booking holidays and flying again in large numbers. At the same time, the hundreds of enormous cruise ships that had been lying at anchor for two years slowly started moving again. Another industry that had been flattened.

There was a bottled-up desire for holidays and by March 2022 our flights to major holiday destinations were full again, particularly in the premium cabins. We were running not one, but two B777s a day to Barbados. That's well over 500 people, just with BA, arriving at Grantley Adams Airport. There were strict procedures still to be followed though, with proof of a full Covid vaccination required, along with evidence that you'd paid a vast amount of money and had somebody in a drive-through testing centre shove a stick up your nose to make sure there wasn't a virus lurking there. It was all worth it though.

By now I had just nine months before compulsory retirement on my 65th birthday on 12 December 2022. I had mixed feelings.

I'd enjoyed my enforced time at home getting into a routine and spending time with the family. We now had a small boat moored on the Thames at Shepperton, so days out with friends in the summer were a delight, often mooring up right outside Hampton Court Palace to pop the cork on a bottle of champagne and tuck into a light lunch that Lynne had prepared at home.

I was going to miss the flying though and, more than anything, the people. It was a stressful job at times, challenging and extremely responsible, of course. But it was still fun. I found I didn't have so much in common with the young crew nowadays, but life was still fairly sociable. I'd never have trouble finding enough people to join me as crew aboard a yacht out of Long Beach, California, for example, or I'd rent a car in Orlando and go waterskiing. I enjoyed mixing with my passengers too, although social interaction with surgical masks covering half your face was somewhat inhibiting.

Things gradually got better though as the year went on, despite the fact the Russians had invaded Ukraine on 24 February 2022 and the world watched the appalling atrocities unfolding. Large blocks of airspace were closed and the share price of most airlines fell again.

GROUNDED BY A LUMP IN MY GROIN

By September 2022 I had just three months to go until retirement. It had been over forty-six years since I'd joined British Airways through that advertisement on Capital Radio for a summer holiday job before going to university. The university that I never went to.

I found myself with a bit of a dilemma. I'd developed an inguinal hernia, a fairly common condition, particularly in men of a certain age. I'd been told I ought to get it fixed fairly soon, but it wasn't too urgent. One of the perks of being an airline pilot with British Airways was that we had private medical insurance. That would cease when I retired. So, do I have surgery through the private sector while I still can, but have more precious time off work, or do I take my chance on the NHS waiting lists when I retire?

My research indicated that these type of hernias can often be repaired with minor keyhole surgery, recovery time was minimal and I'd probably only need a couple of weeks off work. I'd seen a consultant back in June and he had advised not delaying it too long, even expressing some surprise that I was allowed to fly with this noticeable bulge in my groin. There's a joke in there somewhere.

The date was set: 28 September 2022, now just under eleven weeks before retirement. Meanwhile, I was planning my last few trips. Where did I want to visit one more time before my wings were clipped? Barbados, St Lucia, Cape Town and New York all came quickly to mind. Did the family want to join me on any of these last trips?

Natalie came to Barbados at the end of August. By way of captain's privilege, I put her in first class both ways. One happy young lady, so she came to St Lucia with me just a couple of weeks later. Why wouldn't she? She had to make do with business class on that one though!

On 24 September, just four days before surgery, I flew the B777 to New York. Arriving in JFK was always special and took me back to Concorde days, of course. We had a particularly quick flight time due to the favourable wind patterns over the Atlantic. Just six hours and forty-five minutes, so we'd be an hour early if we left on time. I still couldn't help thinking though that this was still over twice as long as it had taken every day, twice a day, for twenty-seven years in an aeroplane that first flew in 1969. Fifty-three years ago.

My co-pilot flew the aircraft out. We take it in turns and knowing I was going to have a couple of weeks off work with my surgery, I thought I'd fly back to minimise my risk of going out of currency. You'll remember that, as a captain, we have to do a landing every thirty-five days. We arrived in New York late afternoon with our inbound routing giving us some of the most spectacular views of Manhattan I've ever seen. I could see Concorde 'AD' sitting next to the flight deck of the USS *Intrepid*, moored in the Hudson River not far from where Sully had parked his Airbus. I'd already decided to pay her a visit in my spare time tomorrow.

Jeff and I went for a beer and a burger in The Perfect Pint, just a couple of blocks from the hotel. We put the world to rights, shared flying stories, as pilots often do, and had a good time. I tried not to dwell too much on the thought that this was my last night in New York. Ever. A British Airways captain crying in his beer isn't a good look.

We had most of the next day free. The bus was due to pick us up at 5 p.m. to take us back to JFK for the flight home. It was a gorgeous start to the day but with some rain forecast to move in after lunch. I signed out one of our BA crew bicycles and set off around Manhattan, probably a somewhat dangerous mission in itself. Central Park was one of my favourites.

I'd spent time in the park in Boston, just before being rushed to hospital with seafood poisoning, and eaten deer food in the park in Osaka, but had never really had any dramas in Central Park. There were thousands of people walking, cycling, rollerblading and some doing nothing apart from watching the squirrels busy squirrelling away, burying their acorns ready for winter. I took it all in and revisited Strawberry Fields, the memorial park opposite where John Lennon had been gunned down outside his home in the Dakota building.

All too soon it was time to move on. If I wanted to get to Concorde I had to get those pedals turning. Downtown Manhattan was busy. Very busy. Life had certainly returned to normal. The last time I'd been to New York had been two years ago during the peak of the Covid pandemic. It had been closed then. Completely. Entry to the United States was prohibited. We flew occasional cargo flights and were confined under strict security to an isolated approved hotel in the airport complex.

I took the cycle lane south down Seventh Avenue and then, once safely through the mayhem of Times Square, turned west along 45th Street and there she was. Towering above the surrounding streets, the USS *Intrepid* has, for over forty years, been the home of the Air, Sea and Space Museum.

Concorde G-BOAD was flown to JFK for the last time on 10 November 2003. After 23,400 flying hours and 7,010 supersonic flights, her Rolls-Royce Olympus engines wound down for the last time. She was lifted on board an enormous barge, originally used for transporting Space Shuttle external fuel tanks, and shipped up the Hudson. She remained on the barge as an exhibit initially, before being lifted to her permanent home on the pier right alongside *Intrepid*.

G-BOAD holds a special place in the Concorde story. She features in the iconic footage flying with the Red Arrows down the Mall, before pulling up into a steep climb over Buckingham Palace as part of the Queen's Golden Jubilee celebrations.

She holds the transatlantic speed record, a record still standing today and unlikely to be broken for a very long time. Captain Leslie Scott, Senior First Officer Tim Orchard, my former flying instructor and PPL examiner, and Senior Engineering Officer Rick Eades launched from JFK on 7 February 1996 and touched down at Heathrow just two hours, fifty-two minutes and fifty-nine seconds later. I last flew her on 7 May 2000 from Heathrow to New York.

She was pleased to see me. I could see a tear in her eyebrow window as I approached her from the front. Or was it a thin streak of rust left from the last rain shower? Either way, it was good to see her and I must confess to a tear in my eyebrow window.

I kept a low profile as the crowds gathered for the pre-booked 12.30 p.m. tour. Tours run every thirty minutes and often sell out for the day quite quickly. I caught the attention of the tour guide and was kindly welcomed to tag along behind. Sitting at the back of the group, I could hear all around me the gasps from the audience enthralled by the facts and figures being shared by the knowledgeable guide. Facts and figures that are simply incredible and relate to an aeroplane that has been sitting dormant now for nearly twenty years.

When the tour group had departed I was kindly granted a quiet minute or two of silent reflection back in the flight deck before it was time to leave 'AD' behind me for the very last time. Thankfully, nobody had nicked my bike and I cycled quietly and thoughtfully back to the hotel just as the first drops of rain started to fall.

THE FINAL CURTAIN – NOT A DRY EYE

The 25th is a date that has featured heavily throughout my aviation life. My PPL arrived in the post, my CPL was issued, my first Concorde flight and then the dreadful Concorde crash, of course. My final command check with the 'graunchy nose wheel' and my PPL revalidation at Blackbushe in Mike's Bulldog for starters. All significant dates. All the 25th.

Just a few minutes before midnight (GMT) on 25 September 2022, I released the brakes on B777, G-STBN, and set off on the BA176 scheduled service from JFK to LHR. Despite the earlier rain, the sky was clear and we had some wonderful views of the lights of Manhattan and Long Island as we turned north towards Boston after departing from Runway 22R.

I hand flew the aircraft for quite a while. She was a delight to fly, light on the controls with just fingertip gentle inputs required to settle her on her way. With that distinct busy chatter from New York air traffic control in our ears, we climbed up gently towards our initial cruising altitude of 33,000ft and Mach 0.82. It wasn't surprising that my mind drifted back twenty years to when I would hand fly Concorde to nearly twice that altitude and two and a half times that speed.

I'd just left New York behind for the very last time in my flying career. Gulp!

I went into hospital as planned three days later on 28 September. The surgery went well but rather than minor keyhole laparoscopic surgery, I'd had to have an open incision as the area of attention was too close to my earlier Crohn's surgery and associated scar tissue.

It dawned on me afterwards that the recovery time, as far as being fit enough to fly was concerned, was likely to be longer than the couple of weeks I'd planned. Would I ever fly again?

Once you've undergone a full surgical procedure the CAA become involved. Your medical certificate is revoked. Reports need to be written and reviewed before you're cleared to fly again. After thirty-five days I'd run out of currency and would have to return to the simulator to revalidate that. The clock was ticking. I'd planned to revisit my other favourites for one last time. My forward roster had now been published and read like the ultimate holiday brochure. Mauritius, Boston, Cape Town, the Maldives and Antigua, and a few blanks yet to fill. Would I be declared fit in time to visit any of them or had I, thankfully without realising it, just operated my last ever flight, on the 25th and from New York? Most poignant, if that was to be the case.

Coming up past Boston that clear night, climbing through 25,000ft, I looked down and could see the lights of the city twinkling back up at us. I knew the natural hook of Cape Cod curved way down to the south and back north again with the historic Provincetown stuck right on the end. It was here that the pilgrims on the *Mayflower* had gained their first glimpse of land and come ashore in November 1620. I'd had the privilege of being able to view this natural wonder from the edge of space from the flight deck of Concorde and it always reminded me of some mystical giant flexing his right arm and clenching his fist where Provincetown sat. We'd had some wonderful holidays down there in years gone by.

We settled into the cruise that night at 33,000ft and sent a message ahead to Gander air traffic control seeking our oceanic clearance, our permission to follow a specific route across the ocean that night on NAT track 'Victor'. While we waited on that approval we completed fuel and system checks, reviewed the weather forecasts for crucial potential diversion airfields en route and took up the invitation of another cup of tea and some leftover first-class starters from Peter, the steward up front. Most of the first-class passengers just wanted to get straight off to sleep in their flat beds that night, so there should be plenty of leftovers, he told us. The menu was both extensive and exquisite.

I soon found myself thinking about the time I'd spent in Boston. It was one of my favourite cities in the USA. Slightly quieter than New York, it had culture, character and much history. It also brought back some pretty scary memories, one of which I alluded to a few pages back. Food poisoning in the park.

Flying into BOS, Logan Airport, could be a challenge in the winter. There was often snow and strong winds and Runway 27, facing west towards the city, was the shortest on our route structure, so a challenge to land a big aeroplane like a B747 or a B777, particularly as the approach at night was over the dark sea, with poor lighting making the visual perspective challenging. In the summer though, it was a delight.

The stopovers were normally twenty-four hours, with BA operating several flights a day. So like most US destinations, we'd arrive late afternoon or early evening their time, grab a beer or two before a good night's sleep and then spend the following day doing whatever took our fancy. I'd normally try and be back in bed two or three hours before the scheduled alarm call for the night flight home again.

A typical day for me in Boston was to take out one of the BA bikes and cycle down to and through Boston Common and on through the downtown area to the waterfront near the aquarium. I'd watch the comings and goings in the harbour for a while, the whale-watching boats going out with tourists and the ferries coming in and out serving the neighbouring islands. Then I'd go for lunch.

Boston is famous for its seafood and while not a great lover of it myself, I had become quite partial to the local clam chowder and took my regular seat at the counter in the well-known chain restaurant on the waterfront this particular day. It was a simple lunch, just a bowl of chowder and a couple of bread rolls.

Before long it was time to start heading back. It was a gorgeous late-summer afternoon, 4 September in fact, so I stopped in the Common, the park, on the way back, laid the bike on the grass and watched the world go by for a while. The boats on the boating lake were drifting by. The ducks were quacking and the squirrels were squirrelling, just like their cousins in Central Park. Then it struck me.

Like a shot going right through me, I felt a sharp stabbing pain in my stomach. I started to sweat and feel nauseous. This wasn't good. I was straight back in the saddle and pedalled as fast as I could the mile or so back to the sanctuary of my hotel room. What happened next was rapid and messy. And very scary. In no time at all, apart from other ghastly symptoms, my body started convulsing uncontrollably and I felt as if unconsciousness wasn't far away. I managed to get myself to the phone and dial 911.

I came to in the ambulance outside the hotel lobby with an oxygen mask clamped to my face, the rear doors open and I was aware of onlookers peeking in at me, mainly hotel guests returning with their latest purchases from the nearby shopping mall. I realised that I was about to be driven away to hospital and nobody, nobody, knew who I was or where I was going. Just before the doors to the ambulance slammed closed I spotted one of my cabin crew walking past and managed to get a message to him along the lines of 'Tell BA what's going on'. There's no way I was flying that plane home tonight. And it was fully booked.

They took good care of me in the local hospital, stuck needles and drips in my arms and cleaned me up a bit. Severe food poisoning or an allergy was the likely cause.

Once I was a bit more compos mentis I had the presence of mind to put together a plan to save my flight being cancelled. Always putting my passengers first, that's me all over. As luck would have it, I'd bumped into a friend of mine, another BA 777 captain, on holiday that morning in the hotel. We'd had breakfast together and he'd told me how he was flying home as a passenger with us that night. Not for much longer he wasn't. I'd even remembered his room number and managed to get a message through to BA operations and suggested they called Howard and asked him to swap his seat in the cabin for one right at the front on the left. Ironically, they got hold of him enjoying a late lunch at another branch of the same seafood restaurant where I had succumbed to my food poisoning. He readily agreed. After all, he wasn't going to get home that night unless he flew the plane himself.

After a few hours of treatment and rest I was declared fit enough to be discharged. I had no clothes though. Let's just say those that I'd arrived in were no longer fit for use. I was discharged and sent out into the street in a pair of hospital scrubs. You know the blue ones that the nurses wear in the operating theatre. I still have them as a memento of that horrific day. I had to take a taxi back to the hotel, keep the driver waiting when I got there and queue up at the reception desk to draw out some cash to pay him. In my blue scrubs. Thank goodness the world didn't know I was a British Airways captain.

You think that was bad? My other 'Boston event' was really what you might call serious. Life threatening in fact.

It started with a splinter.

We'd sold Natalie's bed on eBay and I was busy dismantling it. It wasn't even a dirty splinter but there it was stuck firmly in my left hand. Most of it came out easily and life went on. I kept an eye on it and it became slightly angry over the next couple of days. Nothing to worry about. Or so I thought.

I flew the scheduled service to Seattle and by the time I arrived I had a thin red line working its way past my wrist. Possible infection and blood poisoning, somebody suggested; so when we got to the hotel I called Global Lifeline, an organisation based in the USA that we, as airline crew, can call any time of day or night for medical advice. They arranged for me to go to the local A & E department to get it looked at.

It can't be that serious, I thought, so went for a beer with the boys first and when they went off to bed, I walked round to the hospital. 'Nasty infection,' they said. 'You'll need antibiotics,' and prescribed something called Septrin.

The rules have changed since what I'm about to tell you, but at the time there were no restrictions on me flying home. That's exactly what I did, popping these rather large tablets down my throat at the prescribed intervals.

Two days later, on 21 December, I flew B777 G-VIIK to Boston. The pills were working. The infection was clearing up. Now, it'll not come as a great surprise if I tell you that when we got to Boston, we went for a beer. Just a quick one, and then I fell into that big comfy bed that American hotels do so well.

I awoke in the early hours with a funny sensation in my mouth. I went to the bathroom to investigate further and was horrified to see several large blood blisters on the inside of my cheeks. They looked like purple slugs. I'd also obviously scratched my back in my sleep but the scratch marks were vicious. It looked like a wild tiger with dirty claws had leapt upon me in the night.

Global Lifeline sent a doctor round to see me. 'I've never seen anything like that before,' he said (which didn't exactly fill me with confidence), after inspecting my mouth and when presented with the scratches on my back, offered, 'Are they from passion?'

'I should be so lucky,' I replied, trying to keep the mood quite light-hearted, but then he disappeared into the bathroom with his phone.

As if he thought I couldn't hear him, he embarked on a private conversation with a friend of his who was a dentist. He returned and asked if I was taking any medication and I explained the antibiotics and the infection from the splinter. He said I could stop taking them as it had healed up nicely. Now, I always thought you should complete a course of antibiotics but he was adamant I didn't need to. That was a life-changing moment.

His dentist pal had suggested I'd probably just been munching my cheeks in my sleep and should seek dental advice when I get home. 'Bollocks,' I thought. Am I allowed to write that? I just did because that's exactly what that diagnosis was.

The day went on and, feeling absolutely fine, I donned my uniform at the allocated time and boarded the bus with my crew for our short journey to Logan Airport. We departed on time with a full flight.

A couple of hours into the night, soon after coasting out close to Gander, with a healthy tailwind helping us along, I suddenly developed a spontaneous nose bleed. The co-pilot hadn't thumped me, nor was there any other obvious cause, but I handed over control of the aeroplane and excused myself. Thankfully, most of the passengers were asleep so I could slip into the bathroom without being noticed. The captain coming out of the flight deck looking like he came second in a boxing match isn't a good look.

While doing the obvious with tissues I noticed a bruise on my arm just below my short sleeve ending. Further investigation involving the removal of my shirt revealed I was black and blue all over. WTF! Then I started bleeding from my anus.

Apart from being rather scared, I felt fine. I managed to stop the bleeding from both orifices. We were by now in the middle of the Atlantic so a diversion to another airfield wasn't really a serious consideration, although in hindsight, it might have been wise. In actual fact, it was foggy at Heathrow so we had to do an autoland in 500m visibility.

I knew this wasn't a dental problem by now but phoned my friendly dentist as soon as I got to the car and it was no great surprise when she told me to get myself to a hospital straight away.

Urgent blood tests revealed a severe and potentially fatal reaction to the Septrin. And I'd stopped taking them by now. My blood platelet count was down at 21,000 per mcL and it was on the way back up by now. The normal range is 150,000 to 400,000 per mcL. A severe case of thrombo-cytopenia (a platelet count so low that internal bleeding was occurring) had been brought on by the Septrin. I later found out that this particular drug is rarely used in the UK because of this potentially lethal side effect.

And to think I'd been in command of a B777 over the Atlantic when the problem manifested itself. There's been a joke in our family ever since if I was going to Boston. 'Be careful now', as I left home with a cheery wave.

I had a final Boston trip scheduled for mid-October 2022, less than two months before retirement. It was a particularly attractive one with a full day off in the city and a daylight flight home, rather than the usual flog through the night back across the Atlantic. Boston is gorgeous in October with the leaves on the Common turning that lovely golden colour and the squirrels being more active busy squirrelling than ever. I'd taken some spectacular photos in Boston in the fall when I used to lug my big SLR camera around the world with its whopping zoom lens and was looking forward to doing just that one last time.

The question was, though, would I be back flying in time to do it, and if so were there any more dramas lined up for me?

Sadly the answer was 'no.' I had my review with the consultant who had undertaken my hernia surgery on 12 October. He was impressed that I'd walked a couple of miles two days earlier, which is a lot for me at the best of times, and cut the lawn the day before. 'Just avoid heavy lift-ing a bit longer,' was his advice, but otherwise, he saw no reason for me not returning to work. The CAA have a most cautious approach though. Quite understandably, they worry about blood clots, so a full six weeks between any kind of open surgery and returning to flying was imposed. A lovely five-day trip to Mauritius and that attractive Boston adventure disappeared from my computerised roster and were replaced with the abbreviation SK (sick).

It was probably for the best though. I would have needed to wrap myself in cotton wool and shut myself away in my room in Boston to ensure a safe return given my track record. And then I would probably have been bitten by a poisonous spider that had smuggled itself back from Mauritius the day before, had I been on that trip.

A full six weeks' recuperation would take me through to 9 November. There was a BA rule whereby I had to be back in the UK a full two days before I retired, just to allow for any disruption down route and so I would be able to hand back the uniform and various bits of equipment before being escorted off the premises. That meant I'd only have exactly a month left. I'd also be out of recency, as we call it, so would have to get back in the simulator before I could fly. That would take time to organise. It really looked like I'd blown it. Some might have been glad of this effective early release, but not me. That's not how I wanted it to end after forty-six years in the business.

I've always found, and I've had plenty of dealings with them over the years, the CAA medical department to have a sensible and pragmatic approach to things and when I explained my predicament, my aero-medical examiner (AME) came up trumps. After checking thoroughly that I was really fully fit, he used his discretion and dropped the six weeks to just under five. That meant I could fly on the thirty-fifth day since my last landing, that one back from New York. I was scheduled to go to Antigua on that thirty-fifth day, so by the skin of my teeth I was back in the game, without having to go back in the simulator.

After that Antigua, I managed three more wonderful trips before it was all over. The last time I was on BA premises was on 9 December 2022 to swap my access all areas security pass for a retired staff ID card. Then I went home.

Prior to that, though, I'd had three wonderful trips to finish on. A six-day Mauritius with a lovely crew and a wonderful Cape Town, with Barbados as the grand finale.

The flight down to Mauritius was through the night and very long, reminding me of why I was perhaps getting a bit too old for this job. Funnily enough, just a couple of weeks prior to this, my grandson, Harvey, had been set some homework. He was tasked with doing some research into an African country of his choice. We sat down together in my study and looked at the map. He chose Madagascar and with the help of a well-known online search engine soon answered all the questions about the population, religion and language. When it came to the capital, I did laugh out loud though. 'You've chosen a good one there to test your spelling,' I told him, as between us we tried to figure out how to pronounce 'Antananarivo'. He got the last laugh though. I had to speak to the air traffic controllers there as we flew over the top on the way down to Mauritius. Thankfully, they abbreviate it themselves to 'Antana'. I could just about manage that.

Whatever you want to do as an adrenaline junkie, you can do in Cape Town. Whether it be diving with great white sharks, paragliding, riding in a US Army Huey helicopter from the Vietnam War, or heading up through the mountains on a rented Harley-Davidson, you could do it all. We only had just over forty-eight hours to cram it all in though, and on top of all that there's some fine food and wine to be enjoyed. With global inflation running wild and everything everywhere being vastly expensive, South Africa was still one of the few places in the world where everything was still good value and much cheaper than back home. So the more you did, the more you ate and drank, the more you saved.

The early morning arrival into Cape Town is nothing short of spectacular. The lenticular cloud, known as 'the Tablecloth', sits atop the natural wonder that is Table Mountain and the vibrant city is already teeming with life as we descend towards the coastline and make our final approach to land.

One of my co-pilots on this flight actually lived there, so he was off home after we landed to sit on his veranda and gaze at the ocean.

The Cape Town trip, while not my last, was my official retirement trip. I'd been, like any retiring pilot, permitted to 'extract it'. That means that, on just that one occasion in your career, you can pick any trip you like, before they go out for bidding by the rest of the fleet. You are guaranteed to have it. It's yours. It's special. In days gone by, you could pick all your crew too, but that's not practical nowadays. Some of the cabin crew I'd flown with before though had successfully bid for it. This was a plum trip, leaving Heathrow on the Monday (21 November 2022) and getting back early on the Friday morning, so guaranteeing a weekend at home either side as a bonus.

It's the people that make this job so special, and boy was I lucky this week! I had a wonderful team of people who really made it a special and emotional event for me.

The action-packed adventure stuff didn't happen. The wind was too strong even for the sunset catamaran cruise we had planned, let alone the parachuting and helicopter rides. We had two wonderful evenings out though, just me and eight lovely ladies, including one of my two co-pilots. I was in my element.

I met another captain in the hotel bar early one evening who I'd known since my Dan-Air days back in 1987. He was having a beer with his two male co-pilots and told me he couldn't wait to retire in two years' time. He suggested I'd probably miss this, referring to sitting at the bar with two other guys putting the world to rights and talking flying stories. I told him 'no'. I'd never been one for that sort of thing. I winked and said, 'That's what I'm going to miss,' as I nodded in the direction of 'John's harem', as they'd called themselves, the eight lovely ladies, all dressed up to the nines, whatever that means, ready for a fine dinner in yet another lovely restaurant.

The final day, the flight home, was special, very special. After some lovely team photos in the hotel lobby we headed for the airport.

We pushed back off the gate in B777 G-YMMG. It was late afternoon and I was marvelling at another wonderful African sunset forming in the west, my last. As we taxied out towards Runway 19 for take-off with my co-pilot, Joanne Segebarth, at the controls, I had time to look out of my side window and see all the ground staff, the baggage handlers and tug drivers, seemingly filming us. I could see a mass of torches on their phones, like a scene from a Robbie Williams concert. Being rather slow on the uptake as usual, I said something like, 'Why are they all filming us? It's not like this doesn't happen every day,' referring to the daily BA58 departing for Heathrow. I'd seen a couple of fire engines on the move, but discounted the relevance of that too, until Rahul Bajpai, my other wonderful co-pilot, leant forward from the third seat behind me and said, 'This is for you, John.' Living in Cape Town, as he did, he knew some powerful people at the airport, and had arranged this most moving 'guard of honour' for me. I was in bits. A captain in tears on take-off isn't a good look and it was all I could do to regain my composure as we launched 265 tonnes of 777 down the runway and turned west across the cape and looked down on the suburbs of Camps Bay and Clifton for the last time.

After all these years, it never ceases to amaze me. Flying around this wonderful planet of ours, that is. Coming home from Cape Town took eleven hours and thirty-nine minutes. And nine hours and twenty-three minutes of that was over Africa. At 500mph. That's some 4,700 miles over one continent, more than the maximum range of Concorde. And then we hopped across Europe home.

As I've already said, we have three pilots on these ultra-long flights, anything over about eight and a half hours, so we can have some in-flight rest and not be too tired for the crucial bit at the far end. So, after take-off, the third pilot, Rahul in this case, snuck off upstairs to the flight crew overhead bunk area. You'd never know it was there, concealed in the ceiling above the forward passenger cabin. The cruise period of the flight is divided by three, so we had about three and a quarter hours each up there, snuggled up under the fine duvets and pillows you'd normally find in the first-class cabin.

When it's time to swap over, we can use the internal phone system to ring a handset right by your pillow. Those familiar 'bing-bong' chimes you hear in aircraft cabins are normally plenty to wake you. Except they weren't in my case. I'd taken the last break, so it was an hour before landing. The cabin crew were slightly concerned when they saw Rahul opening the secret door to the bunk area, explaining as he climbed the stairs that there had been no response from John.

I was fine, just in a deep sleep, and a gentle shake of my arm was all that was needed. Thankfully, Rahul already knew about my dodgy legs and the fact I wore orthotics to be able to walk. I appeared fully dressed, 'booted and spurred', a few minutes later and said, 'I bet that's the first time you've had to clamber over a captain's artificial legs to wake him in the bunk.'

We were one of the first flights to land in Heathrow at 4.32 in the morning, just after the night curfew. We shut down as normal and I bade my usual fond farewell to our 226 passengers in my usual manner over the public address system. Then, as is my custom, I left the flight deck, wearing my jacket and hat, to stand in the doorway and say goodbye to each of them personally as they disembarked. What happened next had me in bits again.

I heard Rahul introduce himself over the PA and, still being a bit slow on the uptake, feared initially that something untoward was occurring. He continued something like this, though, in a most eloquent style: 'As you disembark this morning, ladies and gentlemen, you'll see a rather distinguished looking chap in the doorway, your captain. After forty-six years, including being one of only a handful to have flown Concorde, he's retiring …' The rest was lost in the applause and well wishes that I received from everyone leaving the aeroplane. There were hugs, handshakes and selfies. Once again, I was in bits.

Normally, once all the passengers are off, the crew scarper, eager to get home, but this morning they didn't. They started to muster in the front cabin. I was finally getting a bit quicker on the uptake by now. Not much, but enough to realise that perhaps we weren't done yet.

They'd had what we used to call a whip round and presented me with an assortment of gifts and a card, all to be opened when I got home. I was encouraged, though, to take a closer interest in one particular gift. They'd bought me a retro, fatigued-style 'I love Cape Town' baseball cap, which quickly replaced my platinum-braided captain's hat. Not only that, but they'd all signed it and written messages of best wishes. I wore it with great pride as I disembarked and we joined the crowd of hundreds of early morning arriving passengers in Terminal 5.

BA had recently launched a new advertising campaign. It had been filmed way back in February on a very cold, windy but sunny morning. It was bloody freezing. I knew that because I was there with many other staff. A selection of cabin crew, pilots, engineers and check-in agents had been invited to feature in this promotion. The world was finally getting back to normal after the Covid pandemic and 'A British Original' was the theme thought up by the clever marketing agency.

We'd spent the day trying to keep warm, apart from anything else, drinking coffee in the bus, but dashing out into the cold when called upon to walk or stand in various positions, including high up on an enormous gantry normally used for servicing the aircraft at high level. All very strange, but we were assured it would look good once the experts in the editing suite had done their magic.

As we got off the inter-terminal train at the final stop for 'arrivals, baggage reclaim and flight connections all terminals', as the tannoy kept telling us, I saw for the first time the final production. There, in enormous glory, was a picture of one of our brand new Airbus A350 aircraft, but as she'd never been presented before. There was I, along with several other staff, standing on top of the wing. So one final photo opportunity presented itself, with me standing under the picture pointing up at 'mini-me' in full uniform, including the platinum-braided hat, as opposed to the 'I love Cape Town' cap I was now wearing. Passengers were once again wishing me well and snapping away on their phone cameras.

Wow. What a night that had been.

Four children had died across England, one in a neighbouring town. Was this the start of yet another pandemic we wondered?

There was an outbreak of a bacterial infection called Strep A, often leading to scarlet fever, with particularly severe symptoms in children. Our grandson, Harvey, now 8, was taken most unwell less than a week before we were all due to go to Barbados, on my last ever trip on 3 December. His temperature shot up to 39.4°C, dangerously high. Our GP, once again, was fantastic. He confirmed scarlet fever, had him on antibiotics in no time and he bounced back fairly quickly. Then his mum, Jenny, went down with it too. It was touch and go if they'd both be fit enough to travel.

It literally went down to the wire. The antibiotics they were now both on were most effective and the doctor said the night before we were due to go that they were no longer infectious and it was OK to travel.

Natalie had had those two wonderful Caribbean trips with me back in August and September and, as we can only have three nominated people on our travel concessions, it was time for Lynne, Jenny and Harvey to come away with Grandad.

As luck would have it, there were three seats left in first class. Now I'm normally fairly good at adhering to rules and regulations; I'm a pilot after all, so that's a good discipline to have, but the rule about 'no children under 12 in first class on staff travel' was there to be broken on this unique occasion. It really was a once-in-a-lifetime opportunity, Harvey's first and last flight with Grandad in a big plane.

We were allocated B777-300 G-STBI for the BA255 service that day. It was an early departure from home but we were nearly an hour late leaving Heathrow with ground-handling issues. Once all the passengers were seated, though, I took to the public address system and extended my captain's welcome to everyone. Apparently, Harvey's face was a picture, in the front row of first class, when I gave him a special personal welcome by name. By the time I went on the PA for a second time, though, to explain the delay, he'd figured out the entertainment system and was already engrossed in his first movie. My interruption to said entertainment was apparently met with, 'Oh no, Grandad's got the ultimate pause button!'

We had a lovely crew and lovely passengers, 280 of them, and I enjoyed meeting many of them during the day. A few shared with me how, in a bygone era, way back in the mists of time, they had flown this same route in a fraction of the time in an aircraft that's been in a museum for twenty years.

Today our flight time was planned at eight hours and eight minutes. We'd loaded 67 tonnes of fuel, enough for the oceanic crossing, plus 5 per cent for unforeseen contingencies, avoiding bad weather and being battered by stronger than forecast headwinds, for example. We also needed to have enough left to be able to divert to St Lucia, should anything untoward prevent us from landing in Barbados, and then be safely on the ground there with half an hour's worth, about 3 tonnes, left in the tanks.

I'd flown this route in Concorde on 8 April 2000. The flight time had been just three hours and forty-three minutes. We'd accelerated through the sound barrier at our standard 'accel point' in the Bristol Channel and settled at Mach 2 some forty minutes after take-off. We reached our service ceiling, 60,000ft, more than 11 miles above the surface of the earth, somewhere to the south of Bermuda. We'd left Heathrow at 9.30 a.m. and arrived in Barbados at 8.30 a.m. local time, an hour before we left and in time for breakfast. Today, in the B777, after an actual flight of eight hours and eighteen minutes, we made it just in time for sunset.

We'd had a perfect flight out though. The weather was good all across the Atlantic and we'd made up most of the lost time. The passengers were happy to be going to the Caribbean at this time of year, leaving the cold weather behind in the UK. I'd asked the co-pilot to operate the sector out, which meant he would do the take-off and landing and I'd fly the approach from leaving cruise altitude, the top of descent point, some 110 miles from touchdown, until 1,000ft and lined up with the runway. This was BA's standard operating procedure (SOP) and was known as a monitored approach.

Once the island was in sight we asked air traffic control for a visual approach. That meant basically we could do our own thing. I knew the area well and I'd been doing this regularly for over thirty years, but talked it through in great detail with my co-pilot first. I knew I was one of the few remaining old-school pilots who still did this sort of basic flying. Most nowadays preferred to leave the automatics coupled up and fly a radar-vectored (instructions from ATC) approach using an instrument landing system (ILS) or a GPS-based procedure that took them miles out to sea before returning to land towards the east on Runway 09.

Grantley Adams International Airport is on the south-east corner of the pear-shaped island and it's normal to land into wind, towards the east.

We approached the island from the north-east, not having seen any land since we coasted out over Land's End in Cornwall over seven hours ago. Once I had the east coast of Barbados in sight, I switched off the autopilot and asked the co-pilot to disengage the flight directors. The automatic throttles remain engaged throughout, as is standard practice, so they move back and forth on their own to achieve and maintain the target speed I had called for and the co-pilot had set on the instrument panel.

We crossed the east coast at 4,000ft and 400mph, having requested and been granted a dispensation from the standard speed limit of 250 knots (290mph) below 10,000ft. That had been introduced as a result of that very near miss I'd had thirty years ago in a 747, but there really was nobody else about today. It took seconds to cross the island and I gently extended the speed brake with my right hand, by raising the big lever alongside my right leg as I rolled on 20 degrees of bank crossing the west coast so we could parallel it southbound towards the capital, Bridgetown.

We went past the luxury five-star hotels, where many of our passengers would be shortly, at 300mph and in the descent towards 2,000ft. It's mandatory to keep the island on your left all the way in to minimise noise, so I hugged the coastline past Bridgetown and the crew hotel at 2,000ft, and with idle power on the enormous General Electric engines, the speed trickled back nicely on target to 180 knots (207mph).

We had two stages of flap extended by now and as we reached 7nm (nautical miles) from touchdown, I asked the co-pilot to lower the undercarriage and the remaining flap so we could reduce to our final approach speed of 150mph and descend on the 3 degree glideslope to the runway, now clearly visible ahead. At 1,000ft, as is standard procedure, the co-pilot confirmed that everything was stable for the final approach and called, 'Visual. I have control.' I released the control column on my side as he took up the reins from his seat and took this 230-tonne B777 down to a perfect touchdown and onwards the short distance to our standard parking spot on Gate 13. As the roles would be reversed going home, I'd just flown my last approach in my thirty-five years of professional flying.

We had three lovely days in the Caribbean sunshine but all too soon it was time to prepare for that final flight home. I'd managed to swap with another pilot and extend my stay for a day longer than scheduled. It was my pal Howard, in fact, the same chap who'd kindly saved the day after I was rushed off to hospital in Boston. He went home a day earlier than scheduled.

As I was with another crew, I was hoping to keep a low profile, but in fact it was quite sweet really that they knew it was my last flight. Incredibly, once again, there were just three spare seats in first class. That's really rare on this route at this time of year. It was meant to be. I worry now, though, that Harvey's expectations for future flights are far too high.

I had a lovely message from Barbados air traffic control as we taxied out towards the setting sun. And off we went. For the very, very last time. We had 296 passengers and needed 60 tonnes of BP's finest as we had prevailing tailwinds going home and a flight time of just seven hours and twenty-five minutes. That's slightly less than average but still over twice that of that noisy old museum piece that is no longer.

One of the big things I'm going to miss is the interaction with my passengers. We had some lovely people in that front cabin as usual and I had fun with them all. A lovely elderly lady was being treated to her first trip in first class by her daughter, who sat alongside her. She looked great in my captain's hat as I posed for a photo with her. Another couple in the front row spotted my Concorde tiepin and they had travelled supersonically twice, so we had some great time reminiscing. Out of the blue the gentleman asked, 'When's your book coming out?' I told him, 'It's nearly finished. When we get home tomorrow morning, I can write my last paragraph.'

The flight, thankfully, was uneventful. There's always that lingering fear that something nasty might be waiting to catch you out in the closing minutes. Even as I turned G-STBE on to Gate 542 at Heathrow's Terminal 5 at 5.39 a.m. (eleven minutes early), I said aloud, 'Careful now, John. It ain't over yet.'

One of our stewards, young Ben, who by coincidence I'd met in Cape Town on my formal retirement trip a couple of weeks earlier, was the voice on the PA for all the routine announcements. As we taxied in, he made all the standard calls along the lines of, 'Welcome to Heathrow and don't dare get up until the seat belt signs are switched off. Or else.' And then he went off-piste. Armed with some facts and figures from Lynne, including 'forty-six years in the business' and a list of all the aeroplanes I'd flown, he paid me a wonderful and moving tribute that solicited a round of applause we could hear through our bulletproof door. I responded once we'd parked up with my usual farewell but added a heartfelt thanks to Lynne for her support along the way and for buying my first flying lesson over forty years ago. My last ever words on the public address system of a

British Airways aeroplane were, 'Now I'm going to go home and cut the lawn.' That got a laugh, so in my book, a great way to finish.

I was the last off the aeroplane and, unusually, there were no ground staff present, so it was my responsibility to close the aircraft door. I gave it a fond, gentle pat as I did so.

And then I walked away.

The house was cold when we got home. Temperatures had plummeted to just above freezing while we'd been away and the last of the leaves were scattered across the lawn, leaving us in no doubt that, global warming or not, winter had arrived. The mail had piled up while we'd been away. Isn't there always a glimmer of excitement when you open the white envelopes and a drop of fear when you open the brown ones? The first white one I opened was a lovely flyer, featuring elderly, smiling models, possibly from my former part-time employer, Ordinary People, promoting 'compassionate care and luxury living' at a new retirement home.

Not yet thanks, matey.

I sat quietly and put the last entry in my flying logbook. I was on my fifth by now. Each line represented a cherished flight, not one ever taken for granted, and was written neatly in ink from my best fountain pen.

The first entry was a trial lesson on 15 June 1981 in a Piper PA-38 Tomahawk at Booker.

The last entry going in my logbook on 6 December 2022 was in a Boeing 777 from Barbados to Heathrow.

Total flight time (after forty-one and a half years): 18,116 hours and forty-eight minutes.

THEY SAY IT'S ALL OVER – IT IS NOW

12 December 2022. My 65th birthday.

That was it then. My career was all over. It's the only profession left in the world whereby, rightly or wrongly, retirement is compulsory at precisely that age. Not a day longer, regardless of your level of fitness. I get it, I suppose. There have been numerous respected studies about levels of fitness in an ageing population and the data was there for all to see. The statistics show that the number of people having sudden and serious cardio or vascular events over the age of 65 stood at an unacceptable level for people over that age to continue as airline pilots.

To be honest, I hadn't really expected to make it that far with my medical issues along the way. I'd been lucky.

It's been good. It's been fun. It's been rewarding and challenging. Above all, it's been a great privilege. It's gone by in a flash though. I've travelled all across this wonderful planet of ours and met some amazing people along the way. I made friends with some of the poorest, the children in the slums in India. I've flown millions of people safely from one place to another, whether it be for pleasure or business. I've met pop stars and actors, carried a couple of James Bonds and members of the royal family, a Beatle and a Rolling Stone and they've all been absolutely lovely.

I've flown small aeroplanes and big aeroplanes. I've flown slow aeroplanes and fast aeroplanes. I've flown Concorde. Did I say that out loud? I don't often, to be honest, but without doubt, that was the highlight of my career. I start my Concorde talks by *suggesting* to the audience that Concorde was perhaps the greatest icon of the twentieth century. I end an hour later, with a big theatrical finish and everyone agreeing that she was.

Leading up to my retirement, people always asked, 'What are you going to do when you retire?' I'd answer simply, 'Plenty.'

This page: Collecting G-YMMT from the factory, 26 June 2009.

Back on G-BOAD in New York, September 2022.

A few of 'John's Harem' in Cape Town, 25 November 2022.

With the new ad in T5. Like the hat?

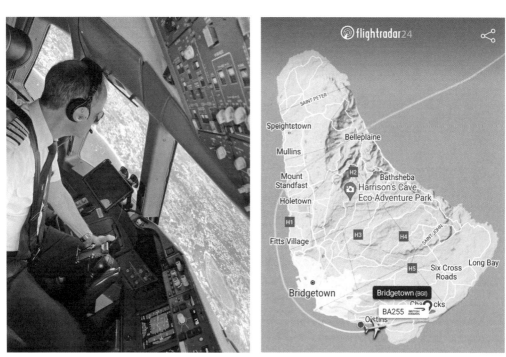

My last ever hand-flown visual approach into Barbados. (Map courtesy of FlightRadar24)

Take your grandson to work day, December 2022.

With Lynne, Jenny and Harvey in Barbados.

Clockwise from top left: Closing the door on a privileged career. Did I put the cat out?; a ski on my 64th birthday, 12 December 2021. Very cold!; a Harley for the day in Los Angeles, 1 April 2021.

'Your move, Grandad', 17 August 2020.

'Ready for a race, Grandad?', 31 July 2023.

7

From the Orphanage
(1957 to 1959)

MUM WAS SPECIAL

All mums are special but mine was the best. Erica Tye was born on 29 May 1927. She was an only child and her parents, my grandparents, lived locally in Shepperton when I was small. I remember them well. Grandad Clark had a wonderful head of thick white hair with teeth to match. He was well known in the village riding his immaculate bicycle with a cheery wave for everyone.

Mum and Dad did a wonderful job bringing Lucille and me up through the 1960s and '70s. Doubtless, they had some sleepless nights along the way, but I don't think we were too bad.

Mum was always very active in the local community and the church. She was always helping others and running the elderly to their hospital or hairdresser appointments. Even though as time went on they were much younger than her.

That generation was different. They'd been through the Second World War and it was very much a case of the man did the work and the woman had his dinner ready when he came home. As such, Dad needed quite a lot of looking after. He didn't cook or clean the house. He did some gardening and tinkered with the car, but Mum always seemed to be rushing around shopping, cleaning, cooking and looking after others.

Mum and Dad had been through any parents' worst nightmare. Their only natural child, Karen, had died at just 6 months old. They didn't talk about her much but I know it affected them terribly. It's something you can never really come to terms with and despite Mum's involvement in the church she, quite understandably, doubted her faith at times.

And then it happened again. My adopted sister, Lucille, had gone to live in France with her first husband when she was in her 20s. Even though that marriage failed, she remained living in the French Alps, working as a ski instructor to start with. She eventually met a lovely quiet French man, Jean-Paul, and they had two wonderful children, Bryan and then Axelle. We'd see them once a year or so, either us going there, or vice versa. Mum would often go alone, quite a feat for a lady in her 70s who didn't have much experience travelling.

In 2011 we got word that Lucille wasn't well. She'd been diagnosed with cancer. She received wonderful treatment but went downhill rapidly and we all went to visit her in hospital in France. She had always been a strong character but this was a fight she sadly couldn't win. She passed away on 29 January 2012, just after her 51st birthday. Her children weren't even teenagers.

Jean-Paul did a wonderful job guiding them through the trauma and grieving period and they've both grown up into fine young adults. Lucille would have been very proud of them.

I was the examiner conducting a line check on a 777 crew to Orlando the day Lucille died, a future coincidence in the making.

Dad had died quite suddenly right after the Air France Concorde crash in July 2000. Mum grieved, of course, and often spoke of 'Dear Ronnie', but after a while, she flourished. She gained a new lease of life. Dad didn't travel, nor was he comfortable socialising much outside our immediate family. Mum rekindled her connection with various local social groups and even though many of her contemporaries had gone, seemed to have an active social life.

Mum was fun too, and a good sport. Because our surname is made up of just three letters, I'd easily and fairly cheaply bought personalised car registrations for Lynne, the girls and me. It had seemed a good idea at the time, but Mum would often say how she felt left out when she came round and was the only person who didn't have one.

Her face was a picture when the following Christmas we presented her with a flat rectangular gift, which she quickly realised was really making her part of the family. It wasn't long before she was complaining though, albeit in jest, that everyone knew who she was now and she couldn't park anywhere without being noticed.

She was always bombing around in her little car, her face seemingly peering over the steering wheel and her nose pressed up to the windscreen. She'd be talking away non-stop to her passenger, normally an old lady from the village, much younger than her, who was being chauffeured to an appointment somewhere or other.

In the Queen's New Year's Honours list at the end of 2015 it was announced that Mum had been awarded the BEM, the British Empire Medal, for her services and dedication to the community of Lower Sunbury.

In her normal modest and humble way she had tried to turn it down, insisting it must be a mistake. The rest of the family were just overflowing with pride and had no doubt that she was a most worthy recipient.

The ceremony and presentation took place on 17 May 2016, just before her 89th birthday. She was in fine form as always, bright and bubbly, cheeky and chatty, and it was a wonderful afternoon.

Mum died seven months later after a short illness on 5 December 2016. We thought she was recovering at the time.

I was the examiner conducting a line check on a 777 crew to Orlando the day Mum died, just as I had been when my sister passed away. The only two line checks I had ever conducted to Orlando.

So That's *Really* How it all Began

I knew very little about my natural background until now. I never had any real interest in tracking down my natural parents. I knew I was the result of an illicit affair between two people in early 1957 and that my father was married. And that was about it.

Mum always told me, though, that she would tell me everything she knew and show me the supporting paperwork if ever I wanted to know more. I had enjoyed such a wonderful, supportive and loving upbringing that I had no desire to look under large boulders that had metaphorically, been gathering moss for over fifty years. If I had turned up on somebody's doorstep unannounced, it was likely I could have ruined other people's lives. After all, I was a secret. Secrets are for keeping.

There are many lovely television programmes that tug at the heart strings and bring a tear to your eye that reunite long-lost families, particularly children given up for adoption, with their natural mother or father. I bet for every one of those, though, there are several disasters. Lucille was reunited with her natural mother briefly and it didn't go that well.

Christmas 2016 wasn't great, to be honest. Mum's funeral was scheduled for three days later on 28 December. We did have our grandson, though, young Harvey, who was 2 by now, to brighten things up somewhat.

Once the festivities were over we set about the awful task of sorting out Mum's and Dad's things. This had been the family home for sixty years, so it wasn't going to be easy. Not that it was cluttered or untidy, just the opposite in fact, but it was the memories and emotions that were set alight with each drawer that was opened. My mouth organ that I had when I was 3, not that I could ever play it, and Lucille's tin toy drum, reminded me of the din we must have made. Dad's watches and Mum's best brooches were all preserved in ancient tissue paper. I'm sure anybody who has been through this can relate to how I felt.

And then we came to the brown suitcase. It looked like something Paddington Bear would have carried around, but much larger and had clearly been well used back in the day. I knew that this held the key to my background. The secret that had always been locked away.

I couldn't open it there and then, so we took it away, back to the comfort of our own home, and sat on the floor in the lounge. I couldn't do this without Lynne, but eventually I popped open the two catches and raised the lid. It must have been a very long time since daylight had last entered this case, but there it was, history all laid bare, all neatly bundled and tied up with string.

I started going through some of the papers and picked up a few nuggets of information, but was soon overwhelmed. I couldn't face it there and then and closed it back up again, earmarking it for a rainy day when I'd retired.

Come mid-October 2022 I was still waiting to hear if and when I was going to get my medical reinstated and get back flying for my last six weeks. It had been raining quite a lot, so rather than waiting for a rainy day in retirement I popped the catches on the old brown suitcase again. Five years after I'd last peered inside at my past.

Wow! I learned a lot. It would seem nobody, but nobody, from my birth family apart from my mother and father ever knew I existed. And my mother never even saw me. Ever.

I now know the names and addresses of my natural parents. I know they are both deceased and have been for quite a while, but I'll still keep this somewhat vague to protect any future generations of both families.

I always had the impression my father was a successful businessman, possibly even a politician, although I'm not quite sure where I got that idea from. It could explain a lot though.

My father lived in a small village in Derbyshire. I won't name it publicly. He was married but they had no children of their own. He was 39 when he had a relationship with a 35-year-old unmarried woman in the village who lived with her mother. I was conceived.

It would seem that, in an attempt to hide her pregnancy, my mother was secreted away to a flat in London, right opposite the Queens Park Rangers football ground. I'm not sure at this stage how that came about, but I've seen reference to her living with some friends.

My mother was admitted to West Middlesex Hospital in Isleworth, London, towards the end of her pregnancy but according to the report Mum had filed away in the old brown suitcase, my mother 'was so definite that she didn't want to see the baby, that alternative arrangements were made. It was then that she went into a nursing home to have the baby and he was delivered by one of the hospital obstetricians.'

It would seem I remained in this nursing home with my mother living nearby in Loftus Road, but she 'maintained her decision not to see the baby', so it would seem we never met. After a few months in the orphanage, I was placed with a foster mother, a Mrs Blake. It's on record that at birth I had a 'displacement of my right toe' and was seen on two occasions by an orthopaedic specialist. He predicted it would 'right itself shortly'. Wrong. That was clearly the start of something more complex.

My mother worried about me and kept in constant contact with the nursing home (orphanage). She asked that I be registered with the Children's Society agency for adoption.

I was named John Philip Scrimshaw, taking my mother's surname. The report, written when I was a few months old and sent to the Children's Society as part of the application process, includes a wonderful and revealing paragraph:

Miss Scrimshaw is a rather bonny-looking woman of 36. She has until recently, always lived at home with her mother, to whom she is very deeply attached. Her main concern throughout has been that her mother should learn nothing of this pregnancy. Apparently Mrs Scrimshaw has always been very sorry her daughter has not married. She (her mother) knows the putative father but has no knowledge of the association. Miss Scrimshaw has known the putative father for four years, though there has not been an intimate relationship through the whole of that period. He is alleged to be unhappily married, although I gather there has never been any question of a divorce. Miss Scrimshaw is now busy trying to detach herself from their relationship, although during her pregnancy, he has visited and seen her regularly. She says, and I believe her, that in spite of the effort not to get tied up with the baby, she would have liked to have kept him and very much regrets that she cannot, but she feels that both for her family and for the putative father's and also for the baby's sake, it is extremely important that he is adopted.

Later on, this application to the Children's Society, written by the Special Services Almoner at the Middlesex County Health Department, talks of my mother's desire for me to have a good university education, something she longed for herself. The almoner writes: 'I have seen Miss Scrimshaw on many occasions and I think she has undoubtedly decided on adoption. She is a sincere and essentially decent person, and I hope you will accept this application.'

I have now learned (in February 2023) that the application to the Children's Society to put me on the 'available for adoption' list was actually withdrawn.

While all this was going on, Ron and Erica Tye, less than 10 miles away in Sunbury, were grieving over the loss of their own daughter, Karen. Erica wrote several letters seeking out children for fostering or adoption and in March 1958 there were talks with the Middlesex County Council Children's Department based in Twickenham.

A 'holding letter' dated 19 March 1958, includes the text: 'up to the present time we have not admitted a baby to care who could have been placed with you', and then 'if you are still able to take a baby perhaps you would ring Miss Stokes at this office, so that she may arrange to visit you.'

Thankfully, Erica must have made that call. There are handwritten notes about a call regarding a 4-year-old, but for whatever reason that didn't materialise. I believe Ron and Erica wanted a younger child so they could pick up where they had left off with young Karen.

By June 1958, so aged 7 months, there's evidence that I was with Ron and Erica at Sunbury. I believe they had taken me in while my original foster mother, Mrs Blake, had a holiday. Goodness knows where I would have ended up if they hadn't. Certainly not counting backwards from three at the controls of Concorde.

A letter dated 17 September 1958 (I'm 10 months old) reads:

Dear Mrs Tye,
I was glad to hear baby John has settled down well. If you continue with the idea of adopting him, I should be very happy to see you, and give you such details about his parents as I can.

I think for the time being, you should accept the money paid by the mother.* She is only too willing to make the payments, as long as he is well cared for. She is interested in his welfare, although she has never seen him. Her main anxiety is that he should be happily settled with people who give him love and security.

---

* There is evidence that my mother sent postal orders to the value of £5 and 5 shillings every now and again towards my care.

I am glad to hear that John is going to remain with you, at least until his appointment at Great Ormond Street.*

By March 1959 my birth mother had signed the relevant papers consenting to my adoption and then I came across a letter dated 15 April 1959 addressed to Erica, advising her that my father had also now signed the consent form. It's the only source of information I have about my father, a somewhat faded sheet of A4 paper.

At first read it was quite a shock. Now I find it makes me smile. Remember the bit about 'a successful businessman?' Let me read some of it to you.

Referring to my father, the Special Services Almoner writes:

I saw him yesterday. He is a man of 39, very much overweight – which may be due to beer – but alert and intelligent, and I should think a jolly good bookie!

Well that brought me back to earth with a bump.

The certificate 'In the matter of the adoption of John Philip Scrimshaw' is dated 15 June 1959. And I guess that was the start of life as I know it.

* *A reference to the famous children's hospital, where doctors were already taking an interest in my unusual feet and legs.*

Mum and Dad with baby Karen. She only lived for 6 months.

Karen Erica Tye.

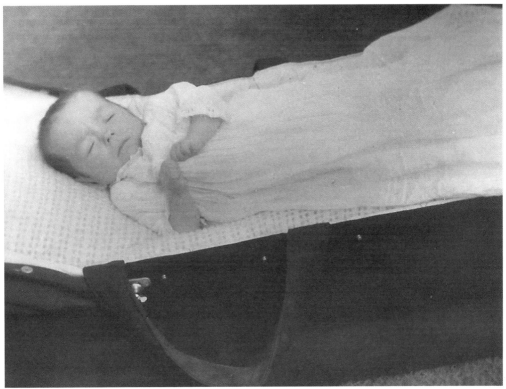

First pictures of me, 10 months.

… and 12 months.

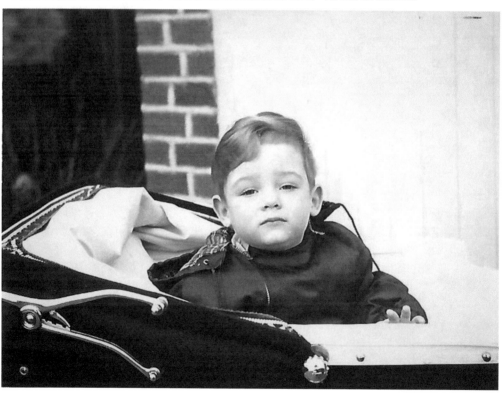

Epilogue

I started this work in March 2020 and it took me three years. Why did I do it?

Well, three main reasons really.

I never knew what Dad did in the war. It was something rather secret and one of my retirement projects is to investigate that further. My children know what I've done with my career. Of course they do. That's far from secret, but future generations of my family won't.

My grandson, Harvey, wasn't even 6 when I started this. He couldn't read and his writing was quite basic. Now I've finished, he can read it himself and does proper 'joined up writing'. He probably thinks I'm a bit of a silly old fool, though, who's not that good at getting goals past him in the back garden. One day, he and any others who come along, and their children too, ought to know that Grandad went 'From the Orphanage to the Edge of Space'. And that it was actually something quite special way back in the twentieth century.

Another reason is that I wanted to inspire others. Of all ages.

Starting out in life, at school or college, regardless of disabilities, wealth or background, go for it. You've only got one life. It's not a dress rehearsal. Make the most of it. I know I have and I ain't finished yet.

I met so many children who looked up at me in my uniform with big wide eyes and probably dreamed of doing what I've done. Well, if you've got the ability, you can. Of course, ambitions need to be realistic (I could never have been a ballet dancer), but I've been most fortunate and privileged. I never say lucky because I've worked hard for it and I've had amazing support from Lynne along the way. Yes, I've had some good luck. Right place, right time and all that, but I've had more than my share of bad luck too. And it's how you deal with that which is important. Pick yourself up, dust yourself down, think, 'Now, where was I?' And carry on.

Thankfully, we're much more aware of mental health issues nowadays. Reading this, you might have got the impression I was always full of beans, loving my job and having a lot of fun, and that I have lived a wonderful life. I've had my bad times too, as we all do. Not least the last few months of my career, when I was rather down in the dumps. It's how, within your family, you support one another that's important. And Lynne's always been there to support me, through thick and thin, for which I'm eternally grateful.

I'd hope to inspire adults too, particularly any other airline pilots reading this. I've always put my heart and soul into my work, as anyone who knows me will testify. As an instructor and as a captain I've tried to do my best for everyone I come across.

As a British Airways captain my primary task was to take an aluminium tube full of people from A to B safely and ideally on time. That was it in a nutshell and there's many out there who, quite happily, do that very well. But only that. I've always been of the mind that, the more you put in, the more you get out.

I've taken much pleasure from interacting with the passengers whenever the opportunity presented itself. I would ask the cabin crew to let me know if they came across anyone who was nervous. And there are plenty, believe me. I'd go and talk to them in flight, explain what causes turbulence, sit with them and make them laugh and invite them to visit the flight deck when we'd landed. I've changed people's lives by doing such a small thing and I've got a lot out of it.

Pre-Covid we used to give ice creams out on the holiday flights in the economy cabin. I'd go and do that personally. Not just so I could get any leftovers, as I was sometimes accused of, but so I could put a smile on hundreds of faces in a few minutes. It was easy, most effective and jolly good fun.

I'm known for going round the premium cabins having a friendly chat with our customers. There's a way to do it and a degree of judgement required, of course. Many people just want to be left alone but there were plenty who loved the fact the captain came and spoke with them personally. All this has kept me motivated and young at heart. Stopped me from becoming a grumpy old git like some I could think of.

There are young pilots out there, just starting their careers, who may well be the next generation to take fare-paying passengers supersonic again. The role of an airline captain will undoubtedly evolve further in years to come. Planes will one day fly themselves, perhaps even being controlled remotely from the ground. The captain, perhaps the only pilot on board, will be there to manage the operation, but won't be allowed to touch anything, except in extremis. His or her role may well be more of a figurehead, perhaps even hosting dinner like captains on cruise ships. Those PR skills I've tried to drum into, I mean subtly develop in, others, might come in handy one day.

The third reason I wrote my book is that I found it quite therapeutic. That's how it all started back in Covid lockdown. And in the three years since, I've felt the urge every now and again to put pen to paper, or whatever the electronic equivalent thereof is?

They say there's a book in everyone. Well, there's mine, out in the open now. I started by saying how I hoped that future generations of my family, and you, dear reader, will find this story inspiring, moving and at times amusing.

If you've got this far, I hope you have.

Now what shall I do?

Acknowledgements

My thanks go to all the friends and colleagues at British Airways who laughed politely at my funny stories and mishaps and said, 'You must write a book.'

To those who read my first draft and gave me honest feedback and guidance to help me tidy it up, my thanks to Jane Barrett, Martin Carter, Mark Lucas, Mike Bannister and, of course, my wife, Lynne.

All images are my own unless otherwise stated. Particular thanks to Michael Regan in New York who kindly let me use the Concorde instrument panels.

The cover picture is with my deepest gratitude to the photographer, Adrian Meredith, www.concordephotos.com